SCHOOL
&
SOCIETY

School
&
Society

Learning Content
Through
Culture

EDITED BY

HENRY T. TRUEBA
&
CONCHA DELGADO-GAITAN

PRAEGER

New York
Westport, Connecticut
London

Library of Congress Cataloging-in-Publication Data

School and society.

  Bibliography: p.
  Includes index.
  1. Educational anthropology. 2. Socialization.
3. Minorities—Education—United States. I. Trueba,
Henry T. II. Delgado-Gaitan, Concha.
LB45.S355   1988   370.19   87-32880
ISBN 0-275-92860-8 (alk. paper)

Library of Congress Catalog Card Number: 87-32880
ISBN: 0-275-92860-8

First published in 1988

Praeger Publishers, One Madison Avenue, New York, NY 10010
A division of Greenwood Press, Inc.

Printed in the United States of America

The paper used in this book complies with the Permanent
Paper Standard issued by the National Information Standards
Organization (Z39.48—1984).

10 9 8 7 6 5 4 3 2 1

As a token of our gratitude and in recognition of the philosophical, methodological, and theoretical contributions they have made to our personal and professional growth, these pages are affectionately dedicated to Professors Louise and George Spindler. Their past and present contributions to the field of educational anthropology continue to inspire systematic research and creative thinking about the relationship of culture to knowledge acquisition and about the role of teachers in understanding how culture affects learning.

On behalf of the contributors, as well as the many students and friends who have received intellectual guidance and encouragement from Professors George and Louise Spindler, the editors want to celebrate the more than 30 productive years of efforts the Spindlers have devoted to educational anthropology. These efforts have resulted in the writing or editing of nearly 300 volumes, to say nothing of the hundreds of scholarly pieces and dissertations that have been developed with their support. This celebration also marks the beginning of challenging new ideas being explored by the Spindlers, their colleagues, and students. Indeed, some of the chapters in this volume reflect a new direction in educational anthropology, a direction inspired by the recent work of George and Louise.

Contents

Tables and Figures

Acknowledgments

We are indebted to the scholars who contributed original research to this volume. Their pioneering efforts in the application of anthropological research methods to a variety of educational problems across cultures have paid off in the form of significant insights into theoretical and methodological advances in educational anthropology. We are particularly grateful to all of the contributors, who went to the trouble of implementing our suggestions in order to comply with size and format requirements while managing to meet pressing deadlines. A word of thanks to our colleagues who helped us conceptualize the structure of the book and gave us feedback for some of the chapters, especially Terry Denny, Richard Duran, and Roberto Rueda.

Without the clerical assistance and organizational skills of Mary McConkey and her staff, particularly Beatriz Jamaica and Carol Benson, this volume would not have been possible. Finally, we want to thank the anonymous readers, reviewers, and editors for their excellent suggestions.

Henry T. Trueba
Concha Delgado-Gaitan

SCHOOL
&
SOCIETY

Introduction

Henry T. Trueba

Over the last 30 years, educational anthropologists have engaged in systematic efforts to explore the organizational structure of schools and their relationship to society, in order to shed some light on the complex processes of acquisition, organization, and transmission of cultural knowledge. Related to this issue is how the internalization of cultural values inculcated in school influences learning. This linkage between values and academic success can be better understood when we examine the notion that culture, as the Spindlers have written recently, consists to some extent of the organization of activities that bring people satisfaction, power, possessions, recognition, and status. By implication, what we as Americans choose to do, and the kinds of specific activities we prefer, are chosen because of their presumed function in enhancing expected cultural values.

Work by the Spindlers has helped researchers focus on the role of teachers in the culture of the schools. Teachers act as cultural brokers who, through the process of cultural transmission, may perpetuate or change the existing social order. One of the most significant contributions made by the Spindlers and their associates has been the study of student socialization in school. The contributors to this volume have focused on the cultural knowledge and values required for participating actively in the educational process. This volume gathers the contributions of many recognized scholars, who collectively have unique expertise relevant to the peoples of Germany, Israel, Mexico, Latin America, Iran, Japan, Indochina, and other areas from which today's ethnic minority groups in America come. The concerns of this volume include the need to provide a field-based, well-documented cultural environment for the many groups of children who face cultural conflict. Most of these children have been uprooted and must acquire not only communicative skills in a new language but also new cultural values. Issues such as the "hidden curriculum," the task of making the strange familiar, the need to engage students in critical thinking activities, and the help teachers may receive through cultural therapy have triggered research and thinking in many other scholars and practitioners. This volume represents some of the current thinking and the ongoing dialogue between the Spindlers, other researchers, and practitioners.

The volume is divided into three parts. Part I includes the first three chapters and deals with general issues of methodological and theoretical trends in ethnography, especially as it is used to document the ethnohistorical context of political socialization. In Chapter 1, Harry P. Wolcott warns us about the pitfalls of initiating ethnographic inquiry without acknowledging that we bring our cultural biases into the research arena. "Ethnography" should be reserved, Wolcott insists, for studies clearly concerned with cultural analysis and interpretation, not just with methods for data collection; and it should be an interactive process affecting each phase of the research as it progresses, from the moment of conception to the final report on findings of the ethnographers. Wolcott discusses qualitative research as an interactive process that extends from the onset of the study throughout the data-gathering, analyzing and presenting, to the final point of incorporating feedback from responses to final accounts on the research. In conclusion, he suggests that the formulation of a research question is crucial to finding an answer for it.

Chapter 2, written by Robert R. Alvarez, presents a dramatic ethnohistorical account of a court case, the *Roberto Alvarez v. the Board of Trustees of the Lemon Grove School District* (1931) in Southern California, which helped defeat the infamous Bliss Bill. The Bliss Bill had requested "the power to establish separate schools for Indian children of Chinese, Japanese, and Mongolian ancestry" and argued that Mexican and Mexican American children, since they were Indians, should also be placed in separate schools (Indians were legally segregated). Judge Chambers clearly stood for American democratic values when, in ruling against the Bliss Bill, he stated, "I believe this separation denies the Mexican children the presence of the American children, which is so necessary to learn the English language." Alvarez presents the sociolcultural context of local and state racial biases during the 1920s and 1930s, and helps us understand the historical significance of his unique discovery.

Chapter 3 is written by Richard A. Navarro. He presents an ethnographic account of the complex political processes that united Chicano constituencies in favor of bilingualism during the period 1967-80 in California. This Chicano solidarity resulted in the formation of an Hispanic pressure group that participated actively in the formulation of policy issues and became conscious of its political power. Chicanos also became collectively aware of political patronage, state power structures, formulation of policy propositions, steps in the political process, and the cultural values and norms behind American democratic institutions. This case illustrates an intensive period of successful transmission of cultural values related to the political process.

Part II has four chapters dealing with the early periods of socialization and cultural transmission across various cultures. Chapter 4 is written by Mariko Fujita and Toshiyuki Sano, who jointly present a cross-cultural comparison of the American and Japanese day-care centers. Their focus is on cultural transmission and culturally constructed meaning systems, with special reference to child socialization in independent behavior. Using the Spindlers' "Reflective Cross-Cultural Interview Procedure," as well as their "Culture Dialogues," the authors examine American and Japanese teachers' interpretations of each others' day-care systems. American teachers saw Japanese day-care centers as too noisy, chaotic, and out of control. Japanese teachers, on the other hand, saw American teachers as distant, lazy, and rigid (treating children as if they were adults). American teachers felt they were training children to be truly individualistic, while Japanese felt they were training children to be cooperative and respectful of traditions. The authors point out that the most profound philosophical differences between American and Japanese teachers is regarding the concept of "children" and "teachers."

Chapter 5, written by Nancy H. Hornberger, describes the early experiences of Quechua-speaking children in Peruvian schools. She offers, in some detail, the sociolinguistic context of Quechua and Spanish language distribution in two school settings: Spanish-only and bilingual. In the bilingual instructional settings, there is more extensive and spontaneous use of Quechua and more active, meaningful participation of students in the instructional process. In contrast, Hornberger observes that in the Spanish-only setting children copy sentences without understanding their content. Hornberger's well-documented study raises questions about the linkage between language and culture, and the ineffectiveness of literacy activities in a linguistic and cultural vacuum.

Chapter 6 is written by Christine Robinson Finnan and illustrates the impact Southeast Asian refugees have had on some American schools. Originally, Southeast Asian refugees from Vietnam, Cambodia, and Laos were calculated to reach 150,000 people by 1975. By 1986, however, this population exceeded 800,000. Finnan's fieldwork was conducted in California (Orange and San Francisco counties), Louisiana (New Orleans), Kansas (Wichita, Sedwick County), and New York (Rochester and Ithaca, Monroe and Tompkins counties). Schools did not seem to be negatively influenced by the arrival of Indochinese refugees, despite their special needs and the limited resources of schools. ESL (English as a Second Language) classes, special programs, and bilingual instruction were provided by aides, making it possible for regular teachers to continue their normal duties. In fact, refugee children stimulated other children with their example to try harder.

Chapter 7 is written by Richard L. Warren and discusses the relationships between parents and teachers in three elementary schools. The first school was in Rebhausen, a rural German village; the second school was Campbell, in Westland, a low-income California town near the Mexican border; and the third school was Calhoun, in Dennison, a middle-class suburban-industrial city of 100,000 in northern California. In Rebhausen, the teacher dominated the instructional process rigidly through mechanisms such as physical punishment, shame, public denunciation, and peer censorship. Teachers and parents had adversary relationships and teachers were threatened by parents, who were part of the working class and were associated with labor unions. At Calhoun, teachers played a more traditional and distant instructional role, and had no cooperative relationships with parents. At Campbell, teachers were competent and professionally secure; their bilingual-bicultural model emphasized individualized and small group instruction through curriculum management systems and criterion-referenced tests. Teachers there had the best working relationships with parents.

Part III deals with cultural transmission and conflict in high school youngsters. Chapter 8, written by Diane M. Hoffman, offers a unique cross-cultural comparison of Iranian and mainstream American students in American high schools. She explores the dimensions of cultural conflicts in interethnic interaction as based on different values and assumptions. Iranians are described as a cultural group in the United States that does not consider itself an ethnic minority group. Iranians are generally highly educated, wealthy, successful professionals who see themselves as unwilling exiles. In the Los Angeles area alone the Iranian population is about 200,000, and of those 60,000 are students in the schools, thus forming the largest foreign student group in this country. Iranian students are often characterized by their peers as obnoxious, arrogant, and dishonest. Hoffman describes the refusal by Iranians to accept American culture with its norms, values, and laws as an expression of a very strong ethnic identity, which also explains their success in professional careers.

Chapter 9, written by Steven Borish, uses George Spindler's notion of compression and decompression periods in the life cycle. He studied for 18 months the Kibbutz Gan HaEmek, which was organized 30 years ago by Jews from England, in the Upper Galilee region of Israel. Children there were seen as speaking an inferior type of Hebrew because of the unusual grammatical and phonetic structures they used. Childhood on a kibbutz was a time of cultural decompression, unhindered self-expression, development, and spontaneous enjoyment, that is, a time for the formation of Jewish identity. At age 13, kibbutz youngsters were required to work, increasing to a full day's work by age 17. Compression started with the Bar Mitzvah ceremony and continued through high school years. Youngsters developed ways of coping with the conflict and demands of kibbutz work; all shared common knowledge and one year of army duty following high school, which is viewed as imminent. The postarmy decompression years required a postponement of career decisions, but gave young people the opportunity to travel throughout the world visiting former kibbutz peers. The boundaries between success and failure had collapsed in the kibbutz. "Adolescence on Kibbutz Gan HaEmek is the winter of their discontent...soon followed by the year of service and then by the army," in Borish's eloquent terms.

In Chapter 10 Henry T. Trueba presents his study of a high school dropout prevention program for minority students in central California, and discusses the psychosocial dimensions of academic socialization of "high risk" minority students. The socialization starts by helping youth interpret previous negative school experiences and preparing them to meet academic demands. Students describe their experience prior to the prevention program in terms of degradation incidents that leave them with feelings of alienation and low self-esteem. These feelings, and their lack of knowledge and skills needed for full participation in academic activities, are translated in low academic achievement. The program offers them interactional settings in which they may experience rewarding learning growth without degradation, and in which they develop individual personal relationships with peers and teachers. This chapter takes the position of the Neo-Vygotskians, who view academic underachievement not as an individual failure but as a social phenomenon caused by social-structural factors isolating and alienating minority students, thus preventing them from acquiring the cultural values and/or knowledge required for academic success. Using George and Louise Spindler's notion of instrumental competencies, Trueba analyzes program activities in which students move to higher levels of literacy and reach higher levels of achievement motivation.

These chapters recognize the contributions of the Spindlers throughout their 30 years of intensive and systematic intellectual efforts. Their writings and teaching have provided a deeper understanding of the relationships between school and society, of the role of schools in the process of cultural transmission, and of the relationships between teachers and students. The Spindlers have invited serious reflection about American society with its democratic values, and how they relate to the cultural pluralism and ethnic diversity that are America's quintessence. The Spindlers have long observed the cycles of rapid change along with the persistent continuation of cultural values in American social institutions, particularly in school. In their final analysis, they direct our attention to the very conception of culture and the need for "cultural therapy," something they had suggested back in the 1950s. This time, however, they remind us that the very survival of American democracy will hinge upon our ability to resolve cultural conflict, especially in school.

The Spindlers also invite us to view American culture as a diachronic dialogue between an egalitarian philosophy based on democratic (political and economic) values, struggling to remain intact in an internationally based technocracy that bypasses our complex system of checks and balances. The "dialogue" or diametric opposition between individualism and conformity, consensus and debate, continuity and change, is at the heart of American democracy, regardless of progress, and it will continue to be reflected in educational controversies.

The Spindlers have distinguished the deeply rooted "enduring self," which includes the ideal-romantic rationalizations associated with images of traditional American life (land, village life), and the "situated self" associated with the pragmatic adaptation to modern societal constraints (urban life-styles in an industrial complex society). Engaging in the dialogue between idealism and realism, Americans remain highly flexible by adapting to modern demands and yet are deeply attached to traditional values. As Americans, we manage to maintain a high self-esteem through complex mechanisms. As part of the situated self, individuals develop self-efficacy in areas of experienced success and exhibit "instrumental competence" to perform certain tasks. This is particularly relevant to the American school setting, because school is generally the setting for first encounters with children from other social, cultural, linguistic, and ethnic backgrounds. Adjustment to the new educational setting requires a complex reorganization of cultural priorities as well as the acquisition of new instrumental competencies in children.

George and Louise Spindler offer us a revised notion of cultural therapy made relevant to the schools. This therapy has important elements common to the intellectual efforts of Freire and other philosophers. Their approach, however, requires that a conscious effort be made to understand one's own cultural identity in its historical, social, and political context, while searching for the linkages between the cultural adaptation of individuals and the successful acquisition of academic knowledge. The key in the process of adaptation is individual willingness to acquire cultural knowledge and internalize the cultural values that form the foundation of school activities. These activities are expected to lead to the mastery of instrumental competencies and cultural goals. In turn, these goals are consistent with culturally preestablished priorities. The role of the teacher as a cultural broker is crucially important to the process of cultural therapy.

While the Spindlers do not claim to have answers to the problems of American schools, they have made us aware of the difficult task teachers face as they see themselves isolated, silenced, concerned for their personal safety, and lacking the support they need to teach effectively. The Spindlers are turning back to teachers with the confidence that teachers, in a team with researchers and other experts, can create better learning environments for all children, if only they are given a fair chance. As the Spindlers (1987:5) explained:

In any social scene within any setting, whether great or small, social actors carry on a culturally constructed dialogue. This dialogue is expressed in behavior, words, symbols, and the applications of cultural knowledge to make instrumental activities and social situations "work" for one. We learn the dialogue as children and continue learning it all of our lives, as our circumstances change. These are the phenomena that we believe we study as ethnographers—the dialogue of action, interaction, and meaning.

Teachers in the United States, as representatives of modern industrial society, maintain the social order and help promote our technological and military position. However, they would like to see themselves as intellectuals and cultural brokers, and would like to enjoy additional flexibility and support for fulfilling their mission. To many teachers, this mission consists of helping students acquire critical thinking and communicative skills and the knowledge necessary to improve their quality of life. In the final analysis, the Spindlers' contributions amount to a vigorous quest for a more humane school learning environment for all children, through a better understanding of the relationship between culture and successful schooling. George and Louise Spindler know that if we fail to see this relationship, we will end up converting schools into brutal machines for social exploitation.

REFERENCE

Spindler, G. and L. Spindler (1987). Cultural Dialogue and Schooling in Schoenhausen and Roseville: A Comparative Analysis. *Anthropology and Education Quarterly* 18:3-16.

PART I
ETHNOGRAPHIC TRENDS
AND THE POLITICS OF THE
EDUCATIONAL PROCESS

1
"Problem Finding" in Qualitative Research
Harry F. Wolcott

Just tell me the steps I should follow in doing qualitative research. What should I do first? What should I do next? And so on... until a study is completed. No theory. Just the steps!

Queries about qualitative research are relatively new among educational researchers, but they are coming from an ever-widening circle. My original purpose in writing this chapter was to try to address an underlying question (and some accompanying misconceptions as well) about this seeming newcomer to educational research. In turn, that led me to reflect about the question itself, including just who might be asking it today, and why they would ask it of me. By way of introduction, let me start with the last point. That will also allow me to explain how I came to be a contributor to this Festschrift (volume in honor of the Spindlers).

THE CONTEXT OF
QUALITATIVE RESEARCH IN EDUCATION

What once was little more than reluctant tolerance for "qualitative" or "descriptive" studies in educational research, and today borders on academic respectability, has, to a great extent, coincided with the period of my own career in academia, dating from doctoral studies begun at Stanford University in 1959 in what has since materialized as the field of anthropology and education. In the ensuing years I have played some role in helping qualitative approaches in general, and ethnographic approaches in particular, achieve recognition in educational research by contributing a number of studies that have passed critical muster. But the nurturance and opportunity for work done in these two decades were provided by earlier academic generations. Let me quickly review that history, taking ethnographic research as my primary focus.

Margaret Mead's sustained interests in child rearing and in formal schooling, plus the occasional but nonetheless substantial forays of other established anthropologists into related topics among the peoples they studied or the texts they produced (e.g., Ruth Benedict, Dorothy Eggan, Meyer Fortes, Melville Herskovits, Dorothy Lee, Margaret Read, Melford Spiro), coupled with occasional bursts of attention from maverick anthropologists like C.W.M. Hart, Jules Henry, or Ashley Montagu, helped pave the way.

As a recognizable intellectual pursuit, anthropology and education made its real gains in the next academic generation. This effort was spearheaded at Stanford by my mentor, George Spindler—working always in concert with Louise Spindler—and by Solon Kimball, who was then at Teachers College, Columbia University. Their individual efforts on the West and East Coasts, respectively, were augmented by other anthropologists who acknowledged education as an important—if not necessarily the central—dimension of their work and discipline, together with some educators who early recognized the potential contribution of anthropology. (For fuller accounts of the anthropological contributors to this field and the roles they played, see Eddy 1985; G. Spindler 1984; for an account of the early dialogue among individuals representing the two perspectives, see G. Spindler 1955.)

Looking back, the increasing popularity and status accorded to ethnography and other forms of qualitative research in education today appear the result of a natural evolution, smooth and inevitable, but I can attest personally that the progression was neither so smooth nor so inevitable as it seems in retrospect. Those of my academic 'generation' willing to commit themselves to the anthropological potential in education—including Mark Atwood, Ximena Bunster, Jacquetta Hill Burnett, Frankie Beth Nelson, and Gerry Rosenfeld, studying with Kimball at Teachers College, and A. Richard King, Ted Parsons, John Singleton, and Richard Warren, my fellow students studying with Spindler at Stanford—were not altogether sure whether our anthropological training would open any doors or serve us intellectually except as a personal resource. Among our respective cohorts of doctoral students we were not numbered among the real (i.e., quantitative) researchers. Rather, we were identified through our minor discipline as "anthropologists," a doubly unsatisfactory label as we realized that our investigative efforts were dismissed by fellow educators as "experiences" instead of research ("Going off to spend a year with the Indians," in my own case) while often-aloof colleagues taking degrees in "pure" anthropology found us too education-focused to be convincing as social scientists.

In obtaining my first full-time academic appointment after completing the Ph.D. program at Stanford in 1964, it was my interdisciplinary background rather than my prowess at field research that led to job offers. The newly funded Research and Development Center at the University of Oregon that recruited me did not have another village and school it wanted me to study (in the fashion of my just-completed dissertation), but it did want an anthropologist to help validate its interdisciplinary commitment. For my initial research assignment, I was seconded to a senior sociologist engaged in a semistatistical survey that produced numerical values for a seemingly endless list of professional role expectations for teachers and administrators that we generated in seemingly endless meetings in a staff room in the basement of the Sociology Department.

I extricated myself from the project (and basement) by suggesting that I might make a more valuable contribution by conducting an ethnographic inquiry in the schools, an idea growing out of extended dialogue with the Spindlers. I proposed a study of one elementary school principal, whom I intended to follow about as though he were an Indian chief. My intent was to explore what school principals actually do by describing in careful detail what one of them did during a sustained period of anthropological field observation.

My proposal was not met with wild enthusiasm, but neither was it dismissed as unworthy or inappropriate to the broad charter of the Center to focus on issues in educational administration. If it was unclear exactly what was to be gained (What is to be learned by following *one* principal around?), it was also evident that not a great deal could be lost other than part of the time of one very junior faculty member. Other projects being conducted under auspices of the Center had cadres of assistants and support staff, as well as additional budget for data processing and outside consultants, so my modest (and inexpensive) project went virtually unnoticed as it lumbered along into a third and fourth year when, at last, there was tangible evidence of scholarly productivity.

If the quality of my completed study of the principal (Wolcott 1973), something largely under my control, is rather good—and I maintain rather unabashedly that it is (compare Wolcott 1982b)—my timing for proposing and conducting the research, something quite beyond my control, was exquisite. Had the study stood entirely alone, perhaps it would have made little mark. But in that era there were many individuals across the United States—particularly in other Regional Educational Laboratories and Educational Research and Development Centers funded under President Lyndon Johnson's efforts to achieve a Great Society—carrying out qualitative and descriptive studies.

Those with whom I was earliest and closest in touch oriented their studies according to ethnographic research practices. Others in what was becoming a rapidly expanding network of qualitative researchers found their inspiration and disciplinary precedents elsewhere. Maverick sociologists like Howard Becker and his colleagues took license to do participant observation from "Chicago-school" sociology and provided some of the earliest fine-detailed studies of educational institutions and processes (Becker et al. 1961, 1968). Maverick psychologists like Roger Barker and H. F. Wright turned to natural settings for studying individual behavior. Maverick educational psychologist Louis M. Smith, reacting to the "dust bowl empiricism" of his formal training, addressed the complexities of classroom life head on. Maverick educational sociologists like Dan Lortie began listening carefully to what teachers said. Out-and-out mavericks like Philip Jackson and Phil Cusick within the educational establishment, Martin Meyer and Robert Coles outside it, or Jonathan Kozol and John Holt on its fringes, simply ignored the canons of formal research altogether in favor of looking at what children and their teachers were doing, inside schools and out, because that was what they wanted to learn about and bring to the attention of a wider audience.

Commercial publishing houses found a lucrative market for journalistically oriented critiques of education popular in the late 1950s and 1960s. Academics doing descriptive studies searched for arenas in which to present their work and for publishers to print their admittedly less flamboyant but nonetheless critical studies. Students and established researchers contemplating new work provided a ready-made—if modest—market for the completed work of their qualitatively oriented associates. Independently, the Spindlers and Solon Kimball introduced case study series in education and anthropology in the late 1960s (see, respectively, Spindler and Spindler 1983; Eddy 1983). Under the direction of David Boynton, its capable college editor for those two separate fields, the publishing company of Holt, Rinehart and Winston opened the way not only for publication of the Spindler-edited Case Studies in Cultural Anthropology introduced in the late 1950s but to two parallel series, the Studies in Anthropological Method and the Case Studies in Education and Culture, as well as to descriptive case studies offered by other astute observers of the educational scene such as Phil Cusick, Philip Jackson, and Louis M. Smith mentioned earlier.

As an insider in the evolution of this descriptive complement to educational research, it would be comforting to report that we ourselves accounted for the great inroads that qualitative research has made in these three decades. But all I can say for sure is that as interest grew, the studies were there, ready and waiting. For all our efforts on behalf of qualitative research from outside the establishment (e.g., in the mid-1960s there was no real niche for educational researchers like myself in the American Educational Research Association, and the American Anthropological Association flatly denied early applications for Fellow status from several of us because our doctorates were in education), the real impetus for acceptance probably originated from *within* the ranks of those hard-nosed researchers whom we believed could never be dissuaded from their psychometric persuasion.

In the 1960s and 1970s, inspired and subsidized to a great extent by the same circumstances and agencies that opened the way for qualitative research, quantitative research in education also enjoyed a heyday. As its ranks and strengths increased, so did its skeptics. Any long tradition has its share of Young Turks, along with a predictable proportion of the perennially disenchanted. But educational psychology found another group of powerful critics among those most adept in measurement and statistical procedures. As my quantitatively oriented but qualitatively sympathetic friend and fellow Stanford alumnus Len Cahen used to say of the statistical approaches with which he worked, "We're shooting ants with cannons." In the obsession with measurement, method in educational research became an end in itself: formal guarantees of *statistical* significance assuaged personal misgivings as to significance of any other kind. Tests and measurements became the marching order of the day.

More recently, educational research has come of age to seek a better balance in its accepted ways of knowing. Among those who best understand the potential of rigorous design and measurement studies are a comforting number who also recognize some critical limitations in them. One of the worst things that could happen to qualitative approaches would be to have too-eager proponents step into the breach and boast that we can succeed where quantitative research has failed. At best, qualitatively oriented approaches offer a necessary complement to quantitatively oriented ones, not a substitute for them. At worst, they may prove, to the critical eyes of educational practitioners, little more than further demonstration of research irrelevance. We still do not have an adequate clientele for our work, and we still have paid too little attention to demonstrating how—or whether—our studies help.

To me, the attraction of qualitative approaches is that they offer other ways of looking. They invite us to look at things not ordinarily looked at, from perspectives not ordinarily taken. If we seldom offer "solutions," we should be able at least to offer useful insights. Under what circumstances, for example, do so-called slow or below average students become rapid learners? What knowledge *is* valued by youth who do not value school knowledge? If most young people of some identifiable ethnic group or social class drop out of school or college, how might we achieve some breakthrough in our thinking if we were to regard those who *remain* as deviant? What kinds of questions are we *not* encouraged to pursue in our efforts to understand schools and school processes? How do efforts to educate sometimes become miseducative when we become preoccupied with restricting rather than enhancing educational opportunity (e.g., by raising entrance requirements), or when we inadvertently lead students to feel less rather than more competent under too-careful tutelage?

When our insights help teachers, administrators, or even other researchers to understand the social systems in which they live and work—paradoxes, contradictions, antithetical goals, and all—we believe we are making a contribution, even though we cannot exactly point the way out of the dilemmas. And that raises the immediate question: Are these the kinds of concerns that bring you to this reading?

Why the Surge of Interest in Qualitative Research?

If you recently have become interested in qualitative approaches, the point of the preceding discussion is to remind you that you didn't exactly invent the idea, that 30 years ago what may seem today to be a natural inclination toward qualitative research would have been channeled differently, and that in following that inclination you still run the risk of being identified as a second-class researcher, especially if your interest in qualitative/descriptive work belies a fear of statistics or a refusal to gain sufficient grasp of design-rigorous approaches to understand the common research language of educators. On the other hand, if your interest stems from a healthy skepticism about aggregated numbers, a humanitarian concern for what happens to individuals both during research and as a consequence of it, or a sense or need to expand your own orientation beyond the texts and training you received in an earlier day, then allow me to say more.

My impression is that devotees of experimental design still remain conveniently unaware of the critical role of social context in classroom learning and teaching. Len Cahen, mentioned earlier, liked to underscore a major paradox of so-called educational experiments, that in practice we never have true *control* groups, only *treatment* groups. It would be unthinkable for us as educators to deny *any* group the opportunity to learn merely for the sake of experimentation. We would never dream of an educational experiment in which the control group was systematically denied access to basic instructional processes and materials. We are obliged to do our best for all. At most, our experiments are *treatments* in which the experimental group gets some small dose of something "new" or extra while a so-called control group receives "only" what was previously accepted as standard practice.

If ethics permitted, we might learn a great deal from even a few cases if we could deliberately *not* educate. What, for example, might we learn from observing children persistently denied opportunity to hear normal speech, or denied any form of instruction in reading or arithmetic? The nearest we come to such circumstances is to make detailed case studies of instances resulting from events beyond our control, just as we learn from brain-damaged individuals but stop short of damaging brains to satisfy the conditions of rigorous experimental design. We ordinarily learn all we can from *certain kinds* of cases, a reminder that qualitative approaches and small Ns are not unknown in educational research. Cowed by the powerful contempt for generalization that characterizes much scientific posturing, we limit unduly the extent to which we accept individual cases as legitimate sources of professional knowledge.[1] We quite forget how little encumbered we feel by similar conditions in our everyday lives as we constantly generalize from small samples, fully realizing that our generalizations or stereotypes may later prove incorrect or ill-founded. With awakened interest in qualitative research, the answer to a question once posed as implicit criticism, "But what we can learn from a single case?" is now more helpful: "All we can!"

Research Itself as a Problem

There is yet another facet to the dialogue about qualitative research. It concerns educators who are potential recruits to research but whose limited experiences and overwhelming anxieties have led them to wonder if they are, or ever can be, researchers. This disquieting speculation may come at the very moment when they realize that if they are going to pursue successful careers in higher education they must achieve and demonstrate research competence. For them, "qualitative" or "quantitative" is not the issue as much as whether they have sufficient grasp of the research process to be able to demonstrate competence in *any* form of it. They see research more like an exclusive club, in which the requirements for membership are vague and mysterious, than as an extension of normal human curiosity accompanied by systematic rather than casual observation. Qualitative research offers their only hope for claiming identity among the coveted ranks of researchers, not because they really see themselves as researchers but because they see no alternative.

Those suffering the most agony may not be new recruits in graduate study or doctoral students currently completing dissertations as much as those who have completed doctoral studies and for whom that initial experience at demonstrating research competence became a personal demonstration of quite the opposite—that they are not researchers at all. The supposed "opportunity" for pursuing further research has become instead a call for a performance they fear they cannot give.

I am concerned that the untoward interest we are witnessing in qualitative research is prompted by factors that have little to do with any particular style of research. What this heightened interest may reveal is that research or, more accurately, anxiety about research acts as a negative influence that erodes career effectiveness because too many educators accept the unexamined assumption and normative ideal that everyone in higher education is and ought to be a researcher.

Qualitative research should not have to serve as a forced alternative or reluctant compromise for people who by talent and inclination should not be doing research at all: There are other roles and other skills equally critical to any university's well-being. What qualitative research *may* be able to offer is an alternative for individuals whose problems are genuinely investigative rather than motivational in nature. If research in any form has become the bugaboo, qualitative approaches are probably not the answer, although a guiding question from that approach, "What's going on here?" may help one gain needed perspective.

ASPECTS OF PROBLEM FINDING

Now to the topic as promised, delimited to circumstances where the problem is not only research but researchable. How do researchers whose motives include a compelling urge to know and to help others understand educational processes (although they may also include personal concerns such as seeking promotion or professional recognition) go about initiating research? What are the sources for the problems they select for study? How do they know where to begin or what to look at?

Probably the most serious misunderstanding (and biggest disappointment) about qualitative research is the realization that, just as with quantitative approaches, *we bring our questions with us* to the research setting. We do not sit by, passively waiting to see what a setting is going to tell us. That is why we cannot respond satisfactorily to the plea, "Just tell me the steps..." and why it is difficult to answer even a seemingly straightforward question like, "What do I need to do as a participant observer?" Except for the most global advice, field techniques cannot be distilled and described independently from the questions guiding the researcher or the nature of the research setting. Nor can the art of problem posing be isolated from the complex web of personal motives and persuasions, professional strictures, prevailing paradigms, or current preoccupations inherent in each unique study.[2] Still, some general observations may be helpful.

Objectivity

Although the process in qualitative research of linking ideas in the observer's mind with what one observes is dialectical, with ideas informing observations and observations informing ideas, the first move belongs to the researcher. That point must be emphasized. Whatever constitutes the illusive quality called "objectivity," mindlessness is not part of it. Observation cannot proceed without a sense *in the observer's mind* of what one is to look at and for in qualitative any more than in quantitative research. The idea of "pure" description, referred to lightheartedly as "immaculate perception" (compare Beer 1973:49), cannot exist in fact. If you are tempted to insist that you expect to proceed as an unbiased observer, eager and obliged to observe everything, stop and reconsider. For only one classroom, or even one individual in it, could you—and for any reason would you ever want or need to—record *everything*?

With educational research's scare words "reliability" and "validity" lurking everywhere, and no seemingly satisfactory way to counter the charge that if we already know what we are looking for, how can we ever claim to be objective, I once portrayed myself as a Flatfooted Ethnographer, devoid of (i.e., uncontaminated by) theory, ready to surrender to any social setting what it told or showed me. In disbelief, a more theoretically inclined colleague offered to examine notes from a field study I was conducting to demonstrate how my observations reveal, however implicitly, that my fieldwork was guided by theory of some sort. Unfortunately for the evolution of my understanding of the nexus between scientific observations and scientific thinking about them, my colleague lost interest in the point he wanted to make. (Or was he unsure exactly how to go about making it, since the demonstration in practice would have been far more complex than the theoretical idea he was trying to illustrate?) He returned my notes after a perfunctory examination, commenting in passing that he was impressed with my notetaking and that although my written observations were not *absolutely* atheoretical, they were as near to it as he could imagine. I mistakenly took his words as a confirmation of my studied objectivity (i.e., theorylessness).

What actually may have impressed my colleague was that my notes reveal adequate appreciation of the difference between what I observe and inferences I make about what the behavior may "mean" to observer or observed. Gilbert Ryle's distinction between "winks" and "twitches" notwithstanding (as discussed in Geertz 1973:6 ff.), in practice if I record that someone "scowls" I recognize that what I have observed is some kind of facial contortion and that the meaning has been imputed. The less certainty I feel about my interpretation, the more closely I distinguish behavior from inference, carefully cautioning myself (or a reader, if I draw upon the notes in subsequent write-up) when I offer my interpretation but recognize that it is not necessarily the only one or even the most appropriate.

Recognizing the difference between observed and inferred behavior is probably the most critical aspect of so-called objectivity for an observer to make and to convey to readers. Egon Guba and Yvonna Lincoln (1981:328) have helped clarify the issue by suggesting that we direct attention to the "confirmability of the data" rather than become distracted with efforts to assess the "objectivity of the inquirer."

Neutrality

For a long time I harbored the misconception that neutrality was another essential element in descriptive research, that to be "fair" one had to regard every human with equal esteem—the anthropological preference for deferred judgment taken to the extreme. An experienced fieldworker (John Connolly, in this case) raised the issue of whether one really needs to be neutral in order to be objective. I've never completely sorted out what being objective means, especially in the subjective and sensitive business of humans observing and interpreting the behavior of other humans, but I was relieved to realize that having likes or dislikes—a rather human quality in which I occasionally overindulge—did not preclude me from doing fieldwork.

I do recall my initial dismay that Jules Henry had allowed himself too free a rein in presenting his "passionate ethnography" of American society, *Culture Against Man* (Henry 1963), but I have since come to appreciate how personal preferences sometimes provide anthropologists the impetus for rendering their ethnographic accounts. The problem, for further illustration, is not that Colin Turnbull (1972) saw little to admire among the Ik—although he has been roundly criticized for his candid portrayal not only of the people but of his disaffection toward them—but that anthropologists too seldom *admit* to strong feelings about those they study unless their feelings are positive.

I take deep and genuine interest in the people and setting I write about. I also have learned to recognize and to appreciate in those feelings a source of energy for conducting and completing my studies. My feelings are not always positive, and I have never known any group of people that did not have its share of rogues and rascals, but I cannot imagine initiating a study in which I had no personal feelings, felt no concern for the humans whose lives touched mine, or failed to find in my feelings a vital source of personal energy.

Theoretical/Conceptual Orientation

Were it considered essential in anthropology to declare firmly on behalf of one theoretical school or another before conducting fieldwork, I might have made a more sustained effort to locate myself within whatever seemed the most compatible (or least restrictive) theoretical orientation. But I'm chary of "-isms" and "-ists." If I sometimes admire the ability of others who can pigeonhole anthropologists into one camp or another on the basis of their published accounts, I am far less enthusiastic when they stick some label on me. If, for example, functionalism in the extreme produces circular explanations of societies in which the customs all fit together too well, are there moderate functionalists who do not exceed reasonable bounds in drawing upon functional interpretations of the societies they study? If I am a functionalist, am I therefore also a structuralist, or are the two positions antithetical? Am I perforce denied *any* appreciation for ecology because I happen not to stress cultural ecology in my interpretations?

Happily, I am free of having to accept one and reject all other Grand Theories in anthropology. Anthropologists and educators alike, together with historians, strike me as underencumbered with concerns for Grand Theory; economists, psychologists, and sociologists, by contrast, seem theory-compulsive. If I am not bound by big theories, however, I must be guided at least by some middle-range theory or conceptual approaches characteristic of anthropological work. What guides my research so that I am willing to lay claim for its anthropological orientation?

In the growing educator receptivity to qualitative research in the 1960s and 1970s, it did not seem to matter which studies and approaches were anthropologically "pure" and which were not, particularly to an educator audience for whom the whole idea of accepting observational or naturalistic studies was something of a novelty. Nonetheless, new questions were being raised for some of us who wondered about educator "adaptations" of discipline-based approaches. Could one distinguish an anthropologically oriented case from cases oriented by other disciplines? Are discipline-oriented studies different from methodologically oriented ones (e.g., participant observer studies)?

A major concern for the anthropologically oriented among us, the consequence of a disregard for disciplinary boundaries sometimes evident in the work of educational researchers, was that the term "ethnography" increasingly was being employed as a generic label for all field-based research. Researchers who were only borrowing a fieldwork technique or two began slapping the label "ethnography" on virtually every completed account. A critical question arose: "What might get lost if educational researchers begin to regard ethnographic research as synonymous with qualitative research, rather than as one particular form of it?"

The critical difference appeared to be not in the way research was conducted, but in what ethnographers customarily look at and for, and whether that is the same as what other researchers look at and for. At risk of being lost was the overriding anthropological concern for *cultural interpretation*.

The resolution was not to seek consensus on a common approach and purpose in conducting field studies, but rather to make sure we did not lose sight of the different perspectives that we could obtain if disciplinary lines were known, recognized, and—under customary circumstances—adhered to rather than ignored. Most assuredly, we did not need to have every qualitative study culminate in a cultural interpretation! Equally, however, we did not want to lose whatever insight can be achieved from an anthropological perspective by ignoring or blurring that traditional ethnographic preoccupation.

Heretofore, ethnography had been under the sole proprietorship of anthropologists, so much so that even ethnographically inclined sociologists studiously avoided the label itself. If an occasional ethnographer drifted a bit, most accounts stayed in the mainstream of cultural anthropology, and the cross-cultural nature of traditional fieldwork invariably precipitated cultural comparisons or frameworks even in those rare instances where the setting itself was not dramatically cross-cultural (e.g., in Jules Henry's or Margaret Mead's writings on American society).

In the 1960s and 1970s, accounts and individuals proclaiming ethnographic affiliation began to assemble under the banner of qualitative research. We realized that we had not given sufficient thought to discussing what ethnography was, how that label implies certain commitments on the researcher's part, or how ethnography provides focus for the kinds of problems one might address and the kinds of interpretations one might expect. In our own way, several of us sought to address a question posed early and cogently by Frederick Erickson, "What Makes School Ethnography 'Ethnographic'?"—a topic that continues to prompt a healthy dialogue and divergence of opinion (compare Erickson 1973; L. Smith 1979; G. Spindler 1974, 1982; Spindler and Spindler 1987; Wolcott 1975, 1982a, 1987).

To anyone embarking on qualitative research who is unsure what ethnography is or whether a proposed study can properly be called ethnographic, I offer two bits of advice that can be generalized as guidelines for any qualitative approach. First, *do not* use the label ethnography—or any other label that implicates a particular style or disciplinary tradition—until you are sure that you have correctly identified that tradition and are conversant with its techniques and with appropriate and exemplary samples of completed work. Second, *do* familiarize yourself with the wide range of labels and approaches that qualitative researchers employ. Examine studies produced by people working in the various traditions, analyze how they approach their research, and proceed from there.

The best way to achieve that familiarity is to read completed accounts of the sort one intends to produce. Qualitative researchers, like all researchers, are inclined toward lofty pronouncements when telling others how research studies "should" be conducted. Would-be ethnographers need to read ethnographies, would-be case study authors need to read completed case studies, and so forth.

A developing literature in qualitative research methods also provides an easily accessible resource shelf. Anthropological approaches, for example, are well introduced by Agar (1980), discussed in detail in Pelto and Pelto (1978), and applied to research in classrooms by Burnett (1973) and in schools and to education more generally by the Spindlers (G. Spindler 1982; Spindler and Spindler 1987). A sociological classic that described and presented a strong case for the "discovery of grounded theory" is a monograph by that title authored by Glaser and Strauss (1967). Bogdan and Biklin (1982) and Jaeger (1987) present useful introductions to qualitative research for educators; Everhart (forthcoming) provides a summary and critique of qualitative research focused on educational administration. For applications of what the authors call "naturalistic" approaches in education, particularly in evaluation research, see Guba and Lincoln (1981). To highlight educationally relevant differences among these approaches, see a symposium entitled "Teaching Fieldwork to Educational Researchers" in the Fall 1983 issue of the *Anthropology and Education Quarterly* (Volume 14, No. 3).

Some educational researchers today elect among loosely defined styles such as case study or participant observer study; others work in carefully specified traditions such as phenomenology, ethnomethodology, or ethnography. (For a brief summary of different styles of qualitative research, see Wolcott 1982a.) Unless you want to make (and are prepared to defend) the claim that single-handedly you invented your approach to educational research, or that you are uninfluenced by the work of anyone before you (in spite of my efforts here to demonstrate that the call to qualitative research in your professional life is rather little a matter of your own doing), you should be well informed about the course of research on which you are about to embark. These waters are not totally uncharted; don't inadvertently repeat or reinvent what has been done when so much remains to do.

The Ethnographic Approach as Example

The comforting thing about using ethnography as one's approach to educational research, taking one's bearings from the discipline of anthropology that one's inspiration from pioneers like the Spindlers, is that one thereby makes a declaration to be working in a particular scholarly tradition. Although this charter is a broad one, ethnographers—even those who define their areas of expertise in terms of geographical region (e.g., sub-Saharan Africa, Oceania)—always know what they are looking for, and that is to provide explanations of human behavior in cultural terms. Anthropologists invariably locate culture among the peoples they study, not because it is lying about waiting to be discovered but because it is the anthropologist's responsibility to put it there. Anthropologists do not "discover" culture as much as they "impose" it on (or, in Goodenough's [1976] better phrase, "attribute it to") the members of the society they are studying. It is hardly a coincidence, therefore, that ethnographers always "find" culture; rather, their work is not complete until they make culture explicit in the social behavior they have observed.

Broad as it is, the culture concept offers form and focus to ethnographic research. Employing culture as my orienting concept locates a manageable conceptual level somewhere between the illusive abstractions of Grand Theory and the nagging concreteness of everyday events. Many scholars fault the culture concept for being too nebulous to serve the needs of theory-building. Perhaps that is what I find attractive about it: the concept guides observational studies of human behavior without implicating a particular theory. My sentiments are with those who favor cutting the culture concept down to size rather than with those anxious to see it pumped up to greater heights, but the most valuable role the concept plays is the dialogue it provokes concerning its definition.

I am hardly going to insist that cultural analysis should be the driving force behind all qualitative research: cultural analysis is *a* way of seeing, not *the* way of seeing. But I do urge (insist, really) that the term "ethnography" be reserved for studies in which culture is the orienting concept. We might call that the "culturally oriented" approach in qualitative research. It is the approach I follow. I confess to being converted to it, but I do not proselyte on its behalf. My commitment probably blinds me from seeing certain other aspects of human behavior, but it also provides a strong sense of what to look at, and for, in any particular setting, even if I have trouble stating what that is in the abstract. However, in an effort to pin down ideas and provide examples, let me try.

Working my own set of questions from broad to specific, and reflecting my concern for cultural interpretation, a basic question to focus my observations in a particular setting is the seemingly straightforward one already noted, "What is going on here?" That question quickly bifurcates into two perspectives dichotomized in anthropology's distinction between etic (i.e., outsider) and emic (i.e., insider) views. What is going on in terms of behavior as I, the presumably more detached and objective outsider, see it? What is going on in terms of the way various insiders see it?

When I am allowed the luxury of giving full attention to cultural interpretation—particularly to examining aspects of cultural acquisition, my keenest scholarly interest at present—other questions come quickly to mind. What do various individuals in a particular setting have to know to make their cultural system work? How has each person acquired the necessary cultural competence? If my research must be related to some pressing educational problem as defined by someone else, there are underlying questions I might pose linking actions to purposes: Does the system achieve what people say they want? What problems are resolved; what problems are created? In what ways does the microsystem reflect the underlying ethos of a larger macrocultural system?

For me, these are persistent quetions, what Malinowski would (I trust) describe as "foreshadowed problems." They help set an initial focus so that even at the outset I don't feel I must observe "everything." They also give me a starting point from which to ponder further questions relevant to a particular setting. You are welcome to use them to initiate your own research, although I would be surprised if you found them exactly the questions with which you would start. From the beginning, our approaches differ—yours and mine— because we would not attend to exactly the same problem.

Theoretical/Conceptual Orientation: Further Discussion

What is critical for understanding qualitative approaches in general is to recognize that the function the culture concept (and my particular set of questions relating to it) plays for me in conducting ethnographically oriented research must be filled by some comparable concept or theory in any approach. Neither method nor setting provides direction: one's guiding theory, or concepts, or questions, or ideas, or hunches (it matters not at all how we call them, only that we have them) must do that.

The more traditionally defined or discipline-based approaches to qualitative research have their conceptual baggage in place, thereby offering the advantage of well-established procedures gained at the cost of prior methodological or conceptual commitment. Conversely, in following a case study or participant observation approach, one is freed from methodological constraint, but that freedom is won at the cost of structure.

Lack of constraint should not be mistaken for greater objectivity; more likely, it ought to portend chaos by rendering observers impotent, overwhelmed by the complexity of any setting in which they immerse themselves. But researchers no more need to be immobilized by the complexity of everyday social life than are the everyday humans who live it. We all go about our activities attending to some small part of the hubbub about us and ignoring most of it. We are all theory builders, and rather effective ones at that. Any researcher who claims only to be "going in to have a look around" can offer a more powerful rationale, provided that no penalty is attached to revealing what you *think* you are looking for. My field notes must, in the end, yield to the charge that the observer who made them did indeed have a sufficient idea of what he was up to that he could get on with it. No compelling and intrusive Grand Theory, but a conscious effort on my part to discern and describe patterns of thought and behavior revealing of an underlying ethos, a consensus about what "ought to be" that enables us collectively to cope with what is.

"I am a camera," reflected novelist Christopher Isherwood in *Goodbye to Berlin*, "with its shutter open, quite passive, recording, not thinking." A passive, unthinking camera must be aimed and shuttered, nonetheless, and the better ethnographers, like the better novelists or photographers, draw our attention for the very reason that they draw our attention. The critical first step in even the most doggedly descriptive research is to make sufficiently explicit (if only to oneself) the sense of problem one is taking *into* the field so that purposeful observation can begin. The problem derives from the researcher, not the researched, even if the original problem identification is subsequently abandoned during ensuing stages of problem evolution, redefinition, and refinement. No social setting, cultural event, or individual ever "tells" an observer how to proceed with an inquiry; the answer is contained in, and only in, viewer purposes.

As with the term "culture," the term "theory" also had to be cut down to size before it became helpful to me. Theory needed to become something sufficiently mundane that I could recognize it in ordinary human lives—my own included— rather than something possible only with the genius of a Darwin (for a successful instance) or a Freud (for a less successful one) or the sociological persistence of a Weber or Durkheim. The explanation that won me over to the ubiquity of theory came in words attributed to William James and called up in Michael Agar's delightful introduction to ethnography, *The Professional Stranger* (1980:23). The telling idea is that one cannot even pick up rocks in a field without a theory. In other words—if the idea needs others' words—behind every conscious human action lies an idea of what we think we are about. *Voila!* At that level, even *I* am a theory builder, not because I am a natural-born scientist, but because *to be human is to be a theory builder*. And "sciencing"—including even largely descriptive endeavors like ethnography or narrative history—is merely being more explicit about certain theories we hold regarding some small sector(s) of human behavior, recognizing distinctions between what *is* and what *ought to be* in some few facets of special interest to us that we might not otherwise attend to so carefully in normal social intercourse.

I've often wondered if Malinowski (1922 [1984:9]) didn't throw fieldworkers an unintended curve with his early pronouncement about fieldwork (in a day when there were few pronouncements to guide neophytes) that "foreshadowed problems are the main endowment of a scientific thinker" but "preconceived ideas are pernicious." Rather than extol students to the positive, creative, and even aggressive act of foreshadowing,[3] Malinowski's words have been misappropriated to serve warning against the danger of ideas well formulated rather than his intended caution against ideas rigidly held. The effect has been not only to make the difference between foreshadowed problem and preconceived idea seem real but to make ideas appear the nemesis in observational science.

We do no violence to objectivity by knowing what we want to look at, by locating ourselves in a setting where we are most likely to see it, by being well acquainted with the work and procedures of others whose methods or focus are of possible relevance to our proposed research, by having theoretical/conceptual frameworks within which to couch our observations, or by having hunches about how we think a system works. We may even hold the arrogant assumption that we correctly have anticipated the answer to what we have set out to know. "Say what you choose," states Wittgenstein, "so long as it does not prevent you from seeing the facts" (quoted in Barnes 1982).

Fortunate indeed is the qualitative researcher who can garner support for a proposed study without having to specify more than the broad direction in which the search will begin. The demands of contemporary proposal writing in the field of education are best suited to studies in which method is both paramount and, somehow, magically disengaged from the methodologist. I have more sympathy than advice for qualitative researchers whose proposals face strong resistance due to their necessary open-endedness, except for the opinion stated earlier that, when pushed to it, we *can* be more explicit about our "foreshadowed problems" and we *can* strengthen our cases (and our cause) by locating our projected studies both methodologically and substantively in relation to the work of others.

If, as Harold Brown (1979:120) insists in his discussion of the new philosophy of science, "concepts, propositions and observations are the elements from which scientific theories are built," then qualitative researchers work with the same ingredients as quantitative ones. The difference as *I* like to portray it is that qualitative research seems more interactive and creative. I recognize, however, that quantitatively oriented researchers argue similarly on behalf of their approaches. If so, maybe we could admit to them that qualitative research is at times tedious and boring. We, too, reach "dead ends." We, too, overstudy the same (usually acquiescent) phenomena. We also devote a lot of time, as detractors are quick to point out, to "making the obvious obvious."

On the other hand, a closer look at what passes as quantitative research— what those so-called number-crunchers or "hard" scientists are really doing rather than what they *say* they are doing—might leave us wondering whether the qualitative–quantitative distinction is ever warranted. Even the most qualitatively oriented researchers number their pages; some who perceive of themselves as quantitative researchers offer little more in claiming that their data are truly "ordered."[4] Not even the most objective of quantifiers can transcend the fact that, regardless of the procedures that may follow from it, the initial determination of problem focus must be entirely subjective.

The Scientific Method

On the wall of my office hangs a sign gleaned from words attributed by anthropologist Roger Keesing to biologist Paul Weiss, "Nobody who followed the scientific method ever discovered anything interesting" (Keesing and Keesing 1971:10). It is hardly surprising that a biologist's comment about the scientific method is offered as solace for anthropologists torn between wanting their discipline to be the most scientific of the humanities and the most humanistic of the sciences. Except when talking with students, or with colleagues outside their discipline, anthropologists, particularly cultural ones, talk about method hardly at all. In small part that is because fieldwork methods, especially in the early stages that lend most easily to recounting, tend to be rather everyday ("hanging around," "talking to people," "getting a sense of what is going on"); in larger part, it is because anthropologists are absorbed in what they are trying to understand, not whether they are going about it properly. As George Homans (1962) observed years ago, research is a matter of strategies, not of morals.

Nonetheless, anthropologists—and qualitative researchers in general—do seem to become self-conscious whenever method is at issue. Perhaps it is time to question more systematically whether *any* scientists really follow the scientific method and, in ethnographic style, to begin to look more closely at how science actually proceeds (see, for example, studies by Fleck 1979; Latour and Woolgar 1986). "Scientific method" provides a convenient gloss for referring to a process that, on close examination, is quite vulnerable to human judgment and social construction. It is the insistent demand of outsiders for the guided tour of the laboratory, the formula for discovery, the "Just tell me the steps I should follow...," that traps researchers of all persuasions into portraying as a neat, linear sequence what is in fact a dialectical process in which ideas inform observations, observations inform ideas, and all *critical* judgments are made by humans.

Honing In

For descriptive social research, in which one is never sure where to draw the boundaries of relevant context, the critical task is not, as neophyte observers often believe, to collect everything or to try to record everything; rather, it is to try to get *rid* of almost everything, of honing the topic and sharpening the focus, so that increasingly there is *less* to be concerned with, and thus what is of concern can be observed with greater attention. If one's perspective is discipline-based, established guidelines provide an initial depth-of-field until the researcher is better able to decide where and how to pinpoint attention. For more open-ended approaches, a useful guiding question that continues to be refined even into the analysis and write-up is, "What is this a case of?" To that end, the answer resides with the researcher and with the ideas guiding the information-seeking, not with the characteristics intrinsic in the setting.

To me, the more convincing among descriptive researchers bring the reader along as they call attention to one thing rather than another in unfolding their accounts. Researchers must know something of themselves as storytellers. They also must know something of the preferences of different audiences for the appropriate ratio of information to explanation (see the discussion by A. Smith 1964:257–258). The balance to be achieved is to provide enough of the stuff out of which observations are made (it is tempting to call such stuff "data," but that label seems a bit pompous for our unprocessed field notes; "data source" might be more appropriate) that readers feel they not only have a sense of the setting but also have sufficient information that they can take issue with the observer's interpretation or offer alternative interpretations of their own.[5] The task is to strike a balance between extremes of telling too little and telling too much. Again, there is no precise formula. For different audiences, as well as for different raconteurs, too little embellishment for one may be too much for another.

One of the pervasive problems in getting classroom teachers and practicing administrators to view and to use qualitative studies as a resource is their preference for prescription and their correspondingly low tolerance for description. Typically, educators feel *too* familiar with the everyday life in schools that qualitative research depicts. "We already know how it is!" the cry goes up. "Tell us what we should do about it."

A basic tenet of descriptive research is that people in a setting do *not* necessarily "know how it is": seemingly everyday or routine behavior is worthy of scrutiny. The obvious is not so obvious after all. We want people to look more carefully, to analyze more critically, and to recognize that things are probably more rather than less complex than they seem, even as we search for ways to reduce that complexity enough to render understandable accounts.

Nonetheless, we must pare our descriptive accounts lest no one reads them at all. Readers often skip quickly through carefully detailed descriptions, impatiently forging ahead to summaries or recommendations rather than availing themselves of the engagement we hoped to precipitate. Our efforts to be "wholistic" present one of our biggest challenges, nicely captured in the whimsical title of a paper Larry Reynolds presented to a meeting of educators more than a decade ago, "Who Wants to Read a 600-page Ethnography?" So the final problem in the process of qualitative research is frequently an unexpected one: presentation.

Completing the Account

Although I stress that qualitative research is an interactive process that begins before one identifies a problem (and continues after the completion of a final draft as we ponder our interpretations), I can identify three stages in which a different activity is dominant: problem finding (which continues into the write-up as problem redefining), fieldwork, and organizing and presenting the final account(s).

Each major task appears formidable until we confront and recognize the magnitude of the next in sequence, when what already has been accomplished appears easy compared to what lies ahead. But no task can be dismissed lightly. Would-be researchers who cannot acquire a "sense of problem" are perforce barred from ever embarking upon the research sequence; we all know graduate students who struggled for months to identify a manageable topic (or, more likely, a manageable aspect of one). As their mentors, we are accountable in part for the problem by failing to underscore the modesty of most dissertation research and by holding up as models studies produced by established researchers at the peak of their careers.

Once a problem is sufficiently in place to allow fieldwork to begin, identifying a research possibility may seem "small potatoes" compared to a new set of tasks that includes site selection and access (the familiar "gaining entrée and maintaining rapport"); selecting appropriately among fieldwork techniques (participant observation and interviewing, in their almost infinite variation); attending to problems of professional ethics and personal reciprocity; arranging as necessary the logistics of transportation, food, lodging, and use of recording equipment; and somehow managing to keep all this secondary to the business of observing, recording, and analyzing a constantly shifting mass of human actions and meanings.

Yet the realization that the period of observations must come to a close, the note-making and early information-sorting give way to a major effort at organizing, analyzing, writing, and editing a final account, can make even the time-and-energy demands of fieldwork appear attractive by comparison. Experienced fieldworkers know the strong "pull" that a field setting can exert once writing looms as the next task. One must guard against the temptation to prolong field observations as an excuse to avoid writing.

For all the talent required of the researcher as conceptualizer in problem finding and as participant observer during fieldwork, the final stage requires the researcher to be a storyteller who can present information in a sufficiently engaging way that readers will read it (or, less frequently in educational research, viewers will view it). We do not have abbreviated findings that can be summarized succinctly or statically recapitulated in charts or appendixes. Too seldom do colleagues make an effort to locate their work in the efforts of others (for a notable exception, see L. Smith 1979). But to render their potential, our studies need to be read in the original and in full. If our accounts are not read, our efforts are essentially for naught.

Recognizing that a well-written account is the ultimate end product of most qualitative research, qualitative researchers ought to "think" writing from the outset. There is no reason that problems of presentation should catch anyone unaware, no reason why statements of purpose cannot also include statements about intended audiences and the probable format for presentation (e.g., working paper, journal article [which journal?], chapter, monograph). I encourage students proposing descriptive studies to provide not only a tentative Table of Contents but also to indicate the number of pages they intend to devote to each section. Page count per se is not the concern; I want students to get some feel for distributing their initial efforts and final page count among such critical components stating the problem, describing fieldwork procedures, citing and incorporating *relevant* literature, presenting an account with adequately thick description, providing analysis and interpretation, and, as disciplinary (and institutional) traditions require, concluding with a statement of implications for practice and/or future research.

The universal problem of data display in scientific research has its own peculiar paradox in qualitative research. We collect a huge corpus of precious descriptive material (e.g., the 5,000 single-spaced typed pages of field notes and interviews in the study conducted by Becker et al. 1961:30), yet in the final account, the less such raw, primary material we put before the reader, the more effective the presentation. (Classic life histories like *Sun Chief* [Leo Simmons] or *Children of Sanchez* [Oscar Lewis] that seem at first blush to provide exceptions actually prove the rule, since these "informants' own stories" are skillfully edited accounts at the "invisible" hand of the anthropologist.) In the end we run roughshod over our most tangible accomplishment—the accumulation of notebook after notebook of finely recorded detail—by editing, abridging, or deleting the very material that is the basis of our endeavor. We eliminate repetitious material in order to spare our readers, thereby leaving to faith that instances we report reflect discernible patterns observed during fieldwork.

Malinowski's advice to ethnographers to prepare a draft while still in the field is good advice for any qualitative researcher: Begin the writing early, while still having access to settings and informants. His concern that fieldworkers might be unable later to fill in the gaps is probably not as critical to researchers in contemporary educational settings that typically are only a telephone call away, but the advice also reminds us to couple writing *with* fieldwork rather than to regard it as something begun only when field research is completed.

To anyone who neither has done prior fieldwork nor written a scholarly monograph, however, the idea of involving oneself simultaneously in two such all-consuming tasks may be unthinkable. Let me confess that I returned from my first fieldwork with only the faintest idea of how I would organize my account. I had decided that a major section describing the village should precede a second section in which I would introduce the school. My organizational strategy, simple as it was, seemed necessary because village and school differed so dramatically that I felt it necessary to describe them separately before introducing the tension between them (see Wolcott 1964, 1967). That was the only idea that guided me as I began to organize my thoughts and notes. Not until much later, when writing had become a regular (and a satisfying rather than an anxiety-provoking) activity, could I follow Malinowski's advice. I repeat it now with the caveat that although the advice is good, a neophyte researcher may find it just one more unexpected problem to be found in qualitative research.

CONCLUSION

Somewhere among my personal store of guiding proverbs and cautioning clichés is the adage that the biggest step one can take toward finding an answer is to begin with a well-formulated question. My purpose here has been to draw attention to what I have heard George Spindler describe as "the 'problem' problem." In particular I have emphasized that research settings do not beckon or speak to qualitative researchers in some mysterious way different from how quantitative researchers approach their work. Problems do not "emerge" in natural settings without critical input on behalf of the observer who identifies them any more than laboratory experiments conduct themselves independently from those who design them. For scientists of any persuasion, as Harold Brown

(1979:81) has observed, "the knowledge, beliefs and theories we already hold play a fundamental role in determining what we perceive." Rather than ignoring relevant work done by others, claiming to be theoryless, failing to recognize the influence of what is current and vogue, or denying the critical input of our own experience, intuition, and hunches in order to lay claim to so-called scientific objectivity, we need to identify as many as we can of these elements and their possible impact and then muster all our professional and personal resources in posing our problems and selecting our settings and subjects.

Our professional commitment already narrows our field of vision by making *educational* concern a focus. We hardly apologize for a lack of objectivity on that score; indeed, we are envied by other social scientists whose charters are even broader. An anthropologist colleague once commented, "Educators are lucky! They always know what they should be studying."

Alas! The educational researcher's charter is still too broad: virtually anyone claiming to do educational research can study virtually anything. We lack what Brown (1979:101) identified as the fundamental requirement for founding a true science of education: a basis for deciding what research problems are worth pursuing.

Soothsayers anxious to foretell an impending paradigm shift in educational research might better spend their time assessing whether we ever achieved a clearly identifiable paradigm to shift from. As a solitary researcher, however, you have not created the problems that characterize the haphazard and essentially noncumulative nature of educational research, and it is unlikely that single handedly you will greatly exacerbate or markedly reduce them. Neither did you invent the social system in professional education that implores you to be a researcher, any more than you came independently to the conclusion that qualitative research is the approach you should pursue. You do, however, need to know the disciplinary tradition in which you are working or, if you must follow the educator proclivity to be eclectic, at least to know what you are being eclectic about!

Qualitative approaches are not without their pitfalls as well as their possibilities. Acquiescing to the seeming objectivity of measurement as we do, I think qualitative research will continue to play second fiddle to quantitative approaches, although their relative contributions to our understanding may be at par. Any individual claiming competence as an educational researcher ought to be politically astute enough to recognize when personality or circumstances require rigid problem specification in advance, precise measurement procedures during, and/or acceptable levels of statistical significance when reporting an investigation.

What I have found encouraging among educational researchers in recent years is their appreciation for more diverse ways to pose questions and to accumulate evidence. It has become fashionable not only to look at what occurs in classrooms but to look as well at less formal educational settings (e.g., parent–child or older sibling–younger sibling interactions, work groups, casual play, adults as learners) in addition to contriving experiences and experiments that emphasize certain aspects of human interaction and learning but ignore most of them.

To the qualitatively oriented researcher, the circumstances of everyday life are filled not with extraneous variables to be controlled but with social contexts to be understood. No matter how basic or "purely descriptive" you may want your work to be, recognize that you bring your question(s) with you to the setting(s) you intend to observe. You won't find your problem there; you must take it there in order to investigate the connections between idea and observation. That is the way of all inquiry.

NOTES

This chapter was originally drafted in 1986 during the author's residence in Thailand as a senior Fulbright Scholar on leave from the University of Oregon. Appreciation is extended to the Thailand-United States Educational Foundation and to members of the Faculty of Education at Kasetsart University, Bangkok, who not only proved gracious hosts but raised basic questions about qualitative research that prompted this writing. Drs. Kitiya Phornsadja, John R. Jungck, and Edwin R. Bingham offered provocative insights at various stages of the writing. Norman Delue facilitated the original editing with newly acquired skill at the word processor.

1. The phrase "contempt for generalization" and its prevalence in and impact on scientific thinking was suggested by Professor Bingham.

2. Professor Jungck informs me that in mathematics, and more recently in physics, two areas in which problem finding is more discrete than in the social sciences, one now sees the phrase "problem posing" (see, for example, Brouwer 1984; Brown and Walter 1983; Walter and Brown 1977). More recently the problem-posing approach has been brought to the attention of biology teachers (Jungck 1985). The idea of "problem-posing education" appears earlier in Paulo Freire's *Pedagogy of the Oppressed* (1970).

3. "But the Ethnographer has not only to spread his nets in the right place, and wait for what will fall into them. He must be an active huntsman, and drive his quarry into them and follow it up to its most inaccessible lairs" (Malinowski 1922 [1984:8]).

4. During my stay in Thailand, a visiting sociologist showed me a questionnaire being used for an "opportunistic" world sample inquiry into career choices. Respondents were asked to make subtle distinctions between "some importance" and "little importance" on global factors like "work independently" or "chance to help people." Admittedly, I am not impressed by this kind of research. I was flabbergasted when the visitor expressed delight at our meeting because, he explained, "I always enjoy talking to you qualitative types." It never occurred to me that he would consider himself a quantitative researcher, although I felt a sense of relief that he did not claim to be a qualitative one.

5. Becker et al. (1961:231) refer to this as the "discounting process" through which readers themselves correct, adjust, invalidate, or even deem inapplicable the information and interpretations supplied by researchers.

REFERENCES

Agar, Michael
1980   The Professional Stranger: An Informal Guide to Ethnography. New York: Academic Press.
Barnes, Barry
1982   T. S. Kuhn and Social Science. New York: Columbia University Press.
Becker, Howard S., Blance Geer, and Everett C. Hughes
1968   Making the Grade: The Academic Side of College Life. New York: John Wiley.
Becker, Howard S., Blance Geer, Everett C. Hughes, and Anselm L. Strauss
1961   Boys in White. Chicago: University of Chicago Press.
Beer, C. G.
1973   A view of birds. In Minnesota Symposia on Child Psychology, A. D. Pick, ed. Vol. 7, pp. 46-86. Minneapolis: University of Minnesota Press.
Bogdan, Robert and Sari K. Biklin
1982   Qualitative Research for Education. Boston: Allyn and Bacon.
Brouwer, Wytze
1984   Problem posing physics: A conceptual approach. *American Journal of Physics* 52(7):602-607.
Brown, Harold I.
1979   Perception, Theory and Commitment: The New Philosophy of Science. University of Chicago Press. [Originally published in 1977.]
Brown, Stephen I. and Marion I. Walter
1983   The Art of Problem Posing. Philadelphia: Franklin Institute Press.
Burnett, Jacquetta Hill
1973   Event description and analysis in the microethnography of urban classrooms. In Cultural Relevance and Educational Issues: Readings in Anthropology and Education, F. A. Ianni and Edward Storey, eds., pp. 287-303. Boston: Little, Brown.
Eddy, Elizabeth M.
1983   Review Essay: The Anthropology and Education Series, Solon T. Kimball, General Editor. *Anthropology and Education Quarterly* 14(2):141-147.
1985   Theory, research, and application in educational anthropology. *Anthropology and Education Quarterly* 16(2):83-104.
Erickson, Frederick
1973   What makes school ethnography 'ethnographic'? [Council on] *Anthropology and Education Newsletter* 4(2):10-19. [Revised and reprinted in *Anthropology and Education Quarterly* 15(1):51-66, 1984.]
Everhart, Robert B.
Forth- Qualitative methods in research on educational administration. In Handbook
com-   of Research on Educational Administration, Norman Boyan, ed. Washing-
ing   ton, DC: American Educational Research Association.
Fleck, L.
1979   Genesis and Development of a Scientific Fact. Chicago: University of Chicago Press. [Originally published in 1935 in German.]
Freire, P.
1973   Pedagogy of the Oppressed. New York: Seabury.

Geertz, Clifford
    1973   Thick description: Toward an interpretive theory of culture. In The Interpre-
            tation of Cultures. New York: Basic Books.
Glaser, Barney G. and Anselm L. Strauss
    1967   The Discovery of Grounded Theory: Strategies for Qualitative Research.
            New York: Aldine.
Goodenough, Ward H.
    1976   Multiculturalism as the normal human experience. Anthropology and Educa-
            tion Quarterly 7(4):4–7.
Guba, Egon G. and Yvonna S. Lincoln
    1981   Effective Evaluation: Improving the Usefulness of Evaluation Results Through
            Responsive and Naturalistic Approaches. San Francisco: Jossey-Bass.
Henry, Jules
    1963   Culture Against Man. New York: Random House.
Homans, George
    1962   Sentiments and Activities: Essays in Social Science. New York: Free Press of
            Glencoe.
Jaeger, Richard M., ed.
    1987   Complementary Methods for Research in Education. Washington, DC:
            American Educational Research Association.
Jungck, John R.
    1985   A problem posing approach to biology education. American Biology Teacher
            47(5):264–266.
Keesing, Roger M. and Felix M. Keesing
    1971   New Perspectives in Cultural Anthropology. New York: Holt, Rinehart and
            Winston.
Latour, Bruno and Steve Woolgar
    1986   Laboratory Life: The Construction of Scientific Facts, 2nd ed. Princeton, NJ:
            Princeton University Press.
Malinowski, Bronislaw
    1984   Argonauts of the Western Pacific: An Account of Native Enterprise and
            Adventure in the Archipelagoes of Melanesian New Guinea. Prospect
            Heights, IL: Waveland Press. [First published in 1922.]
Pelto, Pertti and Gretel Pelto
    1978   Anthropological Research: The Structure of Inquiry, 2nd ed. New York:
            Cambridge University Press.
Smith, Alfred G.
    1964   The Dionysian innovation. American Anthropologist 66:251–265.
Smith, Louis M.
    1979   An evolving logic of participant observation, educational ethnography, and
            other case studies. Review of Research in Education 6:316–377.
Spindler, George D.
    1984   Roots revisited: Three decades of perspective. Anthropology and Education
            Quarterly 15(1):3–10.
Spindler, George D., ed.
    1955   Education and Anthropology. Stanford, CA: Stanford University Press.
    1987   Education and Cultural Process: Toward an Anthropology of Education. 2nd
            ed. Prospect Heights, IL: Waveland Press.

1982   Doing the Ethnography of Schooling. New York: Holt, Rinehart and Winston.

Spindler, George D. and Louise Spindler

1983   Review Essay: The case studies in education and culture from cradle to grave. *Anthropology and Education Quarterly* 14(1):73–80.

1987   Teaching and learning how to do the ethnography of education. In Interpretive Ethnography of Education: At Home and Abroad, George and Louise Spindler, eds., pp. 17–33. Hillsdale, NJ: Lawrence Erlbaum Associates.

Spindler, George and Louise Spindler, eds.

1987   Interpretive Ethnography of Education: At Home and Abroad. Hillsdale, NJ: Lawrence Erlbaum Associates.

Turnbull, Colin M.

1972   The Mountain People. New York: Simon and Schuster.

Walter, Marion I. and Stephen I. Brown

1977   Problem posing and problem solving: An illustration of their interdependence. *Mathematics Teacher* 70(1):4–13.

Wolcott, Harry F.

1964   A Kwakiutl Village and Its School: Cultural Barriers to Classroom Performance. Unpublished doctoral dissertation, School of Education, Stanford University.

1967   A Kwakiutl Village and School. New York: Holt, Rinehart and Winston. [Reissued in 1984 by Waveland Press, Prospect Heights, IL.]

1973   The Man in the Principal's Office: An Ethnography. New York: Holt, Rinehart and Winston. [Reissued in 1984 by Waveland Press, Prospect Heights, IL, with a new Preface.]

1975   Criteria for an ethnographic approach to research in schools. *Human Organization* 34:111–128.

1982a   Differing styles of on-site research, or, "If it isn't ethnography, what is it?" *Review Journal of Philosophy and Social Science* 7(1 & 2):154–169.

1982b   Mirrors, models, and monitors: Educator adaptations of the ethnographic innovation. In Doing the Ethnography of Schooling. George Spindler, ed. New York: Holt, Rinehart and Winston.

1987   On ethnographic intent. In Interpretive Ethnography of Education: At Home and Abroad, George and Louise Spindler, eds., pp. 37–57. Hillsdale, NJ: Lawrence Erlbaum Associates.

2

National Politics and Local Responses: The Nation's First Successful School Desegregation Court Case

Robert R. Alvarez

INTRODUCTION

George and Louise Spindler have always encouraged students to focus on particular patterns of sociocultural behavior and to take into account the actual physical setting and the specific time in which the behavior under analysis occurs. The concept of time and space frameworks from the major parameters of the work presented here. This is a simple concept that reminds us that all sociocultural behavior occurs in specific periods of time and within limited sociocultural constraints, both of which have influences to large or small degrees on how people interpret what it is they need to do to survive in sociocultural environments.

The case presented here uses the notion of the time and space framework, while incorporating concepts from developing theory in anthropology, to interpret the first successful school desegregation court case in the United States. Anthropologists and other social scientists have focused on the explanation of social behavior through the combined analysis of both macro- and micro-level influences (Davis 1985; Fischer 1977; Orton 1984). Central in this view are the macrohistorical contexts that condition "on the ground" behavior. The concept of the "constraint-choice" model is included in such macro–micro analysis because it can be used to examine the larger socioeconomic circumstances and the resultant social relations of that interaction (Davis 1985; Fischer 1977, 1984). The concept, basically, is that people find themselves in socioeconomic circumstances that are particular to geographic regions conditioned by political and economic events. These circumstances provide limited alternatives for social-economic survival. Although limited, people choose the best alternatives and create the social relationships that continue to offer support and social continuity. In the case presented here the macropolitical–economic conditions of the period are viewed as the circumstances that affected the local decisions and politics involved in school segregation.

The history of school desegregation legislation in the United States is not often associated with the Mexican community in Southern California and is usually thought to have begun with the 1954 landmark Supreme Court case of *Brown v. Board of Education*.[1] However, the earliest court cases concerning school desegregation occurred in the Southwest and California in the 1930s.[2] In these cases Mexican immigrants and their communities were the targeted groups of segregation by school officials. A case of particular importance, which has begun to take its place in the social history of civil rights, occurred in San Diego County during the 1930s, in the then rural community of Lemon Grove. This case, *Roberto Alvarez v. the Board of Trustees of the Lemon Grove School District*, was the first successful desegregation court decision in the history of the United States.[3] This case is important in U.S. history, not solely because it occurred but because the community took court action, won the case, and established the rights of their children (of which I am one) to equal education. The community accomplished this despite local, regional, and national sentiment and policy that favored not only segregation, but the actual deportation of the Mexican population in the United States.[4] The case is a testimony of the San Diego Mexican community's rights and its actions toward equality in education not only for its own children, but for the Mexican population in California and the United States.

THE COMMUNITY AND COURSE OF EVENTS

The Lemon Grove Community

In 1930 Lemon Grove boasted a number of attractive businesses centered in the midst of productive agricultural fields. A local newspaper, the *La Mesa Scout* (1926) described Lemon Grove as "one of the prettiest spots in the San Diego suburban district.... the hills surrounding the town are covered with fine lemon and orange groves that are producing hundreds of thousands of dollars ...each year."

Among the advantages of Lemon Grove are an "excellent women's club," one of the finest golf courses in Southern California, paved roads, churches and a "livewire chamber of commerce that will gladly assist anyone who desires to locate here...." In addition to the civic and business opportunities described, Lemon Grove was served by its own grammar school. "A fine new building has recently been completed that offers every facility of the well equipped schools."

In describing the residents, the article stated that "within the Lemon Grove district will be found many of the better class of people who have selected San Diego County as their home. Among these people are professional and businessmen of San Diego...it would be hard to find a better class of people anyplace." This blissful view of Lemon Grove and its prominent residents was overshadowed in 1931 when the Mexican community challenged the school board for the educational rights of its children.[5]

In addition to the prominent citizens, Mexican immigrant families had settled in Lemon Grove just after the turn of the century. Most of the families had immigrated into San Diego County from a number of closely related hometowns in Baja California.[6] Many had meandered through a Baja California mining circuit arriving in San Diego by land. Others had come via steamer from company ports and coastal towns. Families had arrived from San Jose del Cabo, Cabo San Lucas, Loreto, Comondu, San Ignacio, Calmalli, and other towns that today are mere place names in the Central Desert in the Mexican peninsula of Baja California. Most families had endured the migration north together, sharing hardships and family experiences. When they crossed into the United States and arrived in San Diego, these Californios sought help and camaraderie from each other.[7]

For the Californio, as for other Mexicanos, Lemon Grove provided jobs in agriculture, a local mining quarry, a railroad packing house, and relatively easy access to the growing city of San Diego. The community was geographically confined and very similar to the hometowns from which people had come. Some 50 families settled here, most of which were of Baja California heritage. These families included Cesena, Alvarez, Castellanos, Smith, Blackwells, Arce, Mesa, and others who bonded together and formed a community of Baja Californios in Lemon Grove.

Political Action by Mexican Families

The unity and perseverance of the community were tested as never before during the early part of 1931. Most of these families had been in Lemon Grove for a number of years and had offspring who were first-generation American citizens by birth. Seventy-five of these children attended the Lemon Grove Grammar School, where a total of 169 students were enrolled. On January 5, 1931, Jerome T. Green, principal of the Lemon Grove Grammar School, acting under instructions from the school trustees, stood at the door and admitted all pupils except the Mexican students. Principal Green announced that the Mexican children did not belong at the school, could not enter, and instructed them to attend the two-room building constructed to house Mexican children.[8]

Dejected, embarrassed, and angry, the Mexican children left the school and returned home. Instructed by their parents, they refused to attend the so-called new school that had been built for them. In the words of students of the time, "It wasn't a school. It was an old building. Everyone called it 'La Caballeriza' (the barnyard)."[9]

This was a turn of events that the school board had not expected. The board had assumed that the Mexican children and families would act docilely, follow orders, and attend the new school. The Mexican parents rallied together and, through the Mexican consulate, acquired legal counsel and support. The school incident became a test case of the power of the district attorney and the school board to create a separate school for Mexican children.[10]

This separation had been carefully planned by the school board. On July 23, 1930, some six months before the barred entrance, the board met. They discussed the separation, which had received the endorsement of the Chamber of Commerce.[11] On August 13 a special board meeting was called because the situation of the school had reached emergency conditions and the "board wanted a special school for the Mexican children." No attempt was made to inform the Mexican parents, and the board, in a following meeting, decided against any official notice so as not to commit themselves in writing.[12] Twenty days later the children were expelled from the main school. Desks and all personal belongings of students had been moved to the "new" structure.

These actions by the school board were not isolated events but had actually been precipitated to a great degree by the Great Depression and a rising anti-Mexican sentiment in San Diego, as well as throughout California and other parts of the country. In order to grasp the social forces that set this action in motion, it is important to understand the larger socioeconomic and historic events that conditioned the events in 1930 San Diego and Lemon Grove.

Historical Context of the Lemon Grove Incident: Immigration Policies

Prior to any planning or decisions by the Lemon Grove school board concerning the separation of Mexican and Anglo children, there had been several public and officially sanctioned antecedents that set the tone for the actions at local community levels throughout the State of California. Among these were: (1) national changes in immigration policy specifically aimed at curtailing Mexican immigration to the United States; (2) a national repatriation plan geared to alleviate the Mexican alien problem that was viewed as a major cause of unemployment and public welfare costs; and (3) in California, official reports and measures that heightened latent prejudices and fears concerning the growing Mexican population. The events of the times are important here because they illustrate the barriers faced by the Mexican community of Lemon Grove in its attempt at security justice, and the socioeconomic conditions that reached local-level decisions.

Before the turn of the century, Mexican immigration was not a problem in the United States, but by 1920 there was a strong restrictionist campaign in the country. Large influxes of Mexicans into the Southwest and a growing Mexican population stirred public concern about the immigration and settlement of alien Mexicans in the United States.[13] Most large cities had Mexican enclaves by 1924 when government action to control the unrestricted influx was taken. Omaha had a population of 1,000, Detroit's population of Mexicans reached 15,000 by 1929, and significant numbers of Mexicans were identified in Chicago, Kansas City, and other U.S. cities.[14] But the majority of Mexicans were in the Southwestern states of Arizona, Colorado, New Mexico, and California. Consequently, governmental action focused upon this area and, in 1924, a 1917 immigration head tax was enforced for the first time along the U.S.-Mexican border.[15] In this same year Congress created the Border Patrol as a force to combat the entry of Mexicans into United States.

In addition to government action, the national press focused attention on the growing Mexican population. In 1928 the U.S. Senate opened hearings on the Restriction of Western Hemisphere Immigration,[16] and through 1929 the *Saturday Evening Post*, with a circulation of over 2.7 million, published a series of articles in strong support of a restrictionist policy limiting Mexican immigration.[17] In an editorial of January 7, 1928, the *Post* stated: "Every consideration of prudence and sound policy indicated that Mexican immigration must be put under quota restrictions.[18]

Kenneth L. Roberts, who had written a series of articles in favor of European immigration restriction, turned his pen toward Mexicans during this period.[19] Writing in the *Post* he stated: "The brown flood of Mexican peon immigration—the immigration of Mexican Indians and Mexican mestizos, or half breeds—had risen from year to year."[20] Roberts, reporting from California, reported that "in Los Angeles...one can see the endless streets crowded with the shacks of illiterate, diseased, pauperized Mexicans...bringing countless numbers of American citizens into the world with the reckless prodigality of rabbits...."[21]

These actions and conditions had a snowball effect and by 1931, when the local school board had initiated its actions, a national policy of repatriation was in place.[22] President Hoover believed that Mexican aliens contributed to the problem of unemployment by taking jobs from native-born Euro-Americans. He made every effort not only to stop both legal and illegal immigrants but to expel them as well. In 1931 the secretary of Labor proposed a solution to the unemployment problem. Announcing that there were 400,000 illegal aliens in the United States he stated that "under provisions of the immigration laws one hundred thousand of these illegal aliens could be deported.[23]"

In addition to the press, the growing prejudice against Mexican nationals was also mirrored in state government reports. In 1930 the governor of California received a report that he had commissioned entitled "Mexicans in California." The report considered all people of Mexican descent as Mexican nationals and did not differentiate between Mexicans born in Mexico or U.S. citizens of Mexican descent.[24] Divided into four major parts the report provided detailed statistics, future predictions, and warnings of alarming rates of growth of the Mexican population in the United States.

Focusing on Southern California, the authors reported that between 1910 and 1920 the increase in Mexicans for the state at large was 159 percent, and for 12 Southern California cities the increase was 215 percent. The increase for the decade in San Diego was 124 percent. The report supported the restrictionist's stereotyped views of the docile, unassimilable Mexican who had no desire to become a permanent U.S. citizen.[25]

By January 1931 the Los Angeles press, distributed in San Diego, was focusing on articles concerning the alien problem. The *Illustrated Daily News* of January 1931 stated: "Aliens who are deportable will save themselves trouble and expense by arranging their departure at once." The *Examiner* announced that "deportable aliens include Mexicans, Japanese and others without any qualifying details."[26] During the following year city and county law enforcement officials made public raids arresting Mexicans. One such raid included the Los Angeles City Park. The overall result in the United States was the deportation and voluntary repatriation of hundreds of thousands of Mexicans and U.S. citizens of Mexican descent.

Economic Pressure and Prejudice

The economic problems of the Depression created a great debate between those in favor of restricting Mexican immigration, particularly in the Southwestern United States, and antirestrictionists fighting for Mexican and other immigrant rights. Economic insecurity coupled with public attitudes led to the legalized expulsion of Mexicans from the country and targeted people of Mexican descent—regardless of nationality—as the socioeconomic scapegoats in the Southwest. The political climate was not as blatantly restrictionist in San Diego County, but it would be difficult to believe that the national sentiment expressed in both dominant newspapers and magazines of the time, and stressed by state and federal leaders, went unnoticed in San Diego and Lemon Grove.

The nativist and restrictionist attitude fanned by economic troubles of the Depression and the precedent of segregation in the form of the Americanization school, where children were to learn English and the basic values of being American, gave the Lemon Grove school board license to segregate the children. By the time of the school case in Lemon Grove, the segregation of Mexican American children had become widespread in California and Texas. In 1928 the enrollment of 64 schools in eight California counties was 90 to 100 percent Mexican-American.[27] During the 1920s segregation was institutionalized in Texas. Texas school boards created Mexican American neighborhood schools, which then became Mexican American schools. Between 1922–23 and 1931–32, the number of such schools doubled from 20 to 40 in Texas.[28]

...no Southwestern state upheld legally the segregation of Mexican-American children, yet the practice was widespread. Separate schools were built and maintained, in theory, simply because of residential segregation or to benefit the Mexican child. He had a "language handicap" and needed to be "Americanized" before mixing with Anglo children. His presence in an integrated school would hinder the progress of white American children.[29]

Such schools had been built without much opposition elsewhere in California and thus the Lemon Grove board was not prepared for the ensuing contest, which reached the Superior Court of the State of California in San Diego the following month.

On January 8, 1931, the *San Diego Evening Tribune* published an article, "75 Mexican students go on strike." It discussed the action taken by Principal Green sending the children to the new Americanization school and the response of the community, charging the school board with segregation. The following day the *San Diego Sun* published a response: "Pupils back at Desks in Lemon Grove," by the supervisor of attendance, L. H. Lovelace, stating the "matter was amicably settled as far as the school authorities are concerned." According to the article, Miss Ada York, superintendent of county schools, stated that the 75 pupils would return to the Americanization school. H. L. Owens, school board member also said "the difficulties between authorities and Mexican children had been 'entirely ironed out.'"[30]

Although the school authorities felt the school separation had been settled, during the following month the Mexican community went to court and under a writ of mandate from the Superior Court of California in San Diego, they challenged the school board's right to build and maintain a separate and segregated school for Mexican-American children. Prior to the school separation, Mexican children had attended special English classes at the school but the building of a separate school and the total segregation was viewed as a threat to the community.

Organization of Mexican Parents

The Mexican parents organized themselves into the Comité de Vecinos de Lemon Grove (the Lemon Grove Neighbors Committee) and sought help in the Mexican community at large.[31] The community went first to Enrique Ferreira, who had been the Mexican consul in San Diego for ten years. Ferreira responded with strong support and arranged for two San Diego attorneys, Fred C. Noon and A. C. Brinkley, to act as legal counsel for the Lemon Grove Community. Noon spoke Spanish fluently and had worked in San Diego since 1928. In 1930 he had been named California attorney for the Northern District of Baja California and was considered an expert in legal affairs concerning border relations.[32] As a result of Counsel Ferreira's support, and the conviction of the community, a suit was filed against the Lemon Grove School Board. The community chose my father, Roberto Alvarez, as representative of the segregated children. He was chosen because he was an exemplary student and spoke English well.[33]

In addition to seeking help from Counsul Ferriera, the Lemon Grove parents appealed to the Mexican community at large. The parents sought help in the Spanish-language media and reports in both Los Angeles and Tijuana newspapers appeared. On January 25, 1931, *La Opinión*, the leading Spanish-language newspaper in the state, featured a page-one article on the Lemon Grove incident entitled: "No Admiten a los Niños Mexicanos" (Mexican children refused admission). Within the article an open letter from the Lemon Grove Neighbors Committee appealed for the rights of all Mexicans in the United States: "We are not in agreement, which is very natural, nor do we consider just, the separation of our children, without any reason, to send them to another establishment that distinguishes Mexican children from children of other nationalities...." The community made a plea for both moral and material support in order to do "the work necessary to convince the school authorities that they should not continue the segregation...."[34] As a result of this request and support from *La Opinion*, the Lemon Grove Committee was able to cover the costs incurred by the court case.[35]

As the case approached the hearing, school board members appealed to nationalistic sentiment in support of their attempt to separate the children. H. A. Anderson, president of the school board, responding to the article in *La Opinión*, stated that "the strike is being carried on by an intense Mexican national organization which is organized among the Spanish-American elements along the coast."[36] The school board was quoted as welcoming the test suit to determine the board's powers to build the separate school for Mexican children. The district attorney's office had already ruled in favor of the board and had chosen to defend the school board's actions as the legal defense for the school.[37]

State Support for Segregation

The local attempt at segregation was also supported at the state level. On January 19, 1931, California Assemblyman George R. Bliss of Carpinteria introduced a bill to the California legislature that would have legalized the segregation of Mexican and Mexican American students. Bliss, as a school board member, had been successful in establishing a segregated school for Mexicans in Carpinteria under the rubric of an "Indian school." The California School Code of the period provided "the power to establish separate schools for Indian children and children of Chinese, Japanese and Mongolian ancestry."[38] Bliss wanted to extend the clause on Indian children to read: "Indian children whether born in the United States or not," thus allowing schools to separate Mexican and Mexican American children on the basis that they were Indians.[39] The Bliss Bill was defeated, but the introduction of the bill had been attributed to the Lemon Grove controversy. Lillian Hill, Chief of the Division of Migratory Schools in California, stated in 1931 that a Lemon Grove supporter of school segregation had announced: "If this [the attempt to segregate Lemon Grove] fails, we will slip a bill through the state legislature so we can segregate these greasers."[40]

The Mexican community, however, was not deterred and on February 13 issued a writ of mandate to the school board through the Superior Court of California in San Diego, to reinstate the Mexican-American students. The petition stated that "the exclusion was clearly an attempt at racial segregation ... by separating and segregating all of the children of Mexican parentage...

from the children of American, European and Japanese parentage."[41] The community stated that the board had "no legal right or power to exclude...[the Mexican children] from receiving instruction upon an equal basis...." The Mexican parents clarified that 95 percent of the students were American-born citizens "entitled to all the rights and privileges common to all citizens of the United States."[42]

In addition, the community showed its concern for residents and citizens of Mexican parentage throughout Southern California: "a speedy determination of the matter is necessary to prevent serious embarrassment and to determine the legal right under the laws of California, of children of Mexican parentage, nationality and or descent to attend the public schools of California on a basis of equality with other Americans."[43]

Based on this petition (Writ of Mandate) the court indicted each of the school board members for illegal segregation and commanded the admittance of all pupils of Mexican parentage and nationality to the main school.

In answer to the Petition for Writ of Mandate the Board of Trustees denied all allegations concerning segregation or isolation of the pupils of Mexican parentage. The school board's action was rationalized under the pretensions for the betterment of the Mexican children's education. The new school was to be an "Americanization school" in which the deficiencies of the children of Mexican descent could be corrected, avoiding the deterioration of American students as a result of contact with the Mexicans in the main school. English language and American customs would be provided to bring the Mexican students up to standards of the American children. The primary arguments submitted to the court were:

1. That the new school house was large enough to accommodate 85 or more pupils and that a playground was set aside and fully equipped.

2. That the school was built in the northerly section of town (in the main Mexican area) for the safety of the children as they could attend the school without traveling over the main boulevard to the main school.

3. That with one or two exceptions the children assigned to this new school were deficient in their knowledge of the English language, and are older than the other children in corresponding grades and require special attention from the instructors.

4. That the new school was built for the purpose of establishing an Americanization school wherein backward and deficient children could be given better instruction than they could be given in the larger school.

5. That the Americanization school was not intended to be a segregation of Mexican children.[44]

On Tuesday, February 24, the case went to court and was heard by San Diego's Judge Claude Chambers, who was well known in San Diego. He had arrived in 1906 and had served as a city justice, and in the late 1930s ran for city councilman and mayor of San Diego. Although he lost both bids, Judge

Chambers had filed an impressive record in the courts of San Diego. He was a civic leader, establishing the San Diego Tourist Magazine in 1908, and in 1913 was co-founder of the San Diego Advertising Club. He served as president of the San Diego Merchant's Association and formed the San Diego Hotel Association. In 1934 he expressed his views as a judge. His campaign slogan was "Justice tempered with Mercy." "I believe a court should uphold the dignity of the law and respect the rights of all equally, irrespective of whether they be rich or poor, and irrespective of what race, nationality or religion they may belong to....[45] These beliefs were carried into court.

The case focused around a rebuttal of the school board's claims concerning the backwardness and deficiencies of the Mexican American children. In addition to the plaintiff representing the children at large, ten principal witnesses took the stand to illustrate the inaccurate generalizations concerning the scholastic achievements of the Mexican children. But the major questions were levied at the school board and school staff.

Judge Chambers: When there are American children who are behind (in grade level) what do you do with them?

Answer: They are kept in a lower grade.

Judge: You don't segregate them? Why not do the same with the other children? Wouldn't the association of American and Mexican children be favorable to the learning of English for these (Mexican) children?

Silence is the answer.

Lawyer Noon: All the Mexican children were behind (in their work)?

Answer: The older ones behaved themselves; the younger ones gave us a lot of work.

Noon: What was the reason for separating them?

Answer: To provide them with more personal attention.[46]

In concluding Judge Chambers stated:

I understand that you can separate a few children, to improve their education if they need special instruction; but to separate all the Mexicans in one group can only be done by infringing the laws of the State of California. And I do not blame the Mexican children because a few of them are behind (in school work) for this segregation. On the contrary, this is a fact in their favor. I believe this separation denies the Mexican children the presence of the American children, which is so necessary to learn the English language.[47]

Final Outcome

On March 30, 1931, a judgment was handed down in favor of the Mexican community.[48] The judge's finding was based on existing laws and an evaluation of the facts. He refuted each claim made by the school board and the court demanded an immediate reinstatement of the children. The separation was indeed deemed segregation and the court ruled that the school board had no legal basis on which to segregate the children. California law did not authorize or permit the maintenance of separate schools for the instruction of pupils of Mexican parentage, nationality, and/or descent. The children were legally entitled to enter the regular school building and receive instruction on the basis of equality with all other children.

In a final reference to the school separation and the only reference to the court case, the minutes of a post-case school board meeting read: "All members of the board present. On account of having lost the court decision there was some discussion about the return of Mexican (children) pupils but only a spirit of good will prevailed, and it was decided that everything was to continue exactly as it did prior to January 5th."[49] The case was never recorded in school board minutes and even a local history of the Lemon Grove School from 1880 to 1966 by a former school superintendent failed to mention the case.[50]

The Lemon Grove case may appear to be an isolated event of the 1930s, but the segregation of Mexican and Mexican-American children became commonplace throughout the Southwest during the 1930s and in some cases reappeared and was fought as de facto segregation in our major cities as late as the 1970s.[51]

Prior to the Lemon Grove case, the League of United Latin American Citizens (LULAC) selected the Del Rio, Texas, School District as a test case to outlaw similar segregation policy. The case, *Salvatierra v. Independent School District*, challenged the legality of the "complete segregation" of school children of Mexican and Spanish descent. The District Court of Val Verde County granted an injunction restraining the district from segregating Mexican children, but the injunction was appealed by the school board. In early 1930 the Texas Court of Appeals agreed in part with the district court on the school's lack of power arbitrarily to segregate Mexican children, but the court upheld the school district's rights to separate children on the basis of English-language handicaps. LULAC appealed the decision to the U.S. Supreme Court, but the case was dismissed for want of jurisdiction.[52]

The Lemon Grove school case was isolated as a local event and had no precedent-setting rulings affecting either the State of California or other situations of school segregation in the Southwest. Unlike the Texas case, the school board did not appeal the district court's decision and complied with the court's ruling. Given the climate of the period, it is surprising that the case was not appealed. Perhaps more surprising is the fact that other communities in the state did not use the case as a precedent in desegregating Americanization schools and classes that were created for Mexican and Mexican-American children. The case stands as a credit to those in the Mexican community of Lemon Grove who as immigrants used the public system of justice to test their children's rights as U.S. Citizens.

In addition to documenting the nation's first successful desegregation court case, this chapter illustrates the socioeconomic forces that influenced and conditioned the decisions that led to the actions by both the school board and the community of Lemon Grove. Rather than viewing the segregation of the Mexican Americn children as a sole act of local prejudice, the national sentiment aimed at Mexican immigrants and the policy of repatriation were seen here as larger mechanisms affecting local behavior. These political ramifications stemmed directly from the economic circumstances of the Great Depression. At the same time, the actions of the Mexican community in the face of seemingly overwhelming odds illustrate the strategic options chosen by the Mexican community.

NOTES

1. The *Brown* case was the culmination of a long series of tested court actions toward black equality in the United States that began with *Plessy v. Ferguson* in 1896. This case, related directly to railroad car travel and only indirectly to schooling, set a precedent for the "separate but equal" or Jim Crow laws that remained in effect until the 1954 *Brown* ruling. A series of cases directly related to equal education were heard throughout the States after the turn of the century. In 1927 the Supreme Court approved of Mississippi's sending a Chinese child to school maintained for blacks (Shoemaker 1957; Haro 1977; Berman 1966; Humphrey 1964; Select Committee on Equal Educational Opportunity 1972). In the 1930s several cases concerned the rights of blacks to attend state colleges were heard throughout the nation, including Maryland (1936), Missouri (1938), Oklahoma (1948), and Texas (1948) (Haro 1977). In 1954 there were 17 states, all in the South or bordering the South plus the District of Columbia, that by law made segregated school mandatory. Four states (Arizona, Kansas, New Mexico, and Wyoming) allowed varieties of local option in segregating and 16 states prohibited segregation but enforcement was random. The 11 remaining states had no laws on segregation aimed at blacks or Chicanos and most had no reported cases in the courts (Haro 1977). California, however, did by law exclude Native Americans, making it legal to segregate people of Indian descent.

2. Alvarez, 1981, 1986; Balderrama, 1982;

3. I discovered this case while doing field research on the migration and adaptation of Mexican families from Baja California. My own family had come from the South and in interviews with my father and other key actors in the case I discovered that court action had been taken by the Mexican community. A grant from the Spencer Foundation for educational research permitted the actual focus on the case. I am also in great debt to my sister, Guadalupe Alvarez Cooper, who conducted interviews and discovered the aging microfilm containing the court records.

4. Other versions of this study that relate the school case to immigration reform have been presented elsewhere (Alvarez 1981, 1983, 1986). The school case presented here was the basis for a Public Broadcasting Service documentary produced by KPBS-TV in San Diego in 1985. This documentary is the second in a series on the San Diego-Lemon Grove families from Baja California. The first, "The Trail North," was broadcast by KPBS in 1983.

5. *La Mesa Scout*, 1926. This copy was obtained from the Lemon Grove Historical Society. No month or day was given.

6. The settlement and development of this community is described in Alvarez 1987.

7. Ibid.

8. Superior Court of the State of California, County of San Diego, Petition for Writ of Mandate No. 66625, February 13, 1931. This is the only official record of the court case that is in existence. A prolonged search in both city and county records led to the discovery of the school case in the microfilm collection of the Superior Court. The microfilm had deteriorated badly, but was still legible.

9. Interviews with Roberto Alvarez, Sr. and Mary Smith Alvarez, February 1981, San Diego.

10. *San Diego Sun*, February, 10–11, 1931.

11. Lemon Grove School Board Minutes, July 23, 1930. Copies of the board minutes had been saved by my paternal grandmother, Ramona Castellanos, along with old San Diego County newspaper accounts of the case. These proved to be the primary documents that led to the investigation and understanding presented here.

12. Ibid.

13. In addition to their current fear of immigration, Ricardo Romo (1975), states that "during the period 1915–1917 hysteria similar to, and at times even more extreme than that aimed at communists elsewhere was directed at Mexicans living in the United States who allegedly stood on the verge of revolution which would reclaim the entire Southwest for Mexico" (pp. 104–132, Chapter 5, "The Brown Scare").

14. Hoffman 1974:12.

15. Alvarez, 1987; Cardenas 1975; Romo 1975; Scott 1971.

16. Divine, 1957:52–76.

17. Divine, 1957; Hoffman 1974; Romo 1975; Scott 1971.

18. Hoffman, 1974:23.

19. Divine 1957:56.

20. Romo 1975:74.

21. Ibid.

22. Balderrama 1982; Bogardus 1934; Cardoso 1974; Divine 1957; Hoffman 1974; Romo 1975; Scott 1971.

23. Hoffman 1977:39.

24. R and E Research Associates 1930.

25. Ibid, p.59.

26. Hoffman 1974:47.

27. Weinberg 1977:155–165. Weinberg stated that in 1928, San Bernadino had 16 such schools, Orange County 14, Los Angeles County 10, Imperial 8, Kern 8, Ventura 4, Riverside 2, and Santa Barbara 2.

Paul Taylor (1928:83), writing in 1927, stated that in the Imperial Valley, California, Mexican children made up one-third of the population and were separated into Americanization and opportunity classes. "Segregation" he stated, "occurs in every town of the Imperial Valley." Thomas Carter (1970:11), in reviewing the 1930 situation for Mexican children, stated "segregation especially in the early grades was regularly recommended and commonly established.

28. Ibid, p. 155.

29. Moore 1970:70.

30. *San Diego Union*, January 9, 1931.

31. Alvarez 1981; Balderrama 1982.

32. *San Diego Union*, February 19, 1930; November 4, 1961.

33. Roberto R. Alvarez, Sr., interview, February 1981.

34. *La Opinion*, January 25, 1931.
35. Balderrama 1982:60.
36. *San Diego Sun*, February 10, 1931; February 11, 1931.
37. Ibid.
38. Balderrama 1982:61.
39. Ibid.
40. Ibid, p. 64.
41. Superior Court of the State of California, San Diego County, Writ of Mandate, February 13, 1931.
42. Ibid.
43. Ibid.
44. Alternative Writ of Mandate, February 14, 1931.
45. *San Diego Union*, 1934. No date given.
46. Secretaría de Relaciones Exteriores. Tomo I–II, 1930–31, pp. 1786–1787. Translation by author.
47. Ibid.
48. Conclusions of Law, March 1, 1931.
49. Lemon Grove School Board Minutes, March 12, 1931.
50. Netzley 1966.
51. Haro 1977; U.S. Commission of Civil Rights 1971.
52. Balderrama 1982:59; Weinberg 1977:165.

REFERENCES

Alvarez, Robert R.
   1981   School segregation in the 1930's. A Mexican American case. Paper presented to the 82nd American Anthropological Association, Los Angeles.
   1983   Public sentiment and public policy towards immigration reform: A lesson from a 1930 Mexican desegregation case. Paper presented to the Society for Applied Anthropology, San Diego.
   1986   The Lemon Grove Incident: The Nation's First Successful Desegregation Court Case. San Diego Historical Society. Spring.
   1987   Familia: Migration and Adaptation in Alta and Baja California, 1800–1975. Los Angeles: University of California Press.
Balderrama, Francisco E.
   1982   In Defense of La Raza. The Mexican Consulate and the Mexican Community, 1926 to 1936. Tucson: University of Arizona
Berman, Daniel M.
   1966   It Is So Ordered. The Supreme Court Rules on School Segregation. New York: W.W. Norton.
Bogardus, Emory
   1934   Mexicans in the United States. Los Angeles: University of Southern California Press.
Cardenas, Gilberto
   1975   United States immigration policy toward Mexico: An historical perspective. *Chicano Law Review* (UCLA) 5(2), Summer.

Cardoso, Lawrence
  1974   Mexican emigration to the United States, 1900–1930: An analysis of socio-economic causes. Ph.D. Thesis, University of Connecticut.
Carter, Thomas
  1970   Mexican Americans in School: A History of Educational Neglect. New York: College Entrance Examination Board.
Davis, William G.
  1985   Class, political constraints and entrepreneurial strategies: Elites and petty market traders in Northern Luzon. In Entrepreneurs and Social Change, Sydney Greenfield and Arnold Stricken, eds. Society for Economic Anthropology. Monograph 2, Washington, DC: University Press of America.
Divine, Robert
  1957   American Immigration Policy 1924–1952. New Haven, CT: Yale University Press.
Fischer, Claude S. et al.
  1977   Networks and Places. New York: The Free Press.
Fischer, Claude S.
  1984   To Dwell Among Friends. Chicago: University of Chicago Press.
Haro, Carlos Manuel
  1977   Mexicano/Chicano Concerns and School Desegregation in Los Angeles. Los Angeles: Chicano Studies Center, UCLA.
Hoffman, Abraham
  1977   Unwanted Mexican-Americans in the Great Depression: Repatriation Pressures, 1929–1939. Tucson: University of Arizona.
Humphrey, Hubert H., ed.
  1964   School Segregation: Documents and Commentaries. New York: Thomas Y. Crowell.
La Mesa Scout
  1926   Lemon Grove article (copy obtained from the Lemon Grove Historical Society), no month given.
Lemon Grove School Board
  1930   Minutes of July 23, August 13, and December 16.
  1931   Minutes of March 12.
Moore, Joan W.
  1970   The Mexican Americans. Englewood Cliffs, NJ: Prentice-Hall.
Netzley, Byron
  1966   A personal history of the Lemon Grove school district. Lemon Grove Historical Society, unpublished manuscript.
Orton, Sherry
  1984   Theory in anthropology since the sixties. Journal of Comparative Study of Society and History 4:126–166.
R and E Research Associates
  1930   Mexicans in California. Report to Governor Clement Young by the Mexican Fact Finding Committee. San Francisco.
Romo, Ricardo
  1975   Mexican workers in the city: Los Angeles 1915–1930. Ph.D. Thesis. Los Angeles: University of California.

San Diego Evening Tribune
  1931   75 Mexican Students Go On Strike. January 8.
San Diego Sun
  1931a Mexican Pupils Go on Strike in Lemon Grove. January 9.
  1931b Tapia Selects Local Attorney. February 19.
  1934   n.d.
  1961   Fred Noon, 82, is honored on birthday. November 4.
Scott, Robin F.
  1971   The Mexican in the Los Angeles area, 1920–1950: From acquiescence to
         activity. Ph.D. Thesis. Los Angeles: University of Southern California.
Secretaría de Relaciones Exteriores
  1931   Tomo I–II, 1930–31. Publicaciones del Gobierno Mexicano. Mexico, D.F.
Select Committee on Equal Educational Opportunity, U.S. Senate.
  1972   Selected Court Decisions Relating to Equal Educational Opportunity. Wash-
         ington DC: U.S. Government Printing Office.
Shoemaker, Don
  1957   With All Deliberate Speed: Segregation-Desegregation in Southern Schools.
         New York: Harper and Brothers.
Superior Court of the State of California, County of San Diego
  1931a Petition for Writ of Mandate No. 66625. Roberto Alvarez, a minor, by Juan
         M. Gonzalez, guardian ad. litem. Petitioner versus E. L. Owen, Anna E.
         Wright, and Henry A. Anderson. Members of and constituting the board of
         trustees of Lemon Grove School District and E. L. Owen, Anna E. Wright,
         Henry A. Anderson individually and Jerome J. Green.
  1931b Order for Alternate Writ of Mandate No. 66625. Roberto Alvarez, a minor,
         by Juan M. Gonzalez, guardian ad. litem. Petitioner versus E. L. Owen et al.,
         February 14.
  1931c Alternative Writ of Mandate No. 66625. Roberto Alvarez, a minor, by Juan
         M. Gonzalez, guardian ad. litem, Petitioner versus E. L. Owen et al.,
         February 21.
  1931d Findings of Fact and Conclusions of Law. Roberto Alvarez, a minor, by Juan
         M. Gonzalez, guardian ad. litem, Petitioner versus E. L. Owen et al.,
         March 30.
Taylor, Paul S.
  1928   Mexican Labor in the United States: Imperial Valley California. University of
         California Publications in Economics 6(1). Berkeley: University of
         California Press.
United States Commission on Civil Rights
  1971   Mexican American Education Study. Washington DC: U.S. Government
         Printing Office.

3
Cultural Transmission and Adaptation in the Political Arena: Hispanic Participation in Bilingual Education Policy Making

Richard A. Navarro

For the past 20 years, the issue of bilingual education has brought public attention to the poverty of Hispanic Americans, their deficiencies in educational achievement, and their limited participation throughout society. However, despite both federal and state programs in the schools, there exists little convincing evidence that bilingual education has been the most appropriate response to the problems of poverty, attrition, and social integration. The difficulty in understanding the reasons for the accomplishments as well as the failures of bilingual education is complicated by the narrow range of issues affecting language minority groups considered by scholars. Specifically, what is needed is a distinction between the social policy issues, as represented by the social marginality of the population in question, and the language issues, which include research on second-language acquisition and teaching. The study reported on in this chapter focuses on the social policy issues that gave rise to bilingual education policies in California from 1967 to 1980, with a particular emphasis on 1979–80 (Navarro 1983, 1985). It assumes that the political arena is a microcosm of the larger society and that political relations will reflect this interaction. Therefore, this research makes an important contribution to our understanding of social relations between language minorities and mainstream society.

METHODOLOGY

The parliamentary rules, norms of behaviors, patterns of authority, communication styles, and artifacts of legislating all constitute a cultural system within the broader confines of American society. In this study particular attention is given to Hispanic political elites active in bilingual interest groups, whose notion of policy making is transformed to conform to the knowledge, behaviors, and interpretive processes of the dominant members of the process. The purpose of this research is to understand the *meanings* or ways of interpreting reality, underlying the formation of an Hispanic identity and role in the political process. It is assumed that politicians have their own way of interpreting reality that bilingual education advocates have had to learn. Meanings are transmitted not only to integrate new members into the process, but to do so in such a way as to maintain the dominant belief system. Thus one concern is to understand the ways in which new members adapt to the constraints imposed by the norms of the system in order to become effective actors (G. Spindler 1972a, 1972b; Spindler and Spindler 1971, 1978).

Historical and ethnographic research methods were employed to collect relevant information regarding the incorporation of bilingual education interest groups into the policy-making process. Historical methods critically examine and analyze the records of the past. This process is broken down into the following steps: the collection of documents, determining if the documents or their parts are authentic, the degree of credibility of the document, and how the facts are put together in a connected narrative.

The task of ethnographic inquiry is to discover the "sociolcultural knowledge" (G. Spindler 1982:5) of the participants in a particular situational context. First the ethnographer assumes that in order to communicate, carry out a transaction, or relate in any form the actors in an encounter must share some level of cultural understanding. Sociocultural knowledge at its more basic level consists of meanings of actions, events, objects, or living creatures that are shared by the actors in interaction. Culture is not static, but is negotiated and changed through the "interpretive process" people use to understand experience and behave appropriately according to culturally defined norms of behavior (Spradley 1980:5–6). In a complex situation, such as the California State Legislature, actors share cultural meanings appropriate to the setting as well as differ from the interaction in the political arena according to their membership in other groups. Thus culture comprises not only the behavior manifested, but also the sociocultural knowledge underlying the manifested behavior that differs according to the "variants" each actor brings to the encounter (G. Spindler 1982:491).

SYMBOLIC INTERACTION IN POLICY MAKING

The events studied in California exemplify the struggle to improve the conditions of schooling for children who are academically at risk, particularly for those who are marginalized because of cultural, linguistic, or social class differences. The debate on bilingual education, like other programs aimed at improving these conditions, did not occur in the schools, nor in research institutions, but in the heart of the political arena—the California State Legislature. Most importantly for supporters of similar programs and students of interest groups, the survival of bilingual education in the state during the period studied ultimately depended upon the political skills of individuals and organizations willing to defend it, which included adapting to new roles in the policy-making process.

While the political actions of coalitions in the policy-making process were successful in averting proposals that would have repealed laws mandating bilingual education, and actually led to the passage of new laws reaffirming the state's commitment to bilingual education, their apparent victories were symbolic gestures (Edelman 1971) to the Hispanic community to placate the dissension that resulted from efforts to terminate state support for the program. The political achievements of bilingual coalitions active during 1979 and 1980—political patronage, formulation of policy proposals, and participation in the political process—did not significantly alter the power relationships within the political system such that Hispanics had more power to effect change. Instead, these symbols of influence incorporated the participation of Hispanic political elites, thereby legitimating the policy-making process. This issue is of major importance for understanding the structure of political relations in the policy-making process and to evaluate the effect of the politicization of bilingual education on the articulation of minority interests.

THE SYMBOLIC MEANING OF BILINGUAL EDUCATION

Historically, the political activity surrounding bilingual education has been an attempt by Hispanics to achieve the power requisite to make their interest a prominent factor in the decision-making equation. At times the competition has escalated to a heated level. Two elements of the "political field" (Turner 1966) crucial to an understanding of why the competition escalates are the nature of the issue and the nature of the political structure.

The notion of bilingual education has had several different and sometimes conflicting meanings to the participants in the policy-making process. Proponents, particularly Hispanics, have found meaning in the program for their own identification with the educational and political systems; whereas opponents of bilingual education, from Miami to San Francisco, have focused on the language issues and criticized supporters for using the program as a political wedge, a jobs program, and a separatist movement. In addition, the political structure, owing to several economic, social, and demographic factors, was undergoing a transition from a liberal to a more conservative orientation, which affected the political support network that proponents of the program were able to rally. The following analysis focuses on these various forces that came to bear on the formation of bilingual education as a political symbol. Although the period studied ends in 1980, the findings are particularly relevant to understanding the conditions of Hispanics' participation in policy making today.

Political anthropologist Abner Cohen (1974:ix) has defined symbols as "objects, acts, concepts or linguistic formation that stand ambiguously for a multitude of disparate meanings, evoke sentiments and emotions, and impel men to action." Information is ambiguously reformulated into a symbol such that it evokes a series of associations with the past, contemporary conditions, and even expectations for the future. The importance of symbolic analysis in this study of the politicization of bilingual education is the role of symbolic meanings in the adaptation of Hispanic interest groups to the political process.

Bilingual education in this study was first an important symbol of political identification. It provided the basis by which political action by Hispanic advocates had meaning to the Hispanic community. The significance of this symbol was enhanced by the threat to repeal the legal mandate. Thus the symbol of identification also led bilingual education supporters to overcome differences among themselves in order to rally support for the program.

The second illustration of the symbolic meaning of bilingual education was the unification of Hispanics around this one issue. Identity and unity were reciprocal actions that characterized the struggle in 1979. However, although Hispanics began to unify with the first threats to the program, the competition between two Hispanic legislators continued to divide the Chicano Legislative Caucus for several more months. When one of the competitors conceded defeat and withdrew, the Caucus united and the position of the coalition of Hispanic interest groups in the process was greatly advantaged.

The third source of meaning for bilingual education was a symbol of consensus that included Hispanic participation. The controversy began with the exclusion of the bilingual education community in the formation of a State Board of Education proposal on bilingual education. As the competition escalated, bilingual education became increasingly symbolic of Hispanic integration into policy making. The governor, legislators, and other key individuals and mainstream organizations all contributed to the incorporation of Hispanics into decision making and further legitimated political action for resolving conflict and pressing diverse interests (Navarro 1986).

The symbolic meaning of bilingual education also enhanced the political position of the opponents to the program. For instance, one legislator felt that as a result of the politicization of the program, bilingual education constituted the criteria for selecting a political role in opposition to it and other policies that directly affect Hispanics. He stated: "Take a look at anything that deals with bilingual education [on the Assembly Floor] and automatically you are going to get red buttons [a no vote] regardless of whether it is good or bad. Anything to do with bilingual education they [non-Hispanic legislators] are going to be against—that is with Democrats as well as Republicans" (Interview, September 13, 1981). According to this legislator's interpretation, the politicization of bilingual education weakened the articulation of Hispanic interests in policy making by alienating legislators who might otherwise have been more disposed to Hispanic interests if they were not so controversial.

The relationship between the symbolic meanings derived from bilingual education—identity, unity, and consensus building—is illustrated in the following three case studies. The forces that impinged on the series of events described illustrate the power of the symbol to direct behavior, alter patterns of interaction, and conceal contradictions in the process. These meanings were significant to the adaptation and integration of Hispanics into the political system and demonstrate an imbalance of power relations to which Hispanics had to adapt in order to participate.

CASE STUDY I: FORMULATION OF A CAUSE

Throughout the period beginning in 1972 with the first Bilingual Education Act until 1980, bilingual education was controversial in California and policy making in the field was always difficult (Navarro 1983). However, no previous events had stirred bilingual educators and Hispanic organizations to political action like the events of 1979. The State Board of Education action to formulate a proposal to repeal the law mandating bilingual education and the later introduction of the proposal in Assembly Bill (AB) 690 by a Chicano assemblyman, Richard Alatorre, did not simply initiate a reactionary response that died away when the threat was no longer present; these actions set in motion the formation of a cause that became symbolic of bilingual educators' interests in the political process and eventually led to their integration into the system. Bilingual education became such a powerful symbol of Hispanic interests that the governor also advocated it and vowed to veto any measure that divided the Hispanic community (Interview, November 12, 1981). Similarly, the Chicano Legislative Caucus used the issue to enhance its image of leadership among the Hispanic community in the state. The first case study analyzes the relationship of the threat to bilingual education identity formation among program supporters.

Soon after the enactment of AB 1329 in 1976, the first comprehensive law mandating bilingual education in California sponsored by Assemblyman Peter Chacon, important policy-making groups began to exhibit critical postures toward bilingual education. The passage of Proposition 13 in 1978 provided further reason to accelerate actions intended to weaken the mandate. The State Board of Education began in January 1978 to examine the state of bilingual education. Its review highlighted problems with implementing AB 1329. In addition, two consultants from Bloomsbury West, Inc. of San Francisco—Heide Dulay and Marina Burt—were hired to make recommendations for the Board on program options for bilingual education. At the time, the State Department of Education reassured bilingual educators that Dulay and Burt were merely suggesting possible alternative courses. Instead, the Board adopted their proposed program options. In short, within the first three months of 1979, the Board, in conjunction with the State Department of Education, formulated and approved legislation to repeal the existing law and replace it with a more flexible program. The effect was described by a reporter.

No bilingual bill emerged from the Legislature [in 1979], but the effort by Deputy Superintendent Davis Campbell set off a furor between legislators and the statewide network of bilingual educators, split the state education department into factions and polarized feelings throughout the state and in the Capitol over the issue (Castro 1980).

The main disagreement was over the purposes of the reform vehicle and the exclusion of bilingual educators from having input in its formulation. In January the Department established the Bilingual Education Community Interaction Group (an ad hoc committee) at the request of the State Board of Education to discuss ways to improve AB 1329. The committee was headed by the Office of Bilingual-Bicultural Education, and the participants represented diverse opinions regarding the current law. They focused their attention on problems of implementation and were led to believe that their purpose was to recommend changes to be made through departmental regulations. Although the Dulay/Burt proposal had been discussed for several months, one member of the ad hoc committee noted that:

[it had always been done] in the context of possible regulations or guidelines under the existing law. All of a sudden the Department of Education shifted gears and came out with this legislative draft—without community input of any substantial nature, even though the draft had been written or was being written at the time and an all day meeting was occurring in which the so-called Community Interaction Group was discussing the concepts involved (Schilla 1979).

The adoption of the Dulay/Burt proposal by the State Board of Education without community input seriously strained relations between bilingual education supporters and the Department. In defense of the Department action, Davis Campbell wrote to Olivia Martinez, a leading bilingual supporter and member of the ad hoc committee, on March 22, 1979:

The [ad hoc] Committee asked that the Department prepare a package of potential program options and discuss it with them. It became clear to us in the Department that Bloomsbury West [Dulay and Burt—editor's note] had developed under contract with us an exciting set of instructional options.

The committee members denied that there had ever been such a request made of the Department, increasing their suspicion that the Department intended to eliminate bilingual education all together.

The members of the ad hoc committee were not the only supporters of bilingual education who were dismayed by the Department actions. The most vocal and active supporter of bilingual education on the State Board, Lorenza Schmidt, was alarmed by the sudden appearance of the Dulay/Burt proposal in legislative language, as were members of the Office of Bilingual-Bicultural Education within the Department. Schmidt received the proposal the same day it was to be heard before the State Board of Education Specially Funded Programs Committee, which she chaired. Campbell tried to assure Schmidt in a cover memorandum (March 7, 1979):

In order to save time, the recommendations have been written up in legislative format. This will enable the Committee to see how the recommendations could appear in a bill. The Committee, however, will only be asked to approve the major concepts outlined, not specific legislative language.

Nevertheless, Schmidt still advised program supporters of the plan and distributed copies for further analysis. She also expressed her own reservations (March 13, 1979, memorandum):

I am further concerned with the definition of bilingual education... it [Dulay/Burt proposal] defines it almost as second language development... we need a bilingual bill which will reinforce the need for professionally qualified bilingual teachers, not one that uses definition to diminish the opportunities for appropriate linguistic education in California.

The existing law, AB 1329, generally reflected Schmidt's concerns that the education of language-minority children required qualified bilingual teachers at all levels. However, the Dulay/Burt proposal was a clear departure from this precedent and threatened to limit the scope of bilingual instruction, reducing the demand for bilingual teachers.

Also removed from any direct input into the formulation of the language in the Dulay/Burt proposal was the Office of Bilingual-Bicultural Education. In response, the office initiated its own internal analysis. David Dolson, a consultant, reported his interpretation in a staff review of Guillermo Lopez, chief of the office (March 27, 1979). Dolson expressed several critical reservations, particularly the issue of bilingual instruction:

At this time there are a number of provisions that would be detrimental to bilingual education... Many LES/NES [limited and non-English-speaking] students would often be placed with a principal teacher who is not bilingual-bicultural. This provision sets bilingual education back 30 years.

Thus, the State Board's action threatened the survival of the program whose fate would be decided politically.

Supporters of the program were first concerned that the proposal would repeal the existing law. Efforts to postpone action and allow for the discussion and evaluation from the bilingual field that the Department said they sought were fruitless, again adding to the anxiety over the program. Supporters (the California Association for Bilingual Education) wrote State Superintendent Wilson Riles and all members of the State Board of Education, on March 28, 1979 and petitioned him to intervene in the State Board's apparent course: "Your department has already alienated a large number of people by moving too fast on this item. The Board should not be acting... until May or June unless it is intending to ride roughshod over the community which is supposed to be served." Finally, despite strong protest at the meeting, the State Board voted 7 to 2 to endorse the proposed legislation. Schmidt, one of the two votes against the plan, charged that the Department was insensitive to the educators, parents, teachers, administrators, and local board members who had attempted to meet with the Department to outline the deficiencies of the bill it was proposing. She accused members in the Department of working "in conjunction with members of the State Board who intended to write new bilingual legislation which reduced the legal mandate on local districts to provide bilingual education" (Schmidt 1979). Schmidt also raised questions regarding the procedure the State Board followed in making its decision. She argued that the proposed bilingual bill was listed as an information item on the agenda but the Board had treated it as an action item (Schmidt 1979).

Following the endorsement of the Dulay/Burt proposal, the Board along with the Department became the targets of strong criticism from bilingual educators. The appearance of a threat and the party responsible for making it greatly enhanced the formation of a stronger political identity, which included defense of the program for Hispanics. In an editorial, Chacon (1979) wrote:

A careful reading of the Burt/Dulay proposal clearly shows that if the mandates of the 1976 Act are removed...bilingual bicultural programs will no longer be required, rather school districts will have options to choose from. None of these options would require a school district to provide a full bilingual program with a certificated bilingual teacher in the classroom for these children. The result will be districts opting for the easiest, least expensive option.

The assemblyman Chacon's interpretation of the existing law resonated among bilingual education supporters. Olivia Martinez, president-elect of the California Bilingual Education Association, focused on the auditor general's report released in March, which charged "the Department has not fully executed some of its responsibilities in accordance with present statutes" (Office of the Auditor General 1979). Martinez (1980) claimed:

[The] Department's non-support of 1329 is part of an effort to coverup gross administrative mishandling at the highest department level and [is an] embarrassing failure in its responsibility to provide assistance to school districts, issue clear, helpful guidelines, provide for the orderly evaluation of programs and in general support bilingual education. After little more than two years, Department officials have managed to turn the Bilingual Education Act into one of the most controversial, maligned educational programs in the State (Martinez 1980).

Once again Schmidt was vocal in her criticisms of the manner in which the State Board approved the bill. She accused the Board of a politically motivated "act of racism" and "an appalling abuse of public power" whose ultimate objective was contrary to the stated intent. The Board action, stated Schmidt, was actually intended to "cripple the educational opportunities for bilingual communities and hence limited their potential as an active and participatory political interest group" (Schmidt 1979).

When Hispanic activists failed to halt the momentum of the Dulay/Burt proposal to dismantle the Bilingual Bicultural Education Law in the first half of 1979, the Bilingual Community Coalition was formed in June among supporters of bilingual education statewide. The Coalition used its collective action and strength as the "bilingual education community" to seek amendments to AB 690 that would retain the existing law and change only those sections of the statute that would alleviate the implementation problems. The threat to bilingual education and the polarization of sides strengthened the identification of program supporters as both the victims of an unfair policy-making process and the defenders of bilingual education.

As the differences in opinion over the direction of changes in bilingual education escalated, members of the Coalition became increasingly politicized, formulating a purposeful role in the political process through the escalation of competition and intensification of adversarial markers. The Coalition met continuously with Assemblyman Altorre and Dulay and Burt to try to hammer out a compromise. However, as negotiations continued, the participants grew more entrenched in their opposing views on whether limited and non-English-speaking students needed bilingual instruction and the services of bilingual certified teachers. Peter Chacon observed: "They simply did not budge and we were not going to compromise. The positions were very, very hard" (Interview, November 12, 1981).

While the State Board endorsement of what became AB 690 was one catalyst for action, it was not the only factor in the formation of a coalition of interest groups to oppose attempts to repeal the bilingual education mandate. Mixed signals from the Department to bilingual educators, exclusion from participating in the proposal formulation, and the alienation of the Office of Bilingual-Bicultural Education and State Board members contributed to the polarization of sides. Key individuals were involved from the beginning in unsuccessfully trying to dissuade the Department from going ahead with its plan and then in trying to obtain favorable amendments to AB 690. However, the threat to the program and the reaction on the part of bilingual supporters resulting in a broad base of organizational support enhanced the position of the Bilingual Community Coalition within the political process. While there had always been an identification with the program, supporters were disorganized and focused upon local concerns. The *threat* at the state level opened a new channel of political activity and a new identity for Hispanics. After coalescing among themselves, coalition members nurtured the identification of Hispanics with the program and disseminated the interpretation that the threat to bilingual education was a threat to Hispanic interests. Thus, not only was the threat transformed into a cause for political action among Hispanic political elites, but the cause itself was crucial for the grounding of a new Hispanic political entity in the maintenance of bilingual education. The strengthening of purposeful action was followed next by increased cohesion among Hispanic groups to support bilingual education, which served to bring other third parties into the negotiation of a consensus.

CASE STUDY II: SACRIFICE AND UNITY

Although bilingual education has generally been characterized as representing Hispanic aspirations in the economic and political fields, as well as in education, disagreements over the program have sometimes been more intense among Hispanics than between Hispanics and mainstream educators. In 1979 there were two Chicano legislators competing for the reform legislation: Assemblyman Alatorre and Assemblyman Chacon.

Although Alatorre's bill was not widely supported by Hispanic organizations across the state, as one of the leading Hispanic leaders in the legislature with a record of significant victories for Hispanics and other minorities, his sponsorship of the State Board/Department legislation to repeal the bilingual law was particularly divisive to the Hispanic community. Thus, when Alatorre withdrew his bill and, more importantly, when he withdrew from the competition, the position of the Bilingual Community Coalition was strengthened. The defeat of Alatorre's legislation also cued other Hispanic leaders that their own credibility to the Hispanic community might also be brought into question if they did not endorse the program. Therefore, the unity of the Hispanic purpose was greatly increased by the elimination of the competition between Alatorre and Chacon.

The Chicano Legislative Caucus met to try to find a resolution to the issue that was factionalizing the Hispanic political leadership, not only in the legislature, but across the state. But the Caucus was basically incapable of resolving division on an issue in which its members were personally involved. Senator Montoya, the Caucus chairman, remarked that the Caucus was only effective "when doing letters of appointment." But even then, he added, it was on the condition that members did not have a preferred individual of their own—"and that hasn't happened very often in the past few years"(Interview, February 8, 1982).

One problem was that the Chicano Caucus did not have the numbers or the resources required to offer the members incentives to work together and resolve their differences (Interview, June 3, 1982). The Caucus was only a coalition inasmuch as the members shared a common goal that was expressed in and through their participation in the group. Group interests and individual interests had to be consonant for the Caucus to take a united position. In this instance, individual interests took precedence over group values until the Bilingual Community Coalition was successful in compelling Hispanic politicians to support bilingual education.

An observer of the legislature said simply that the Chicano Caucus exists not because the legislators feel they are better able to represent Hispanic interests, but "because Hispanics expect it to [exist]" (Interview, June 3, 1982). In other words, while the Caucus had no political value because of its lack of clout as measured by resources and number of members, it was of symbolic value to the Hispanic community; it represented both unity and the legitimacy of expressing political concerns and interests in ethnic terms. However, based upon Montoya's and other legislators' observations of the Caucus, this symbol had rarely been effective in directing political behavior, because legislators acted first in their own interests and the weakness of the caucus negated any incentive to participate. The Caucus' power to act in the interests of Hispanics, as opposed to their districts, came when the Hispanic community itself was first united around bilingual education. Then, Hispanic leaders could claim a legitimate basis for addressing the concern of the Hispanic community in the legislature.

Several attempts were made to compromise, first in Alatorre's bill, then in resolving the differences between Alatorre's bill and a rival bill sponsored by Assemblyman Chacon, which had the endorsement of the Bilingual Community Coalition. But rather than building grounds for consensus and resolving their differences in the first year, adversaries on both sides of the issue were more polarized. The conflict escalated to a dramatic Senate Finance Committee meeting in which several compromise solutions were proposed, including one by the Chicano Legislative Caucus. The committee members rejected the Chicano Caucus' proposal after Alatorre waffled in his support of the proposal. This action caused both authors to withdraw their bills. The Chicano Caucus and the Coalition succeeded in averting further last-minute attempts to pass a bill to repeal the existing law, thereby stalling a resolution until the following year.

Alatorre claimed that, although his refusal to support the Caucus' compromise during the Senate Finance Committee appeared to be the crucial event that led to the defeat of his bill, he was out of the competition long before. By August when the committee meeting took place, "there was so much controversy that all the Chicano legislators were looking for a political 'way out' that would not make them personally responsible for the program, and one of the ways out was saying, 'If the Caucus supports it, then I support it.'" The Caucus served as a means of concealing the legislators' individual actions while they were endearing themselves to the Chicano community. "Besides," added Alatorre in a description of the way he was characterized as a traitor to the Hispanic community, "they had me...here was an opportunity to embarrass me" (Interview, October 10, 1981). In the end, Alatorre became the scapegoat, the symbolic sacrificial lamb for the Caucus to regroup and unify; Montoya emerged as a more powerful leader defending the Caucus and the Chicano community's cause; and Chacon retained his position as the "Father of bilingual education in California" (Interviews, October 28, 1981, February 8, 1982, May 28, 1982).

The reaction of the Bilingual Community Coalition to the division in the Caucus was consonant with the interpretation the legislators provided them. For instance, following the Senate Finance Committee meeting, the Coalition wrote a harsh letter to Montoya demanding Alatorre's removal from the Caucus (August 23, 1979):

We are incensed and horrified by the lies of Mr. Alatorre with regard to the Caucus' compromise which we vigorously supported. Clearly, he has violated the basic principles of trust and in so doing has betrayed the confidence of the Chicano and linguistic minority community represented by this Coalition. Indeed, his action is unethical, unprofessional and obviously not responsible.

Members of the Coalition felt the senators would have gone along with the Caucus compromise if Alatorre had made a "more firm statement" indicating that "maybe he didn't like it, but he was going along with it and felt they should try it" (Interview, January 25, 1982).

According to Montoya, the struggle for unity among Hispanics polarized them from majority legislators: "I think the conclusion reached by mainstream fellow politicians is we are best left alone or if you are going to deal with us or touch us, it had better be with a ten-foot pole" (Interview, February 8, 1982). But the Coalition's reaction was favorable to the outcome. One member's assessment was that it gave them "more time to talk to a whole lot more people." If the controversy had not been extended into 1980, she felt that they might not have gotten the votes to eventually prevail (Interview, January 25, 1982). Roberto Cruz (1979) president of the California Association for Bilingual Education, echoed the theme of unity: "This move brought about unification among bilingual citizens and also faith in our democratic process." Peter Chacon wrote to supporters to rally support for the Caucus' decision, promising that the events of 1979 had strengthened their resolve to "protect and preserve those programs that are important to our community." In his letter, Chacon cautioned: "This year we have won the battle for bilingual education, but not necessarily the war" and went on to command key Chicanos who participated in the effort (Chacon 1979). As a final gesture of unity, all of the Chicano Legislative Caucus members joined as coauthors of Chacon's new bill, AB 812, for the 1980 session.

These final events of 1979 illustrate a transformation in the Hispanic political identity from one of opposing the threat to the program as represented by such bills as AB 690, to a belief that they had gained some power and wielded political influence in the legislature. Although their actions alienated some legislators, their position was enhanced by Alatorre's apparent defeat; in addition, the sanctions that the Hispanic community displayed toward Alatorre for having been involved in his divisive role further strengthened the cohesion of Hispanics and legitimated their participation in the political process.

The reciprocity between identity and unity is illustrated in the linkage between diverse Hispanic interests with the interests of bilingual educators. This unification not only incorporated a greater number of Hispanic political elites who were willing to support the program, but non-Hispanic politicians were also allured into the fray in support of the program. The ability of the Bilingual Community Coalition to obtain the support of non-Hispanic groups and individuals played a major role in the formation of a consensus and legitimated its own participation in the process.

CASE STUDY III: CONSENSUS AND CONSTRAINTS

When the legislature reconvened in January 1980, the Coalition enjoyed greater political resources from which it could draw to influence decision making. Although legislators and mainstream education groups lamented the lack of a "compromising spirit" on the part of the "vehement advocates of bilingual education" (Interview, October 11, 1981), the members of the Coalition proudly proclaimed that they had "cut their political teeth" (Interview, November 12, 1981) in 1979 and that only when they had "matured politically" were they able to effect the final outcome (Interview, January 28, 1981).

As a result of the influence that Hispanic elites derived from their unification and identification with bilingual education, new patterns of interaction began to emerge. In the second year, political actions were directed toward achieving compromise rather than on escalating the competition. Given the nature of bilingual education as a political issue among Hispanics and the escalation of competition that occurred in 1979, compromise was made possible once Chacon and the Coalition had crystallized their role to influence the final bill and altered their posture from opposition to cooperation. At that time, several third parties helped to further legitimate their interests by developing a basis for consensus.

Throughout 1980 groups continued to compete with limited resources; the Coalition was an all-volunteer, predominantly female interest group of approximately 30 members. Each member depended upon her or his organization to provide funds for expenses or contributed out of their own pockets. Although compared with 1979 they were more organized, the effectiveness of their actions was still heavily dependent upon community support.

Chacon also faced formidable obstacles in the second year despite the backing of the united Chicano Legislative Caucus and other organizations. In addition to Chacon's legislation, another bill, AB 2400, which incorporated the provisions of Alatorre's measure, was introduced by a non-Hispanic legislator, Assemblyman Dennis Mangers. Until AB 2400 died in the Assembly Ways and Means Committee, Chacon had a tough time negotiating with mainstream education organizations (Interview, January 28, 1982). However, when Mangers' bill was refused passage, Chacon's hand was strengthened by the mere fact that his was the only possible reform vehicle in that legislative session. At that time, as one supporter described the significance of the demise of AB 2400, the mainstream organizations "saw the handwriting on the wall" (Interview, January 28, 1982). While Chacon controlled the legislation, mainstream education organizations controlled the political resources to gain the approval of the legislature. Negotiations between Chacon and members of his staff with mainstream representatives were critical to sending the correct signals to the legislature that Chacon was willing to compromise.

Governor Jerry Brown's office was also significant in enhancing the political prestige of Chacon and the Coalition and legitimating their participation in the compromise process. In 1979 the governor had declared his neutrality in the competition between Chacon and Alatorre, indicating only his desire for a solution that included the consent of the Hispanic community. Thus the governor cued non-Hispanic authors in his pronouncements that their bills would be subject to close scrutiny and probable veto if they passed the legislature. One member of the Coalition described the significance of the governor's support as "the strength that keeps you going in times of adversity... it made us feel more powerful" (Interview, January 25, 1982). When the governor announced his support for Chacon in April 1980, following several fund-raising events and receptions sponsored by various bilingual organizations for his benefit, he was ensuring a role for the bilingual advocates in the political process.

Other actors supporting Chacon and working behind the scenes as mediators seeking to bring about a resolution to the conflict were also significant in developing a basis for consensus. Representing the governor's office, the State Department of Education, and one of the major counties in the state, their participation was significant not only for the instrumental functions they contributed to negotiating a compromise, but, more importantly, as actors with considerable political resources identified with Chacon and the Bilingual Community Coalition. Their role was to confine the conflict to legislative action on issues strictly related to bilingual education.

The failure of AB 812 in the Senate Education Committee, despite its broad base of support, was another dramatic illustration of the need for mainstream sponsorship to pass the Coalition-backed bill. Senator Rodda, the chairman of the powerful Senate Finance Committee, then recommended that Chacon's earlier bill, AB 507, which was still inactive before the committee, be resurrected, thereby putting Rodda in a key position to determine the outcome. Throughout the legislature's summer recess, Rodda and Chacon negotiated the provisions of the bill. Finally, in August, Rodda was satisfied that Chacon had acted "responsibly" in accepting "compromise" and supported the bill through its passage in the Senate (Interview, October 28, 1982).

The negotiations between Rodda and Chacon were carried out over a relatively short period of time (approximately one month) during several conferences between the legislators and, more frequently, between members of their staff. The Coalition did not participate in these meetings, nor were they consulted on the changes in the bill. However, Mangers and others, including union representatives, were in contact with Rodda's staff and did have a hand in shaping the final bill, particularly in raising issues that Rodda gave to Chacon in the form of demands for his support (Interview, May 28, 1982). In defense of the exclusion of the Coalition at this state of negotiations, Chacon commented: "The greatest impact that is made on a bill is the day-to-day work that a legislator does with individual legislators in meeting in their office and agreeing." While the Coalition was not a part of the bargaining, Chacon added, they contributed by pressuring the legislature for a resolution through "their continued work in the field" (Interview, November 12, 1981).

With each event, Chacon increased his prestige and enhanced the identification of the Coalition with the influence and power they derived from participating in the policy-making process. Illustrations had been drawn from negotiations between Chacon and mainstream organizations, and the role of mediators such as Tovar, Cervantes, and Foster to focus attention to bilingual education issues. However, for all these negotiations to be successful Chacon and the Bilingual Community Coalition had to adapt to two important principles of the policy-making process. One was that they were not going to get all they wanted; second, they learned that the power to negotiate rested with the party that controlled the greater amount of political resources.

Although Chacon's intention were generally in concert with those of the Coalition, a conflict over teacher protection from layoff demonstrated the pressures Chacon received to secure the support of the mainstream organizations as well as legislators. The dispute centered around the legal definition of competence. The existing law protected certified bilingual teachers from layoff even though they had less seniority than a nonbilingual teacher, providing the bilingual teacher was assigned to a bilingual classroom mandated under AB 1329.

The largest teachers' union in the state, the California Teachers Association (CTA), wanted this section of the law changed. The union originally supported Chacon's bill but it changed its support to "no position" and in March 1980 negotiated its support with Chacon if the language was removed from the bill. Chacon complied with the union's demands and the Coalition reacted negatively, threatening to withdraw its support. The language was inserted and taken out several times. One participant in the negotiations noted: "It went back and forth, back and forth. He [Chacon] didn't seem to be able to take his position and stick to it. It was one of those things where he wanted both groups to support him, yet it was a losing battle if somebody was going to withdraw support" (Interview, January 25, 1982).

The conflict surfaced once more two days before Chacon's bill was scheduled for hearing in the Senate Education Committee. The night before the hearing, Chacon met with those members of the Coalition who had indicated a willingness to take a "moderate position." After several hours of "emotional negotiations," the principal spokesperson for the Coalition, Peter Schilla, conceded that if the bill passed, there would be future opportunities for discussion; he eventually convinced a majority of the members not to oppose the bill and "lose the whole thing." While the Coalition could have withdrawn its support (as several member organizations chose to do), it was significant that it chose to admit that it needed the CTA's support to build a successful consensus, thereby continuing its own participation, but in a more limited role (Interview, December 20, 1981).

CONCLUSION

Symbols operate as selective criteria for receiving information that is meaningful (i.e., consonant) within one's belief system and imparts meaning to the role that one takes in the political process. This chapter has analyzed the role—the meaningfulness of participation in the political process—for Hispanic political elites as bilingual education supporters. Identification, unification, and consensus building are the three most salient meanings attributed to bilingual education that were constructed over the two-year period.

One outcome from the Bilingual Community Coalition's successful formation of identity and unity was the role of third parties to mediate in the articulation of the Coalition's interests. The governor's veto threat, the dominance of the unions over the teacher protection, Rodda's role as a compromiser, and the informal channels of influence used by Mangers and others—established over the years of contact and participation in the political process, both on the "front lines" and in "all the behind-the-scenes kinds of ways" (Interview, May 28, 1982)—demonstrated that in order to continue its participation the Coalition had to recognize the limits of its power and concede to major concessions that were "necessary" to achieve a "compromise." The effect of the concessions on the final outcome was to delimit the Coalition's role to that of symbolic bearers of a bill it was only partially responsible for formulating (Interview, January 28, 1982). Each action leading to a consensus reduced the influence of the Coalition on the final outcome. Without minimizing the significance of the Coalition's victory as the sponsors of the bilingual education reform legislation, it is important to recognize that its sponsorship alone did not ensure that the contents of the bill would reflect its interests. Instead, the Coalition's interests, inasmuch as they were represented in the bill, were there because of the power their actions accorded to Chacon in the negotiation process. Thus the symbol (bilingual education policy) accorded a role for Hispanics in the political process. However, this role did not equate with the political capital to realize the group's interests in policy making. Instead, I would argue, Hispanics are still forming a base for political influence that includes identifying their interests. In short, the dominant mainstream's definition of the educational problems of Hispanics and other language-minority children as a language issue without recognizing the social factors involved was the prevailing orientation of the policy enacted. Bilingual education as a symbol of consensus concealed this reality from all the participants in its formation.

REFERENCES

Castro, M. (1980, June 3). Who should teach? Bilingual education produces Tower of Babel. *Sacramento Bee*.
Chacon, P. (1979). The California legislature looks at bilingual education (p. 5). Unpublished manuscript, Sacramento.
Cohen, A. (1974). Two-Dimensional Man. London: Routledge & Kegan Paul.
Cruz, R. (September 1979). Action Alert. Bilingual Community Coalition Newsletter.
Edelman, M. (1971). Politics as Symbolic Action: Mass Arousal and Quiescence. New York: Academic Press.

Martinez, O. (1980, January). Chronology of events leading to current bilingual legislative activity. Memorandum to the file. Unpublished manuscript.

Navarro, R. A. (1983). Identity and consensus in the politics of bilingual education: The case of California, 1967–1980. Unpublished doctoral dissertation, Stanford University, Stanford, CA.

————. (1985). The problems of language, education and society: Who decides? In E. E. Garcia and R. V. Padilla (eds.), Advances in Bilingual Education Research (pp. 289–313). Tucson: University of Arizona Press.

————. (1986). The role of hispanic interest groups in bilingual education policy formation in California. Unpublished manuscript, Michigan State University, Institute for Research on Teaching, East Lansing.

Office of Auditor General. (1979, March). Bilingual education: Pupil assessment, program evaluation and local program implementation. Report of the Joint Legislative Audit Committee. Unpublished manuscript. Sacramento, CA.

Schilla, P. (1979, March). Analysis of the Heide Dulay/Marina Burt legislative proposal on bilingual education. Unpublished manuscript. Sacramento.

Spindler, G. (1971). Dreamers without Power: The Menomini Indians. New York: Holt, Rinehart and Winston.

————. (1972a). Burgbach: Urbanization and Identity in a German Village. New York: Holt, Rinehart and Winston.

————. (1972b). The transmission of culture. In A. R. Beals, G. D. Spindler, and L. Spindler (eds.), Culture in Process (2nd ed.). New York: Holt, Rinehart and Winston.

————. (ed.). (1982). Doing the Ethnography of Schooling: Educational Anthropology in Action. New York: Holt, Rinehart and Winston.

Spindler, G. D., and Spindler, L. (1978). Identity, militancy, and cultural congruence: The Menominee and Kainai. *Annals of the American Academy of Political and Social Science* 436:73–85.

Spradley, J. P. (1980). Participant Observation. New York: Holt, Rinehart and Winston.

Turner, V. (1966). Ritual aspects of conflict control in African micropolitics. In M. Swartz, V. Turner, and A. Tuden (eds.), Political Anthropology (pp. 239–246). Chicago: Aldine.

PART II
SOCIALIZATION OF YOUNG CHILDREN TO SCHOOL: TRANSMISSION OF CULTURAL VALUES ACROSS CULTURES

4

Children in American and Japanese Day-Care Centers: Ethnography and Reflective Cross-Cultural Interviewing

Mariko Fujita and
Toshiyuki Sano

INTRODUCTION

If "independence" is regarded as a core American cultural value (Fujita 1984; Hsu 1973, 1981; Rapson et al. 1967; Varenne 1977), so is "dependence" for Japanese culture (Doi 1973; Fujita 1977; Kiefer 1970). Early childhood is a period when core cultural values are taught (Caudill and Weinstein 1969; LeVine 1984; Masuda 1969). Therefore, studying educational processes in day-care centers in different countries may reveal different cultural transmission processes.

A cross-cultural study of cultural transmission will immediately put us face-to-face with complex problems. It is, of course, difficult to find two comparable, socioeconomic groups in two different countries. The comparative study, however, involves a more profound and perhaps more important problem. That is, is there a concept such as "independence" applicable to different cultures? Recent developments in cultural theory tell us that the meanings of concepts are culturally constructed (Schweder and LeVine 1984). So how can we compare the educational processes of two different countries, being simultaneously sensitive to the cultural construction of the meanings underlying these two systems? This chapter attempts to answer this question by examining day-to-day activities at American (central Wisconsin) and Japanese (suburban Tokyo) day-care centers. We will take the following steps.

First, we will describe similarities and differences in the American and Japanese day-care centers using participant observations and interviews. Our purpose of this section, however, is not a straightforward comparison of the two cultures. We are trying to show that the American and Japanese teachers do not interpret such key concepts as "independence" in the same way. Our contention is that until we know the difference in meanings of the key concepts, it is impossible and inadequate to determine which system produces more independence-oriented children. Judging two cultures using a single criterion blinds us from systematically understanding the two different philosophies of education operating in these two centers (Frake 1980).

Second, to discern different educational assumptions operating under the two systems, we describe a research procedure, "reflective cross-cultural interviewing," which George and Louise Spindler (1987a) coined. Activities at both centers are recorded on videotapes. Both American and Japanese videotapes are shown to the teachers in these two centers. Watching these videotapes with the teachers, we first interviewed the teachers concerning their explanation of their own activities. Then we asked them to compare the American and Japanese day-care centers shown on the tapes. Therefore, we have used these tapes as evocative stimuli to let the teachers talk about their cultural assumptions.

Then we analyze two sets of "cultural dialogues" (Spindler and Spindler 1987b:1-6) which the reflective cross-cultural interviewing revealed. Both American and Japanese teachers interpret the other's system within their own cultural framework. They are not really comparing American culture with Japanese culture. Instead they are talking about their "pivotal concerns" and contrasting them with what is disturbing within their own educational system. Therefore, the teachers' interpretations reveal two distinct cultural frameworks underlying the American and Japanese systems. We also analyze teachers' interpretations, especially their discrepancies, as clues in understanding the two sets of cultural dialogues and will clarify differences in underlying educational philosophy such as the concepts of "time," "space," "teachers," and "children" between the American and Japanese day-care centers.

The material for this chapter is based on three field studies. The American data are part of our on-going, broader fieldwork jointly conducted in Riverfront City, Wisconsin, from fall 1984 to spring 1986 (Maple Day Care). The Japanese material was collected through observations and interviews at a Japanese day-care center (Kawa Day Care) in the summer of 1986. Sano conducted research on young children's behavior patterns at a different Japanese day-care center (Hato Day Care) in 1978-79 in a suburb of Tokyo (Sano 1980, 1983). During this research, he recorded on videotapes the interactions between teachers and children. The Japanese videotapes shown to the American teachers were the ones that Sano recorded at Hato Day Care.[1]

DESCRIPTIVE COMPARISON:
PARTICIPANT OBSERVATION AND INTERVIEWS

Description of Day-Care Centers

Location. Maple Day Care is located in Riverfront City (population 22,000), Wisconsin, in the American Midwest. The center is as the east end of the city on the border of the residential area and is adjacent to the commercial area. The children come from all over the county. Parents bring children by car.

Kawa Day Care is located in the suburb Tokyo, in Tama City (population 121,000), which is the northeastern part of Tokyo Prefecture. The center is in the southern part of Tama City. It is in the middle of high-rise apartment buildings operated by a semigovernmental housing corporation. It is considered to be one of the most conveniently located day-care centers, because it is only a ten-minute walking distance from a private railroad station whose line connects Tama City to the central part of Tokyo (30 minutes by train). Parents bring children on foot or mostly by bicycle. Cars are rarely used for this purpose.

Maple Day Care is open five days a week from Monday to Friday. The classes are formed in September and are organized by age group. Once the child reaches a specific age, such as two, two and a half, three, four, and five, he or she can move to the next class depending on the teachers' evaluation of the child's growth and development as well as the availability of a vacancy. The parents can choose which days of the week to send the children to the center. A certain number of children use the center only two or three days a week. The parents pay an hourly fee, which is competitive with that of several day-care centers in this city. There is one handicapped child.

Japanese parents bring children every day to Kawa Day Care. There is no part-time system like the one at Maple. The center is open from Monday to Saturday (Saturday is a half day). Parents pay a monthly fee directly to the municipal office, though Kawa Day Care is operated by a private, nonprofit organization. The fee is determined by the official schedule according to both parents' income tax of the previous year. The staff does not know how much each parent pays for the fee. The center accepts a few handicapped children (currently two). The classes are organized by age group. They are formed once a year in April according to the children's ages as of April 1st. If the child's age is between one and two, he or she belongs to the class called "Sumire-gumi" (Violet class) or "issai-ji gumi" (one-year-old class). There are four other classes: two-, three-, four- and five-year-old. Unlike the Maple children, the Kawa children can move to the next class only once a year in April. Most of the children attend this center from ages one to five, until they enter the first grade in an elementary school.

Floor Plan and Playground. Maple Day Care is a two-story building with the entrances at the mezzanine level (see Figure 4.1). At an entrance, there are two stairs; one leads to the lower level where classrooms for younger children (ages one to three) are found. Classrooms for older children are upstairs. Entering or leaving the buildings is not especially easy, for only two doors lead to the outside. Classrooms are connected with small halls and each room is divided into areas for specific activities. The floor is carpeted. People enter the building without taking off their shoes. Bare feet are not allowed by state regulations. There is no staff lounge. However, Maple Day Care has a dining room. The playground is divided into three parts: the largest part is cemented, the next

Figure 4.1
Floor Plan of Maple Day Care

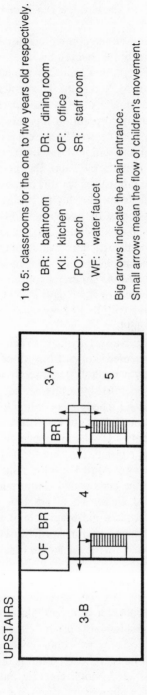

UPSTAIRS

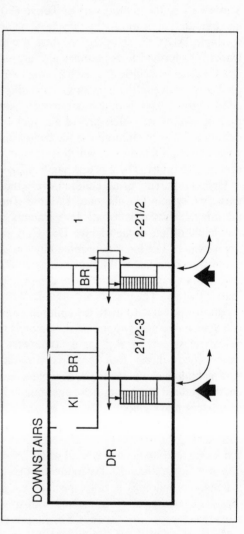

DOWNSTAIRS

1 to 5: classrooms for the one to five years old respectively.

BR: bathroom   DR: dining room
BR: kitchen   OF: office
PO: porch   SR: staff room
WF: water faucet

Big arrows indicate the main entrance.
Small arrows mean the flow of children's movement.

Figure 4.2
Floor Plan of Kawa Day Care

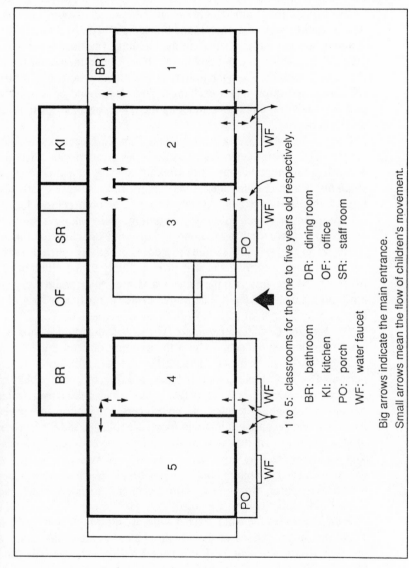

1 to 5: classrooms for the one to five years old respectively.

BR: bathroom   DR: dining room
KI: kitchen   OF: office
PO: porch   SR: staff room
WF: water faucet

Big arrows indicate the main entrance.
Small arrows mean the flow of children's movement.

largest one is sand, and there is a grassy area in front of the building. The playground is fenced. There is a shed for the toys in the sand part.

Kawa Day Care is a one-story building (see Figure 4.2). All the classrooms face the playground with sliding doors that enable children to have easy access through the porch to the playground. The porch of the classroom for the youngest children (age one) is fenced to prevent them from accidentally running out to the playground. Immediately outside of each classroom are water faucets where children wash their hands and brush their teeth. At Kawa Day Care there is a long straight hallway (*roka*) in the building. The floor is hardwood. People take off their shoes and put on "inside shoes" when they enter the building at the main entrance. Going barefoot is permitted. There is a staff room for relaxation and information exchange. The playground is covered with compressed sand. In the playground along the fence are slide, swings, jungle gym, and sand box.

Daily Schedule. The Maple and Kawa Day Care centers have similar daily schedules of general activities. Most activities are performed according to the age group, except in the very early morning and very late afternoon when only a small number of children attend the centers. In those cases, activities are performed in a mixed group. A daily schedule at both centers looks like this: (a) group activity such as singing, painting, and making a story; (b) snack; (c) group activity such as reading a story and dancing; (d) lunch; (e) nap; (f) snack; and (g) free play. Some differences in activity schedule between these two centers are: morning snack is provided only to the children of one- and two-year-old age groups at the Kawa Day Care center, while everyone receives a morning snack at Maple. The Maple center is open at 6:30 A.M. while the Kawa center is open at 7:20 A.M. Both are closed at 6:00 P.M.

Teachers and Child/Teacher Ratio. The staff of the Maple center is all female except for one male teacher who is the assistant director and who also works with the four-year-old group. The staff of the Kawa center is all female. The personnel of the Maple center includes one director, one bookkeeper, seven teachers, three teacher aides, and two cooks. That of the Kawa center includes one director, one head teacher, eleven teachers, one janitor, and two cooks. The American teachers are graduates of four-year colleges and the teacher aides are usually graduates of two-year junior colleges or two-year technical schools. The Japanese teachers are usually graduates of two-year junior colleges or two-year special training schools. Each Maple teacher's aide works with a teacher. Hereafter, we use the term "teachers" to cover both teachers and teacher aides unless otherwise noted.

Table 4.1 shows the child/teacher ratio of both Maple and Kawa Day Care. There are seven classes in the Maple center, which include two classes of three-year-olds, whereas the Kawa center has five classes. The ratio that the Maple and Kawa centers employ is set by local authorities, that is, the State of Wisconsin and the Tokyo Prefecture, respectively. In comparison, the ratio is the same at both centers for younger children (until age three). However, the

Table 4.1
The Child/Teacher Ratio at Maple and Kawa Day Care Centers

MAPLE DAY CARE
Class Group

	One	Two	Two-half	Three-A	Three-B	Four	Five	(Total)
Child	4 (4)	6 (6)	8 (16)	10 (10)	10 (20)	13 (26)	16 (8)	(90)*
Teacher	1 (1)	1 (1)	1 (2)	1 (1)	1 (2)	1 (2)	1 (1)	(10)

KAWA DAY CARE
Class Group

	One	Two	Three	Four	Five	(Total)
Child	4 (9)	6 (16)	10 (21)	25 (25)	25 (25)	(96)
Teacher	1 (3)**	1 (3)	1 (3)**	1 (1)	1 (2)***	(12)

( ) Actual number.

* Average daily number of children. About 120 children are enrolled.

** Since the center is required by regulation to have one teacher for each handicapped child, one of the three teachers is assigned to take care of one handicapped child in both classes.

*** One of the two teachers in this class is the head teacher and called *frii hobo* (free teacher). She substitutes for the off-duty teacher.

Kawa teachers take care of twice as many older children (ages four and five) as the Maple teachers.

Comparisons of Activities

Classroom Activity. At Maple Day Care, each class of older children (from age three) is divided into smaller groups, especially during the morning classroom activities. For example, in the class of the four-year-olds, the children are divided into three groups. The teacher takes care of a group of seven or eight children. He may coordinate these children to jointly create a story. Meanwhile, another teacher (teacher aide) of this class attends to another group of seven or eight children with some instructions for art activities. The rest of this age group are assigned to play on their own with toys in the classroom. The option of playing with toys is set by the teacher. After about 15 minutes, the children rotate and engage in a different activity. At the end, all the children experience all of the three activities provided in this classroom.

At Kawa Day Care there is a single activity for all children of the same age group. Even when there are two teachers, children are not divided into smaller groups. These two teachers help each other carry out this single activity.

"Time-out" is frequently used as a disciplinary measure at Maple Day Care. Whenever a teacher finds a child not engaging in the activity he is supposed to, the teacher tells the child to join the group activity. When the child disturbs other children, or when the child's side activity attracts other children's attention away from the teacher, the teacher pulls this child out of the group and lets him sit on his own and reflect on his conduct. After five or ten minutes, the teacher allows him to rejoin the group activity. However, if the misbehavior is excessive, the teacher asks him why he was disciplined. If the child acknowledges his fault, then he is allowed to join the group and to resume the activity. This disciplinary measure is used several times in each activity session for all the children except for the very youngest.

At Kawa Day Care, though the teachers claim that they sometimes withdraw distracting children from the group activity, this time-out is not recognized as a disciplinary measure and is rarely used. In observing the classroom activities in any age group, we find some children not participating in the group activity. An example from a four-year-old class illustrates the content of a Japanese class. The group activity was to walk on a balance beam designed for children and engage in a game called *jan-ken-pon*.[2] Meanwhile, at one corner of the classroom, two girls were chit-chatting to each other, and at a different corner, three boys and a girl were playing with toys. Three other children were running around the room. The children who were engaged in these side activities were not disciplined by the teacher, as they would be at Maple. The teacher took it as a matter of course that some children did not want to participate in the group activity and that they played on their own. "After all, they are only children. This is not a school, but a day-care center. It is a place to play. They should have happy times."

When the Kawa teachers find a child distracting other children, they use a technique called *kibun-tenkan* instead of trying to discipline the child. That is, they try to divert the child's focus from his preoccupation to other activity. For example, two children were teasing each other by the little pool during their swimming time. Their teacher came, lifted one of the children and jokingly said, "you are so mischievous. I'm going to throw you into the pool!" She pretended that she was actually going to throw this child into the swimming pool. Here everyone knew that she was joking. No one took it that she was emotionally abusing the child by threatening him, as some Americans might interpret the situation. The child also took it as a joke and started giggling. The point here, according to the Kawa teachers, is to change the child's mood rather than trying to teach him what is right and wrong.

The difference between the Kawa and Maple teachers' attitudes is interesting in relation to the issue of "choice." The Maple teachers often stress the importance of children's "choosing" an activity. The American children at Maple are constantly asked to choose one activity from two or three activities. The Maple teachers believe that giving choices to the children will make them sort out their wishes and express their desires to engage in an activity without being forced to do so. Therefore, letting children choose is a step toward independence and freedom. In contrast, the Kawa teachers do not stress the importance of giving choices to the children. They do not make a point of asking their children to "choose" their activity.

However, the Maple teachers do not talk about the fact that the range of "choice" that the children face is always controlled by the teachers. In comparison, the Kawa children are free to participate or not in ongoing group activity. If they decide not to participate, then they are free to choose any activity available to them in the classroom. The range of choice is unlimited as long as they do not disturb or injure other children.

Mealtime. At both Maple and Kawa Day Care, hot lunch is served. The Maple center has a separate dining room exclusively used for eating lunch. A corner of this dining room is the kitchen where meals are prepared. The meals are served in two shifts, one for younger children (ages one to two and a half) who eat first and one for older children (ages three to five). At the Kawa center, lunch is served in each classroom, and children eat by age group.

At Maple there are seven large rectangular tables, where ten people can be seated. The children usually sit with their classmates. The teachers also sit with their own children and eat with them. At the beginning of the meal, they recite a short nonreligious prayer in thanksgiving for the food. Meals are served family style. Each item of the menu is put on a large plate or bowl, which the teachers ask the children to pass among them. The teachers tell children to take a small amount of every item of the menu. If they want to have more, they can ask for seconds. If they do not like a certain food, the teachers ask them to "at least try it."

The Maple teachers regard lunch as a social time. They encourage the children to talk. At the same time, the teachers supervise their table manners.

Unlike at Kawa where the teachers sometimes feed even three-year-old slow eaters, no one, even the youngest child (age one), is fed at Maple. The Maple teachers think it important that each child is able to eat on his or her own using utensils. They regard it as a step toward independence. Feeding children, even if they are slow eaters, is not thought to be a good idea, because they would soon stop making an effort and would expect teachers to feed them constantly. Other children would also want to have the extra attention. Then the whole situation would be chaotic (Fujita 1986).

At Kawa Day Care, each item of the menu is served on a separate plate or bowl for each child instead of on communal plates and bowls. Each teacher brings food for her children on several trays from the kitchen to her classroom. For younger children (ages one to four), teachers set the table for the children. However, among the oldest children, a boy and a girl are assigned this duty each day. These children are called *toban*. They serve the plates and bowls, which are already filled with food, from the trays to each child. Meanwhile the other children are supposed to wait quietly. When the children on duty finish serving, they stand in front of everyone and say *itadakimasu* (which means that I will gratefully receive this food) and others follow. The teacher works on a rotation so that every child has an equal opportunity to be a toban. Each child also knows when his or her next turn comes. The Kawa children do not consider this duty system as an imposition; instead, each one takes pride in being responsible and also in being able to do the task as well as other children do. It is a sign of being a "big child." The Kawa teachers also believe that this toban system makes children responsible.

Although the Maple teachers encourage children to help the teachers, no duty system such as the toban at Kawa Day Care is used at Maple Day Care. At snack time, teachers solicit help, but they think it important that the help come voluntarily from the children rather than being assigned to them. Hence, when a teacher asks, "Who wants to wipe the table?" two or three children usually raise their hands. A Maple child likes to be chosen as a helper. It means that she or he chooses to help the teacher without being forced to do so and that the teacher recognizes her or his willingness. Because children regard helping as a reward of recognition, the teachers say that they see to it that everyone has a chance to help the teachers over a period of time. However, to maintain an appearance of voluntariness, the rotation is implicit and the children do not know when their turn will come. For the children, helping is a competition among them.

Nap Time. Both centers have a daily nap time for all children. At Maple Day Care, the teachers set up portable cots for napping for the children in each classroom. The children do not change their clothes for napping. Setting up these cots is considered to be the teachers' duty and no child helps the teachers.

At the Kawa Day Care, both teachers and children prepare their older children's classrooms for napping. For the oldest group (age five), for example, the teacher first vacuums the floor. Then the children bring *futon* (cotton mattresses) from the closet and set them on the floor. Meanwhile, the children brush their teeth and change from daytime clothes to pajamas. Although not all the children always help, preparing the room for napping is seen as a shared duty between teachers and children. Before the nap, the teacher may read or show one or two children's stories with picture books or videotapes.

Transition from One Activity to the Next. Perhaps one of the most remarkable differences between Kawa and Maple Day Care is the ways in which the teachers move children from one activity to the next. The Maple teachers rely exclusively on verbal instructions. The Kawa teachers in comparison use very little verbal instructions, but they also use nonverbal measures such as music to signal the transition. An example from the class of three-year-olds at Kawa Day Care will illustrate this point. One of the two teachers was reading a book to the children. Then it was time for their swimming. The teacher says, "Let's go swimming. Let's do *basha-basha*" (children's talk for swimming.) Some children know the routine better than others. These children spontaneously go to the bathroom and others follow. The children seem to imitate what the other children are doing rather than following the teachers' verbal instructions. They come back to their classroom and start changing into their swimming suits. Then the children pull out dry towels and the clothes they will wear after swimming from their individual lockers and give these items to the teacher. When the teacher plays a record, the children gather in a circle to exercise before swimming.

The Kawa teachers can expect the children to complete this series of actions without giving a step-by-step instruction. Indeed, when the teachers give instructions, they say only a few words in passing, addressing two or three children nearby. However, the Kawa teachers frequently use music to signal the transition. When one of the teachers announces the snack time, the other teacher starts playing the piano. They have songs for the beginning and end of the snack time, for washing hands, for brushing teeth, and so forth to mobilize children.

At Maple Day Care, on the other hand, teachers find it important to explain procedures verbally to the children before each activity. Every morning at the beginning of the day's activity, the teacher tells her children what they are going to do that morning. Then at the beginning of each activity the teacher repeats what she expects from the children. When the teacher gives an instruction, all the children are supposed to gather and sit down. For example, in the three-year-old class before they go outside to play in wintertime, the teacher gives a series of instructions to the entire group of children. "Now, we are going outside and play. Before you go, I want you to go to the bathroom first. Then, come back here and put on your coat and boots. Don't go outside yet. You must line up in front of the classroom and be quiet. If you are noisy, we are not going outside. Then, we go out together. O.K.? Now, go to bathroom." The teacher waits for all the children to come back to the classroom. "Put on your coats and boots," tells the teacher. She helps some children put on their coats. "Now, I want you to line up in front of the classroom." Those children who have put on their coats start lining up and wait for the others. After everyone lines up, the teacher gives another set of instructions. "Now, we are going outside. When we finish, I want you to come back right away and line up in front of the building, O.K.?" Then the teacher leads her children quietly outside. The children may or may not know these actions, which they routinely perform. However, they seem to wait for the teacher's instructions.[3]

The teachers place different emphasis and importance on verbal instruction in these two centers. The Kawa teachers believe that for the children at this age it is not sufficient just to tell them what to do. It is more important to show them by action, either demonstrating examples for them, or letting them follow some children who can perform the task. The Kawa teachers regard showing by action as a better way of teaching children. They also believe that young children respond better to music than to words. The Maple teachers, on the other hand, believe it important that the children understand why they are doing what they are doing. To avoid blind obedience, it is important for them to explain verbally to the children what they are going to do and why, before the action.

The difference in the teachers' attitudes in regard to the verbal instructions can be seen in the ways they deal with fights among the children. At the beginning of the school year, the Maple teachers set up several lessons to talk about "fights" with the children and establish some rules. For example, they talk about why fighting is bad, how it feels to be hit, and what the children should do instead of fighting. The Maple teachers believe that they can minimize the chances of fighting among the children in this way.

The Kawa teachers, on the other hand, wait for an actual fight to occur before saying anything to the children. They think it important to teach children what is right and wrong in a particular incident, because rules are, according to them, really dependent on individual cases. There is no point in teaching children rules in the abstract. One teacher even said that she did not teach children not to fight, because she believed fighting within a certain limit was a type of communication.

Independence versus Dependence

We have compared some activities at Japanese and American day-care centers through our participant observations. One temptation here is to try to determine which system produces more independent-oriented (or dependent-oriented) behavior among children. However, can we really decide on this issue judging from the decriptions above? First, we will consider several cases to illustrate the difficulty involved. Our contention is that we cannot settle this issue if the meanings of key concepts such as independence held by American and Japanese teachers are different. Second, in the next section, we will discuss the multiplicity of meanings of independence and dependence. We will point out that the Japanese and American teachers interpret the same behavior patterns differently and, therefore, they do indeed hold two different systems of symbols and meanings (Geertz 1973b; Schneider 1972). In the last section, we will analyze the difference in underlying cultural assumptions and conceptions.

The first case to consider is that the American teachers train children to eat on their own by not feeding them from the very earliest stage of development. In view of the fact that some Japanese three-year-olds require occasional assistance and the attending teachers are willing to give that help, the American system seems to produce more independent-oriented children. The Japanese teachers seem to be overprotective of their children. However, the Japanese teachers encourage the children to assume duties through the toban, or by sharing some tasks such as putting down mattresses for napping, or cleaning the classrooms with the teachers. In this sense, they are not overprotective or indulgent. The Japanese system does not necessarily seem to encourage dependent behaviors.

Second, though the American teachers emphasize the importance of having choices for their activities as a key to independence, the range of activities that the American children can choose from is always set by the teachers. If the children engage in activities other than those set by the teachers, the teachers are likely to interpret these side activities as distracting other children and to utilize some disciplinary measures such as the time-out. On the other hand, the Japanese children are allowed not to participate in group activities, and can engage in almost any activity of their choice without penalty. Even though the Japanese teachers do not verbally emphasize the importance of having choices, as do the American teachers, do the Japanese children indeed not have a wider range of choices and find themselves in a less restricting environment than the American children?

Third, though the Japanese teachers give fewer verbal instructions than their American counterparts and do not employ a disciplinary measure such as the time-out, there is certainly an orderly flow of activities at the Japanese day-care center. Even if at each moment the Japanese children are noisier than the American children, programs in the Japanese day-care center are carried out very smoothly.

As the above examples indicate, it is difficult and nearly impossible to determine which system produces more independent-oriented behavior among children without clarifying exactly what we mean by independence. Here we face a fundamental problem, that is, do the American and Japanese teachers share the same meaning of independence? For instance, to an American teacher, a three-year-old being fed by a teacher is a typical dependent behavior. However, do Japanese teachers indeed consider feeding oneself as an essential key to independence as do American teachers? As we shall see below, the Japanese teachers do not interpret independence in the same way as the American teachers. When they do not share the same interpretations of these key concepts, it is not only impossible but also fruitless to try to determine which system is more independent-oriented using a single criterion. Rather, what we should be asking is: What are the underlying assumptions and patterns of meanings that shape their conceptions of "independence" and "dependence"? What we need is to let the informants examine concrete behaviors and to let them make statements that are culturally meaningful. For this purpose, reflective cross-cultural interviewing is a useful step.

REFLECTIVE CROSS-CULTURAL INTERVIEWING

Description of Procedures

In order to conduct reflective cross-cultural interviewing, we have taken the following steps:

1. We prepared viedotapes of several activities. While we conducted participant observations, we recorded on videotapes several activities, such as group activity, lunchtime, and free play. While Sano was videotaping, Fujita took notes of observations, except at Hato Day Care where Sano was the only researcher. We tried to record similar activities at both the Japanese and American day-care centers.
2. We interviewed the teachers by showing videotapes of their own day-care centers. We interviewed the American teachers individually or in pairs while showing the videotapes of Maple Day Care. The interview with the Japanese (Kawa Day Care) teachers was conducted in a group of six while showing videotapes of Kawa Day Care.
3. We conducted reflective cross-cultural interviews. We interviewed the American teachers individually or in pairs while showing the videotapes of the Japanese (Hato) day-care center. The interviews with the Japanese (Kawa Day Care) teachers were conducted with six teachers at a time, while we show the videotapes of Maple Day Care.

Both directors easily allocated the time for interviewing—both during the nap time for one and a half hours. They also decided the place for interviewing: in the dining room of Maple Day Care and in the two-year-old classroom of Kawa Day Care, simply because the Maple dining room was vacant during the nap time, and the Kawa teachers could temporarily move two-year-old children into the one-year-old classroom. We made a request of interviewing teachers individually. The Maple director accepted our request, and made a sign-up sheet so that individual teachers could choose the most convenient day for them. The Kawa director really preferred that we finish our research within a relatively short time (within one or two days), to avoid disrupting their program. We accepted her request and spent two days, one day with the teachers of younger children (ages one and two) and the other day with those of older children (ages three to five). We invited the director and the head teacher to join us in both interview sessions.

Here we should clarify the differences between the first (step 2 above) and second step (step 3) of our interviews. In the first type of interview, we showed the teachers the videotapes of their own day-care center. Having the video-tapes of the teachers' interaction with the children made our interview questions more concrete. As the teachers are usually interested in seeing themselves and their own children on the TV monitor, the videotapes also helped the teachers relax and get involved in our interviews (Erickson and Wilson 1982; McDermott 1976). More importantly, viewing the videotapes enabled both the teachers and us to engage in open-ended conversation. In the second type of interview, a reflective cross-cultural interview, we showed Japanese videotapes to American teachers and American videotapes to Japanese teachers. In this interview, we encouraged the teachers to talk about their impressions, feelings, and interpretations of similarities and differences between an American and a Japanese day-care center as well as between two cultures.

The roles that we as anthropologists played in those two types of interviews were also different. In the first type of interview, we are interviewers of our informants, asking questions in the way anthropologists usually conduct ethnographic research. We asked the teachers what we did not understand in their interaction and activity scenes. As the teachers answered our questions, we paid special attention to how they talked about the children's characteristics, attitudes, feelings, achievements, and sometimes about the children's family members. The first type of interview included some open-ended conversation between teachers and us not only on the specific scenes of the videotapes but also on the more general and broader issue of ways of caring for the children, apart from the scenes on the videotapes.

In the second type of interview (reflective cross-cultural interview), our role was quite different from the first one. We acted as cultural translators, attempting to facilitate a conversation between the American and Japanese teachers. Having the teachers view the videotapes of other cultures enabled them to have a discussion as if the American and Japanese teachers were engaging in a conversation through us as cultural translators. This was done in several ways. First, teachers asked us questions about the scenes of the videotapes. We explained the content of the scenes. We also gave them some basic information about the other day-care center. For example, we mentioned the number of children and staff, the number of days a week when the center is open, the child/teacher ratio, location, and operating organization.

Second, the teachers made professional comments on the performances of the other culture's teachers as if they were observing and talking to them. When that happened, we encouraged the teachers to elaborate on their comments. They also sought explanations for "the other's" way of doing things. We tried to answer the way the teachers of the other culture would answer. For instance, a Japanese teacher remarked on the fact that American children wear shoes while taking a nap, which she thought quite odd and even dirty. Then we explained to her that unlike the Japanese, Americans generally do not take off their shoes inside the house, that going barefoot is not allowed at Maple Day

Care by state regulation, and that children sleep on vinyl cots instead of on futon placed directly on the floor.

Third, we sometimes passed on interpretations that the teachers of the other culture often made. For instance, we said to the Kawa teachers: "American teachers often say, 'We are teachers, and not baby-sitters.' Do you consider yourselves in the same way?" In this way, we opened up the discussion between the Maple and Kawa teachers through us as cultural translators.

Teachers' Views of American and Japanese Cultures

The following is a summary of comments that both the Maple and Kawa teachers made about themselves and the others obtained through our reflective cross-cultural interviewing. We will first examine the views that the Maple teachers had on the Japanese teachers and day-care represented on videotapes. After each comment, we will discuss the Kawa teachers' reply on the same issue obtained through our role as cultural translators in our reflective cross-cultural interviewing. After examining the Maple teachers' views, we will turn to the Kawa teachers' views.

The strongest impression that the Maple teachers have is that the Japanese center is too noisy and looks even chaotic. The Japanese children are talking out loud all the time. Some children are walking and even running around while others are listening to the teacher. The Maple teachers think the reason for these disorderly behaviors must be due to the high child/teacher ratio. With that high ratio, the Maple teachers feel that there is no way the teachers can adequately control the children. One of the reasons for their concern about control is to maintain a safe environment for children.

When we interviewed the Kawa teachers, we raised this issue of the high ratio between teachers and children commented on by the Maple teachers. We also told them that at Maple, one class was often divided into smaller groups. We asked their opinion of having several teachers to lead a class. The Kawa teachers think that two or three teachers would not necessarily make things easier. They believe one teacher can often lead children better, because she can run the whole class in the way she wants and can see the progress of her children better. She can respond to the individual child's pace of development better. The Kawa teachers do not regard their work load as heavy. We should add here that the Kawa teachers were quite surprised when we told them that the Maple teachers thought the Japanese children were too noisy. It was only after they viewed our videotapes on Maple Day Care that they noticed their high noise level.

The American teachers see their Japanese counterparts as working not with but around children by preparing things for them. The Maple teachers think that most of the time the Japanese teachers prepare things for the children rather than teaching them. For example, in the lunchtime, the Japanese teachers set up tables and wipe them, whereas American teachers would let other people such as cooks wipe tables. During playtime, especially outdoors, the Japanese teachers do not supervise the children. There is no one watching what they are doing. The American teachers question the safety of the children.

The Kawa teachers think the American teachers do not play with children. They just sit by them and watch them. To them, the American teachers who do not play with children appear lazy, and not doing a proper job. A good teacher in a Japanese setting, according to the Kawa teachers, is one who can join the children's world, can communicate with the children in the way they understand, and can play with them at their level.

How do the Kawa teachers view the American day-care center? The first impression the Kawa teachers have is that the American children are treated as if they are adults instead of children. They dress like adults. For example, they wear leather shoes and jeans made with tough materials which the Kawa teachers think inappropriate for children. Commenting especially on younger children (ages one and two) a Kawa teacher said: "The material for pants seems so tough. Jeans fit them so tightly. Isn't it awkward, when they [teachers] take children to the toilet? Do they have enough time?" The Kawa teachers think that children should wear something soft and loose for their comfort. They also think that the plastic glasses that the American children use during lunch are not the children's size, but ones that any adult would use.

We point out to the Kawa teachers that the American teachers encourage the children to be self-sufficient as soon as possible. For example, even one-year-old children are expected to eat on their own without any help from the teachers at Maple Day Care. The Kawa teachers think the attitude of the American teachers is strict, rigid and *sparuta-teki* (Spartan), which reminds the director, (the oldest member of the staff) of the educational method in prewar Japan under which she grew up. The Kawa teachers think it acceptable to help younger children to eat, especially slow eaters. They said they used to encourage self-help at an earlier stage. In recent years they changed their policy, because they found out that too much pressure on self-help would make them less motivated in later years, when they reach age four or five. Even though these children can take care of themselves, they refuse to do so. Until the children reach three years of age, it is necessary to provide lots of attention and care, and sometimes to indulge them. "When they are satisfied, they start doing things on their own. But, if they are deprived of care at a very young stage and given pressure to do things on their own, they just lose interest later on." The Kawa director, even though she is running a day-care center, thinks that ideally every mother should stay at home and raise her child until the child reaches three years of age, instead of taking the child to a day-care center, because no one can provide as much love as a mother can.

The Maple teachers have a very different opinion on self-sufficiency, especially in eating, from that of the Kawa teachers. When the Maple teachers saw the videotape of the Japanese day-care center, they took a special note on feeding children, especially the three-year-olds. They asked us whether these children were sick on that day or handicapped. They think it is not a good idea to feed a child, even a one-year-old, if he or she is healthy and normal. The Maple teachers comment on feeding as follows. "If you start feeding a child, other children also want to have extra attention and to be fed. Then, there is no way you can control the children." By feeding them, teachers can spoil the children's self-effort. The children will soon take advantage of the teachers' attitude and stop eating on their own. Being able to eat on their own is the first step toward independence, which should be encouraged as soon as possible.

How do the Maple and Kawa teachers summarize American and Japanese cultures? How do they account for the differences between these two centers?

The Maple Day Care teachers believe that American culture stresses individualism and individual development.

Americans are so individualistic. It is important to teach children to think on their own. For this purpose, children should be given ample opportunities to exercise their choice. However, children at this age need to be closely supervised and be under constant control. As a society, Japanese society is far less individualistic, it is more structured, paternalistic, and traditional. In the videotapes, teachers do not seem to interfere with children. But, because the society itself is so structured, traditional values can control the children and keep the order in the day care center.

The Kawa Day Care teachers believe that things are in stages. They summarize the cultural difference as follows.

Americans seem to have a consistent rule applicable to any age and place. The same rule at school, at home, or in public and for adults as well as for children. These rules are very strictly enforced. For Japanese, rules are relative and not absolute. We tend to be inconsistent in applying rules. Maybe we are indulging children. But we also need to consider particular time, place, and occasion in applying rules. Childhood is a separate stage from the rest of the life cycle. Children are different from adults; they have their own world apart from adults. They have their own way of thinking and acting. And, we should respect that. We cannot impose adult values on them. It is better to leave things to their natural pace of development.

Note here the difference in central concerns on which the Maple and Kawa teachers focus. The Maple teachers' cultural comparison focuses on individualism and the issue of power and control over the children, whereas that of the Kawa teachers focuses on time—for example, time for disciplining, and time of childhood in the life cycle. Now we proceed to analyze the significance of this difference.

AN ANALYSIS OF TWO SETS OF CULTURAL DIALOGUES

We have seen how the Maple and Kawa teachers characterize some aspects of American and Japanese cultures. Are they really comparing the two cultures, or are they telling us something else? To answer this question, we need to examine more closely the ways they describe these two cultures, and analyze their descriptions as texts (Geertz 1973a). What are these teachers telling us when they describe things as the "Japanese way" or the "American way"?

First, we should note here a peculiar feature of their descriptions. Both the Maple and Kawa teachers underplay the similarities between these two day-care centers. They simply omit the similarities. For example, when the Maple teachers talk about the high ratio between teachers and children at the Japanese day-care center, they ignore the fact that the ratio for younger children is the same for both centers. Similarly, when the Kawa teachers describe the American teachers as being strict, rigid, and even Spartan, they do not comment on the affections that the Maple teachers physically demonstrate, for instance, hugging and kissing, toward the children. Both teachers highlight the differences, not the similarities, between these centers.

Let us compare the Kawa teachers' view of the American way and the self-conception held by the Maple teachers. Note the discrepancy between them. The Kawa teachers describe the American teachers as being strict and rigid, and as imposing absolute rules on the children regardless of their stages of development. The way the Maple teachers characterize the American teachers or American way is different from the one described by the Kawa teachers. The "American teachers," according to the Maple teachers, are the teachers who are sensitive to the individual needs of the children and, thus, who give choices to the children. But because of the children's age, the teachers must exercise control.

Similarly, there is a discrepancy between the way the Maple teachers describe the Japanese way and the self-image held by the Kawa teachers. The Maple teachers describe Japanese society as structured, paternalistic, and traditional, and both the teachers and children as being governed by traditional values that are beyond individual power. The Kawa teachers do not consider themselves as slaves of traditional value. On the contrary, their image of the Japanese teachers is those who are sensitive to the nature of a particular situation, who can judge accordingly, and who can respond to the children's pace of development.

Clearly, both the Maple and Kawa teachers misinterpreted each other. It is a misinterpretation in the sense that there is an acute discrepancy between the outsider's interpretation and that of the insider. Our point here is not to criticize either the Maple or Kawa teachers for misunderstanding Japanese or American culture. After all, no one among the Maple or Kawa teachers spent any time in the other's country, or were especially familiar with that country.

Our argument here is that both the Maple and Kawa teachers' descriptions are not a comparison of two cultures, but a contrast between two types of educational philosophies within their own cultural system. The fact that the Kawa director describes the American way as resembling the educational method of prewar Japan is very suggestive here. When these teachers describe the other culture, they are telling us what is disturbing to them. They are establishing their own self-identity by constructing something different from themselves and labeling it as "American" or "Japanese." They are making a sharp polarization within their own cultural framework. They describe the other culture as negating the values of their own culture, and by doing so they are indirectly affirming their own system. What the Kawa teachers are contrasting their system with is the prewar Japanese education, which employed tougher disciplinary measures starting at a very early stage of development. If the Kawa Day Care system is a contemporary form of mainstream culture, what they contrast exists, at least as an idea, as a counterculture model. It is not difficult to imagine some other institutions, including day-care centers, employing a stricter disciplinary policy (Frager and Rohlen 1976). What the Maple teachers contrast their system with is less explicit. However, given that they emphasize individualism and characterize the Japanese society as structured, they are contrasting their system with a more totalitarian system. However, they also emphasize the importance of the teacher's control over children and they view the Japanese teachers as noninterfering. Therefore they also contrast themselves with a more laissez-faire type of education. In Midwest America, the educational philosophy found at Maple Day Care is certainly a more mainstream type.

If the Maple and Kawa teachers' descriptions are not cultural comparisons between American and Japanese cultures, but the ways of talking about their own systems, how do we proceed from this point to an analysis of the meanings of the underlying concepts that shape their systems? The best way seems to treat their descriptions as two sets of distinct "cultural dialogues." Here we adopt George and Louise Spindler's (1987b) definition: a cultural dialogue is "the exchange of patterned meanings and significations among actors in social contexts." The following quotation, which defines an American culture, clarifies what is meant by the "cultural dialogue":

We claim that there is an American culture because since prerevolutionary times we have been dialoging about freedom and constraint, equality and difference, cooperation and competition, independence and conformity, sociability and individuality, puritanism and free love, materialism and altruism, hard work and getting by, and achievement and failure.... It is not because we are all the same (we are not), or that we agree on most important matters (we do not), that there is an American culture. It is that somehow we agreed to worry, argue, fight, emulate and agree or disagree about the same pivotal concerns (Spindler and Spindler 1987b).

When both the Maple and Kawa teachers describe their own and the other's day-care centers and educational orientations, they are undoubtedly talking about their "pivotal concerns." In this sense, their descriptions are cultural dialogues. We should point out here that their cultural dialogues are not the same type, but two distinct dialogues. For the Maple teachers' description uses the idioms of control and power, whereas that of the Kawa teachers' employs the idiom of time. Their central, pivotal concerns are different. Because of the difference in the central themes of the cultural dialogues, they are most likely to misinterpret each other when they compare the two systems, as they actually did.

Given that the Maple and Kawa teachers describe educational philosophy in the idioms of power and control and of time, respectively, what are the meanings of the key concepts such as "teachers," "children," "time," and "space" that shape their educational orientations? How do these concepts influence their action?

The most fundamental difference between the Maple teachers' educational philosophy and that of the Kawa teachers is the concept of "children." The Kawa teachers emphasize the separate and distinct stage of childhood from the rest of the life cycle. They believe that "children" have their own world, their own ways of communicating, and their own rules apart from the world of adults. The Maple teachers do recognize childhood as a stage in the life cycle. However, they also believe that children should not stay in this stage too long, and should learn the rules that are applicable to adults and children alike as soon as they can. Thus, the Maple teachers encourage their children to be self-sufficient, especially in the area of self-care, whereas the Kawa teachers are more willing to offer assistance to their children in the same area.

The concept of "teachers" that the Maple and Kawa teachers have are also different. The Maple teachers conceptualize a teacher as someone who supervises and controls children's behavior. The Kawa teachers, on the other hand, believe a teacher at a day-care center is someone who facilitates and maintains a flow of activities. Rather than a supervisor, the image of a teacher they have is closer to that of a navigator or a guide.

Both the Maple and Kawa teachers use the word "natural" to describe children's behavior. Yet the nuances that they convey are very different. When the Kawa teachers use the Japanese word for nature (*shizan*), they mean something positive. "The children should be left as natural as possible" (*shizen no mama ni*). What they mean by this phrase is that the children are innocent and should be left uninterfered with and unrestrained, and should be left as they are. When the Maple teachers talk about "natural" behavior of the children, they convey that the children are unpredictable and disorderly, if they are left as they are. Their behavior must be supervised and controlled.

The Maple and Kawa teachers' perceptions of "time" and "space" in the context of the day-care centers are also different. The Kawa teachers' focus is the flow of activities over an entire day, whereas that of the Maple teachers is activities in each moment. Thus the Kawa teachers are bothered less by the children who do not participate in a particular group activity so long as they join other activities some other time and as the activities flow smoothly. The Maple teachers focus on each activity. They often give verbal instructions at the beginning of each activity. They supervise the children and strongly encourage them to join in each activity. If a child misbehaves himself in one of the activities, the teacher gives a disciplinary measure such as time-out regardless of the child's conduct in other activities.

The spatial orientations of the Maple and Kawa teachers are different as far as the area of the children's activities is concerned. Although the Kawa teachers prefer that the children stay in their classroom, they do not stop children from going to other classrooms, to the hall, or sometimes even to the playground, as long as they stay within the premises of the day-care center. The Maple teachers expect their children to stay in their own classroom and those who wander around in the buildings are likely to be taken back to their own rooms. The difference in the spatial orientations of the teachers are reflected in the floor plans of the buildings (see Figures 4.1 and 4.2). Each room at Kawa Day Care has several sliding doors, which are usually open during the classroom activities, and the children have easy access to other rooms through the hallway and also through the porch. At Maple Day Care, each room is enclosed and has only one door. The children do not have access to other rooms without going through several doors, which are usually closed during the classroom activities.

CONCLUSION

At the beginning of this chapter we asked the question: How can we compare the educational processes of two different countries, being simultaneously sensitive to the cultural construction of the meanings underlying these systems? To answer this question we have employed reflective cross-cultural interviewing using videotapes, as well as a more conventional ethnographic method—that is, participant observations and interviews—in studying the educational processes at American and Japanese day-care centers. The above analysis has made cultural assumptions and conceptual frameworks underlying the American and Japanese educational processes explicit. The result of this analysis also demonstrates the following.

First, the use of audiovisual and reflective cross-cultural interviewing in addition to participant observations exposes us to fundamental differences in the cultural assumptions and meanings of the key concepts in cross-cultural, comparative research. The conventional participant observations and interviews alone are liable to create a pitfall for researchers. That is, researchers unconsciously apply only a single framework to compare two distinct cultures. Often the underlying cultural assumptions and conceptions are so different from each other, as in the case of the day-care centers in this study, that a straightforward comparison using a single cultural framework misinterprets the cultural differences.

Second, reflective, cross-cultural interviewing allows a greater involvement of informants in cultural comparisons. The use of audiovisual equipment, especially showing comparable scenes from different cultures, greatly facilitates informants' ability to make explicit statements that are culturally meaningful. The role of an anthropologist is reflective, cross-cultural interviewing has an additional dimension to the one found in more conventional ethnographic research. The anthropologist is no longer a simple observer; he/she participates as a cultural translator, and thus facilitates a cultural dialogue in which informants can engage.

Last, reflective, cross-cultural interviewing often helps informants to establish their own identity in a sharp polarization with something different from them—something by which they are disturbed. In this way, this research procedure not only brings the cultural assumptions of the informants to the surface, but also the tension in a wider social context surrounding the informants. Through their characterization of the polarization, we begin to appreciate the tension between mainstream culture and counterculture within a society.

ACKNOWLEDGMENT

This study was supported in part by the Spencer Fellowship, National Academy of Education, which was awarded to Mariko Fujita (1984–87). The authors would like to express their gratitude to George and Louise Spindler, who have always been helpful to us not only as university professors, but also as colleagues and friends, ever since we took their courses at Stanford University. We are grateful to the people of Maple and Kawa Day Care who gave us their valuable time. We also thank Susan Zack for her editorial comments, and Sharon Traweek for the discussion we had.

NOTES

1. The reflective cross-cultural interviews at the American day-care center were conducted in March 1986, before we did our fieldwork at Kawa Day Care. When we went to Japan for research in the summer of 1986, we tried to conduct more intensive fieldwork at Hato Day Care because of the familiarity with this center from the previous research. However, because of many changes in staff and some miscommunication, it was practically impossible for us to resume our research at Hato Day Care. Instead, we chose Kawa Day Care in a different suburban city. Hato and Kawa Day Care share many similarities. The differences between these centers are limited to the fact that the Kawa center is a one-story building operated by a private organization, while the Hato center is a two-story building operated by the city. In fact, both centers have very similar educational philosophies and daily activities, the same child/teacher ratio, identical floor and playground arrangements, similar backgrounds of the children's parents, and almost the same age distribution of staff. Most importantly, the types of activities the American teachers commented about while viewing the videotapes of the Hato center, such as the noise level, help in eating, or the duty system, which we will describe, are also commonly observed at Kawa Day Care. Therefore, we have judged that both sets of videotapes from Hato and Kawa Day Care are adequate for the present study.

2. The children are divided into two groups. The children from each group face each other and walk on the balance beam from the opposite ends. When they meet, each child extends a hand showing one of the following three forms: *qu* (stone, by making a

fist), *choki* (scissors, a fist with the index finger and the middle finger extended), and *pa* (paper, by opening a hand). The stone is stronger than the scissors, but weaker than the paper. The scissors defeats the paper but loses to the stone. So, if child one extends a hand showing paper, and child two shows stone, child one wins; but if child two shows scissors, then child one loses. The child who loses goes to the end of the line and the next child in the group walks on the balance beam to compete with the winner.

3. The difference in the amount of instructions the teachers give in these two centers may be due to the difference in the attendance patterns of the children. The Kawa teachers can expect to see the same group of children every day for their classes and also for the entire year, whereas some of the children at Maple are part-time; they do not come every day. The children can move up a class at their birthdays in the middle of the school year. Hence, the children a Maple teacher has for her class change quite frequently. Repeating instructions for the changing group of children may be necessary.

REFERENCES

Caudill, William, and Weinstein, Helen. 1969. Maternal care and infant behavior in Japan and America. *Psychiatry* 32:12–43.

Doi, Takeo. 1973. The anatomy of dependence. Tokyo: Kodansha International Ltd.

Erickson, F., and Wilson, Jan. 1982. Sights and sounds of life in schools: Research guide to film and videotape for research and education. Research Series No. 125. East Lansing: Institute for Research on Teaching, Michigan State University.

Frager, Robert, and Rohlen, Thomas P. 1976. The future of a tradition: Japanese spirit in the 1980s. In Japan: The paradox of progress, Lewis Austin (ed.). New Haven, CT: Yale University Press, pp. 255–278.

Frake, Charles O. 1980. Plying frames can be dangerous: Some reflections on methodology in cognitive anthropology. In Language and cultural description, C. O. Frake. Stanford, CA: Stanford University Press. pp. 45–60.

Fujita, Mariko. 1977. The concept of *Amae* in Western social science. Unpublished master's thesis (Spring Paper), Stanford University.

————. 1984. The cultural dilemmas of aging in America. Ph.D. dissertation, Anthropology, Stanford University.

————. 1986. Independence and sharing: A symbolic analysis of meal programs for the elderly and pre-school children. In Essays by the second year Spencer Fellows. Cambridge, MA: National Academy of Education.

Geertz, Clifford. 1973a. Deep Play: Notes on the Balinese Cockfight. In The interpretation of cultures, C. Geertz. New York: Basic Books, pp. 412–454.

————. 1973b. Religion as a cultural system. In The interpretation of cultures, C. Geertz. New York: Basic Books, pp. 87–125.

Hsu, F. 1973. Rugged individualism reconsidered. *Colorado Quarterly* 9:145–162.

————. 1981. Americans and Chinese: Passage to differences. Honolulu: University of Hawaii Press.

Kiefer, Christie W. 1970. The psychological interdependence of family, school, and bureaucracy in Japan *American Anthropologist* 72:66–75.

LeVine, Robert A. 1984. Properties of culture: An ethnographic view. In Culture theory: Essays on mind, self, and emotion, R. A. Shweder and R. A. LeVine (eds.). Cambridge University Press, pp. 67–88.

McDermott, R. P. 1976. Kids make sense: An ethnographic account of the interactional management of success and failure in one first grade classroom. Ph.D. dissertation, Anthropology, Stanford University.

Masuda, Kokichi. 1969. Amerika no kazoku-Nippon no kazoku. Tokyo: Nippon Hoso Shuppan Kyokai.

Rapson, Richard L. et al. 1967. Individualism and conformity in the American character. Boston: D. C. Heath.

Sano, Toshiyuki. 1980. Hito no yoji no kodagakuteki kenkyu (An ethological study of behavior of day nursery children). Unpublished master's thesis, University of Tokyo.

_____. 1983. Behavior patterns of mother and child in separation and greeting at a Japanese day nursery. J. Anthrop. Soc. Nippon 91(4), pp. 435-454.

Schneider, David M. 1972. What is kinship all about: In Kinship studies in the Morgan Centennial year, Priscilla Reining (ed.). Washington DC: The Anthropological Society of Washington, pp. 32-63.

Shweder, Richard A., and LeVine, Robert A. (eds.). 1984. Culture theory: Essays on mind, self, and emotion. Cambridge: Cambridge University Press.

Spindler, George, and Spindler, Louise. 1987a. In prospect for a controlled cross-cultural comparison of schooling Schoenhausen and Roseville. In Education and cultural process: Anthropological approaches, 2nd ed. George Spindler (ed.). Prospect Heights, IL: Waveland Press, pp. 389-400.

Spindler, George, and Spindler, Louise. 1987b. Editorial introduction to Part I, Ethnography: An anthropological view. In Interpretive ethnography of education at home and abroad, G. Spindler & L. Spindler (eds.) (pp 1-6). Hillsdale, NJ: Lawrence Erlbaum Associates.

Spindler, George, and Spindler, Louise. (forthcoming). Foreword. In Symbolizing America, H. Varenne (ed.). Lincoln: University of Nebraska Press.

Varenne, H. 1977 American together: Structured diversity in a Midwestern town. New York: Teacher's College Press.

5
Iman Chay?:
Quechua Children in Peru's Schools
Nancy H. Hornberger

When Quechua children arrive at school, they enter a setting of language use and social interaction that is at once very different from and yet consonant with patterns they have known at home and in the community. This chapter explores those patterns of language use and interaction from a number of angles. First, in a brief consideration of language use patterns in the community, I show how both children's language use and school language use fit into the overall pattern. Then I look more closely at actual language use and interaction in school and classroom by comparing children's participation in Spanish-only and bilingual Quechua/Spanish instructional settings. Finally, I consider the consequences of bilingual instruction for Quechua children's learning.

LANGUAGE USE PATTERNS IN THE COMMUNITY

Let me begin by being clear as to what I mean by community. The community I refer to here is the nonnucleated community that may be all or part of a traditional Quechua *ayllu* (community family home). It is a community composed of dispersed homes within a certain geographical area, and it is defined both by the sacred places within sight of and bounding the physical area and by the common descent of the community members.

Furthermore, language ideology helps to define community identity. For Quechua speakers the Quechua language is identified with the physical territory of the community, while Spanish is identified with the cities, mines, and coastal areas to which community members travel outside their communities. It is the community members' perception that Quechua is the language for ayllu and Spanish is the language for everything outside the community, home, and family (see Hornberger 1985:215–323 for detailed documentation of these statements). How does this characterization match up with observed oral language use? Overall, it is a correct but somewhat inadequate and therefore initially misleading characterization.

If it were true, as it probably was at some point in the past, that *all* language interaction within the confines of the community were in Quechua and only Quechua, and *all* language interaction outside the confines of the community were in Spanish and only Spanish, then the foregoing description would suffice to characterize language use by community members. However, such a characterization no longer adequately describes language use in the community. There is today, to a greater or lesser degree from community to community, some use of Spanish within the physical confines of the communities. There are, first of all, domains within the community in which Spanish is either the usual or the accepted language. Furthermore, there is both codeswitching into Spanish in the midst of Quechua discourse in Quechua domains, and strong lexical borrowing from Spanish into Quechua (see Hornberger 1985:344–351).

My purpose in this first section will be to outline the use of Quechua and Spanish within the community in terms of three domains, which I call ayllu, non-ayllu, and *comunidad* (see Table 5.1). I should emphasize that though these

Table 5.1
Three Community Language Domains

Domain	Social Situation		Language
	ROLE-RELATIONSHIP	SETTING	
Ayllu	Member-to-Member	(A) Household-Field	Quechua
		(B) *Faena*	
		(C) *Fiesta*	
		(D) Free Encounter	
Non-*Ayllu*	Member-to-Outsider	(E) District Seat	Spanish
		(F) School in Session	
		(G) Free Encounter	
Comunidad	Member-to-Member	(H) Literacy Class	Quechua
	Member-to-Outsider	(J) *Club de Madres*	and
		(K) Adventist Meeting	Spanish
		(L) School Meetings	
		(M) School Celebrations	
		(N) *Deportes*	
		(O) *Recreo*	
		(P) Free Encounter	

names reflect real categories for Quechua speakers, and the domains them-selves embody categories that are emically derived (that is, from within) from language use patterns in the communities, the domains are not talked about as such by Quechua speakers, nor yet to my knowledge by other scholars of Quechua. Data for the description that follows come from two years of ethno-graphic investigation of language use in the communities of Kinsachata and Visallani, and to some extent in Pumiti and other communities, all in the Department of Puno.[1]

In essence, the ayllu domain includes all those social situations pertaining to "traditional" community life; that is, those aspects of community life that have maintained a continuous tradition since at least the coming of the Spanish to the New World. Conversely, the non-ayllu domain includes all those social situa-tions resulting from the intrusion of the larger, national Peruvian society into the community territory. Social situation is used here to mean the juncture of setting (time and place) and role-relationship.

The ayllu domain consists of all member-to-member role-relationships in the following settings: (A) household and field; (B) *faena* (community work proj-ect); (C) *fiesta* (in both the community itself and the district seat); and (D) free encounter within the community confines, including the school grounds when school is not in session. Within the ayllu domain, Quechua is always spoken. An example of an ayllu speech event in setting A involving children would be the two smallest Alejo Mamani children making up riddles to each other as they wait in the truck cab at their family's field (10-9-82[2]; see Hornberger 1985:328-329 for more examples).

The non-ayllu domain consists of all member-to-outsider role-relationships in the following settings: (E) the district seat; (F) the school grounds when school is in session; and (G) free encounter within the community confines. Within the non-ayllu domain, Spanish is always spoken. An example of a non-ayllu speech event in setting F involving children would be the school-children speaking to the Microregion representatives who have come to demonstrate the planting of the school garden, about how to trim the onion seedlings and plant them (9-21-83; see Hornberger 1985:330-331 for more examples).

These two domains provide the principal contours of language use in the community. In both domains, children's language use is entirely consistent with the overall patterns. Within these contours, however, variation occurs. I said that the definition of each domain depended on the juncture of particular settings with particular role-relationships. There are instances, though, when the settings and role-relationships meet in a mismatch or when the distinction between ayllu and non-ayllu becomes unclear. In these instances, language use becomes variable.

The first instance of variable language use arises when setting and role-relationship do not combine in the prescribed way. In these cases, either the setting takes precedence over role-relationship and the speaker uses the language associated with that setting; or role-relationship takes precedence over setting and the speaker uses the language associated with that role-relationship. For example, in non-ayllu setting F (school in session), school-children in ayllu role-relationships to each other sometimes speak Spanish, the language of the setting: Alberta exclaims to her classmates Olga and Bartola, *¿Quién sabe?* (Who knows?) (V, 3-4; 10-25-83). At other times they speak Quechua, the language of the role-relationship: Cecilia asks to borrow Nancy's pen, *Mañariway lapizniykita* (Lend me your pen) (V, 3-4; 9-26-83; see Hornberger 1985:322-334, 377-380 for more examples).

By far the bulk of observed variation in language use occurs not in these areas of mismatch of setting and role-relationship, however, but in areas where the very distinctions between ayllu and non-ayllu settings and ayllu and non-ayllu role-relationships become unclear. It is in these latter areas where it can be said that a different domain is functioning within the community.

I call this domain the *comunidad* domain because it is that domain in which the community members function together as a "community" in the sense in which the larger Peruvian society defines that concept. This domain is most visible in those situations where community members come together for meetings, celebrations, or recreation in program formats that originated outside the "traditional" community ambience but that have now become incorporated into the community life to a greater or lesser degree. See Table 5.1 for a listing of the settings of the comunidad domain. Within this domain, both Spanish and Quechua are spoken. Examples of comunidad speech events in setting N involving children would be Kinsachata third and fourth graders at high jump practice conversing in Spanish, using short phrases such as *más arriba* (higher), *bajito* (a little low); or Visallani students commenting on their classmates' performance at long jump in Spanish when the school director is there and in Quechua after she leaves (12-2-82; 8-17-83; see Hornberger 1985:337-340 for more examples).

It can be seen then that either Spanish or Quechua may be used in the situations associated with the comunidad domain and in situations in setting-role mismatch within the ayllu or non-ayllu domains. What is striking in all this is the significant role the school plays in the two domains associated with Spanish: the non-ayllu domain and the comunidad domain. The school setting and the persons associated with the school are defining determinants of the one, and major contributors to the other. I now turn to a more careful examination of school language use.

LANGUAGE USE AND INTERACTION IN SCHOOL CLASSROOM

In this section I describe oral language use and interaction in the traditional Spanish-only instructional setting and in the next section compare it to that in a Quechua/Spanish bilingual instructional setting, along with a brief outline of written language use in each case. In describing Spanish-only and bilingual instructional settings, I refer to the domains and to other emically derived analytical categories to characterize pupil language use. The analysis presented here is based on data gathered in Spanish-only instructional settings in Visallani and Pumiti and in bilingual instructional settings in Kinsachata.[3]

Pupil language use at school covers all three domains. In general, at school before teachers call the children to line up and after teachers dismiss the children for the day, schoolchildren speak Quechua with each other in all sorts of interactions on school grounds; these speech events belong to ayllu domain setting D. During class and lineup time, schoolchildren speak Spanish in interactions directly or indirectly including the teachers; these speech events belong to the non-ayllu domain setting F. During school *recreo* or formal *deporte* practice periods, schoolchildren speak Quechua with each other in interactions involving traditional or nonorganized types of play, such as *caretas*, jacks,

Table 5.2
Pupil Schooltime by Language Use Domain

Domain	Activity	Hours	%
Ayllu	Waiting during adult meetings	3.5	7
	Teachers absent	3.5	7
Non-*Ayllu*	Line-up	2.5	5
	Class-time: teacher teaching*	3.0	6
Comunidad	*Recreo*	16.5	32
	Deportes	4.5	9
Non *Ayllu* Setting and *Ayllu* Role-Relationship			
	Class-time: Pupils on own*	9.0	18
	Class-time: Housecleaning	4.0	8
	Class-time: Board work	4.0	8
TOTAL		50.5	100

* This table represents estimated proportions of how pupil school-time is usually spent, based on observations during seven school-days, August 12-20, 1982 in Kinsachata, Puno, Peru.

marbles, or free play; Spanish in interactions involving teachers; and Quechua with some Spanish terms in such nontraditional, organized team sports as volleyball, soccer, and high or long jump. These speech events belong to the comunidad domain settings N and O.

By and large, then, schoolchildren, as community members, follow the domain-constrained patterns of language use. Pupil language use in the ayllu and comunidad domains needs no further description here, beyond noting that over half of pupil school time is spent in these two domains: Table 5.2 shows that approximately 41 percent of pupil schooltime is spent in the comunidad domains, and 14 percent in the ayllu domain.

The two areas that do deserve further comment, however, are those of pupil language use in the non-ayllu domain (11 percent of schooltime) and in the mismatched situations of non-ayllu settings and ayllu role-relationships (34 percent of pupil schooltime). I take up language use in the non-ayllu domain and in the mismatched situations in the following order:

1. Schoolchildren speak to their teachers in class (non-ayllu).
2. Schoolchildren speak to their teachers and the school at large in line-up activities (non-ayllu).
3. Schoolchildren speak to their teachers in regular schoolwide class or other learning activities (non-ayllu).
4. Schoolchildren speak to their schoolmates in class (mismatched situation).

The language used in class by pupils speaking to their teachers is Spanish, with very few exceptions which will be noted below. For the sake of future discussion, I divide pupil interactions with the teacher in class into the following categories derived from participant observation:

1. Content Response (CR): the pupil(s) respond(s) to a question the teacher asks about the lesson at hand. This is usually a one-word response. In the Spanish-only instructional setting, these CRs are most often given in Spanish. For example, pupils respond to Profesor[4] Victor's questions with one-word answers such as *sí* (yes), *bailar* (to dance), *caminar* (to walk), *tomar* (to drink), *haber* (to have), *preceder* (to precede); or the names of the numbers in Spanish (V, 5-6; 8-22-83, 9-21-83).

2. Reading Response (RR): the pupil reads aloud from board or book in response to teacher request. In the Spanish-only instructional setting, an RR is always in Spanish since all reading material is in Spanish.

3. Spontaneous Request (SR): the pupil requests teacher assistance of advice, either directly by speaking aloud to the teacher or indirectly by commenting aloud on his or her *own* work. This is always done verbally, and not, for instance, by raising the hand. In the Spanish-only instructional setting, these SRs are most often given in Spanish. For example, *Siñurita [sic], he terminado* (I'm finished, Miss); or *¿Este cuadrado así se hace, profe?* (Do you do the square like this, teacher?) (V, 1-2; 9-19-83; and K, 3-4M; 12-7-82).

4. Spontaneous Comment (SC): the pupil comments aloud to teacher and class in general on *another* pupil's behavior. In the Spanish-only instructional setting, these SCs are most often given in Spanish. For example, *Siñurita [sic], esta Mercedes está fastidiando* (Mercedes is bothering me, Miss); or *Prufsur [sic], su lapicero de Lucio está agarrando el Feliciano* (Teacher, Feliciano has Lucio's pen) (V, 1-2; 9-23-83; and V, 3-4; 10-25-83). (See Hornberger 1985:373-374 for more examples.)

It is, as I have said, consistent with community language use patterns, and with community expectations about the school, for Quechua children to speak Spanish in class. It is also consistent with the written language that surrounds them there.

All written language at Visallani and Pumiti and in Profesor Mario's and Profesor Manuel's classrooms at Kinsachata was in Spanish, with one exception. The title of Visallani's third-fourth grade *periódico mural* (class news-board) was *El Chasqui* (The Messenger), with Quechua *chaski* spelled according to Spanish orthography, and with the Spanish article *el*.

Written language included posters and decorations on the walls of the class-rooms (e.g., patriotic and religious portraits, the Peruvian shield and flag, the class schedule, labeled areas of the classroom, and an occasional motto), black-board writing (written assignments or summaries of lesson content to be copied by the pupils; in the absence of textbooks and other teaching aids, the black-boards were in constant use), notebook writing (pupils copy from the board into their notebooks), and readers and teachers' guides (usually only the teacher had these). It is worth noting in passing that much of the written language and visual display in the classrooms was not only linguistically but also topically un-familiar to the children.

Outside of the classroom, the school also provides other settings for inter-action. Each school day begins with lineup in front of the school. All of the school children line up by grade in two rows per grade—one boys' and one girls' row. On Monday mornings a flag ceremony is usually carried out, and every day teachers may make announcements, and one student from each grade is asked to "participate" with a song, story, riddle or poem to be said in front of the whole school. This ceremony usually lasts about 20 minutes, but may take from 5 to 40 minutes. Occasionally, an additional lineup is called at the beginning of the afternoon session or at the close of the school day if additional announcements need to be made.

In 25 lineups observed and recorded at Visallani, all pupil participation was in Spanish, with the exception of four individual cases when a child sang a song in Quechua: the song was either "Cabana plazitapi" (In the Plaza of Cabana), or "Sakaywamanpi" (In the Ruins of Saksaywaman), two standard well-known songs at the Visallani school. All other songs sung, riddles asked, and poems declaimed were in Spanish. At Pumiti, use of Quechua in the lineup ceremonies was even more "meaningless" to the pupils. The only Quechua heard at any Pumiti lineup was the daily greeting exchange modeled on the greeting said to date from Inca times and popularized during the Velasco government: *Ama qilla, ama suwa, ama Ilulla* (Be neither lazy, a thief, nor a liar) spoken by the teacher or leader with the group responding *Qanpis hinallataq* (and the same to you).

In schoolwide activities, too, pupils use Spanish in direct and indirect interaction with their teachers, a use that is entirely consistent with the domains of community language use. For example, when Alberto was reprimanded for running around rather than working during a period of schoolyard cleanup one afternoon, he said to his classmate Tin, in the hearing of the teacher, *Tú también estás correteando* (You're running around too), hoping to divert the teacher's attention to Tin (10-25-83).

With these clarifications and amplifications of the pupils' use of Spanish in the non-ayllu domain, I turn now to discussion of their language use in the case of a non-ayllu setting mismatched with an ayllu role-relationship. I refer here to the case of pupils interacting with each other in class while the teacher is either absent, engrossed in work with other pupils, or at his or her own desk. As shown in Table 5.2, time spent in this way constitutes a large proportion of the pupils' school time (34 percent) and therefore merits consideration.

As mentioned above, in these mismatched situations, at times the setting takes precedence over the role-relationship and Spanish is spoken, while at other times the role-relationship takes precedence over the setting and Quechua is spoken. In general, however, my observation was that these interactions occur more often in Quechua. Impressionistically, it seems that when pupils interact in Quechua they are interacting as equals and/or commenting on the task at hand. When they use Spanish, the dynamic is often one of creating distance among themselves by insulting or showing off. At other times the use of Spanish is associated with certain lexical domains (such as numbers) or simple phrases. Compare, for example, the following four speech events.

1. Santos tells Percy in Quechua *Llakikusharqayku qanmanta* (We were worried about you) when Percy returns to school after an absence of several days (V, 3-4; 12-6-83).

2. Mercedes comments to Basilia in Quechua, *Imachá kanpis?* (What could it be?) as they look at the wall picture (V, 1-2; 10-28-83).

3. Grimaldo usually interacts in Quechua but on one occasion comments in Spanish, *Facel es [sic]* (It's easy) to his classmates in general (V, 1-2; 9-19-83).

4. Santos announces as he begins work on the class assignment, *Aquí está mi lapicera [sic]* (Here's my pen) (V, 3-4; 12-6-83).

Here, as in the case of community language use, language use becomes variable when domain constraints are loosened. In light of the ample possibility of interaction with their ayllu peers, pupil language use in the traditional classroom is by no means limited to Spanish only.

Patterns of language use at the traditional community school can be summarized as follows. Pupils follow community norms of language use in the ayllu and comunidad domains, which combined occupy about 55 percent of their schooltime. In non-ayllu settings, pupils use Spanish with their teachers (about 11 percent of their schooltime) unless the teacher explicitly solicits a Quechua response; and they use both Spanish and Quechua with their peers (about 34 percent of their schooltime). In the latter case, the use of Quechua predominates.

QUECHUA/SPANISH BILINGUAL INSTRUCTIONAL SETTINGS

How do language use patterns in the bilingual instructional setting compare to those just described? Pupil language use in the ayllu and comunidad domains at Kinsachata is essentially the same as that of pupils at Visallani and Pumiti. For example, the patterns of their language use before and after school and at recess parallel the patterns at Visallani. Remember also that these two domains account for more than half of pupil schooltime.

It is in the non-ayllu domain, which accounts for about 11 percent of pupil schooltime, that significant differences in pupil language use appear. These differences are directly related to differences in teacher language use and written language use in that domain. Consider the following examples of pupil talk according to the categories referred to above.

1. Teacher asks in Quechua, *Imapaqmi allin?* (What is it good for?); (CR) Pupils respond in Quechua, *Kaltukunapaq* (It's good for broth).

2. Teacher asks in Quechua, *Iman sutin kaypata?* (What's this called?). (CR) Pupils respond in Quechua, *Ukuku* (Bear).

3. (RR) First graders read in Quechua from *Kusi*, repeating after the teacher (11-8-82; 12-6-82).

4. (RR) Second graders read in Quechua from *Ayllunchis* (8-18-82).

5. (SR in Spanish) The most common SR is the bid to be called to the board or called on: *yo* (me), *yo, yo, yo* (me, me, me), *profesor* (teacher), *yo sabo [sic]* (I know) (8-12-82, 9-14-82, 10-11-82).

6. (SR in Spanish) *Ya, profesor, ya he terminado* (There, teacher, I've finished) (9-14-82).

7. (SR in Quechua) *Iman chay?* (What's that?) (9-14-82).

8. (SC in Spanish) *Este Luciano mi ha pigau [sic]* (Luciano hit me) (10-12-82).

9. (SC in Quechua) *Askhata hap'ishan Mercedes* (Mercedes has a lot) (9-15-82). (See Hornberger 1985:429-430 for more examples.)

Because information content in the bilingual class is largely in Quechua, pupil talk categories Content Response and Reading Response almost automatically are in Quechua more often than in Spanish. On the other hand, pupil

Spontaneous Comments and Spontaneous Requests to the teacher are often still offered in Spanish, even in the bilingual classroom. SCs seem to occur much less frequently here than in the Spanish-only classrooms, but when they do occur, the language used is often Spanish.

As in the Spanish-only instructional setting, Quechua children's language use in the bilingual instructional setting is consistent with the written language that surrounds them. In the bilingual classrooms, written Quechua was observed, to a greater or lesser extent, in all four categories.

Quechua was used in posters and decorations on the walls. Displays or classroom areas were labeled, for example: *Willayniy* (My news items); *T'ikanchis* (Our flowers). A Quechua motto, *Ama suwa, Ama Llulla, Ama Qella* (Be neither a thief, a liar, or lazy) was observed in more than one classroom.

Blackboard writing also included Quechua. Both Sr. Sergio (first grade) and Profesor Victor (second grade) noted that they had never written Quechua before participating in the Bilingual Education Project (PEEB). Observation revealed, however, that now they had largely mastered the rules of Quechua orthography and used written Quechua correctly on the blackboard. This contrasted with spellings of occasional Quechua words by non-PEEB teachers, which usually followed Spanish orthography, as in: *El Chasqui (chaski)*, or *Aclla Huasi (aqlla wasi)* (House of the Chosen Maidens).

As in the case of the traditional classrooms, notebook writing was a direct reflection of blackboard writing. Therefore, notebook writing in the bilingual classrooms included a good deal of writing in Quechua.

Textbooks were provided by the PEEB and were all in Quechua. This was a marked difference from the traditional classroom. Not only were the textbooks in Quechua, but each student had his or her own copy because they were provided by the PEEB.

In sum, whereas written language in the Spanish-only instructional settings was restricted almost exclusively to Spanish, in the bilingual instructional settings all four areas of written language included a considerable amount of Quechua.

Outside the classroom, at lineup and other schoolwide activities, more use of Quechua was observed among pupils at Kinsachata. At the 25 observed lineup times, the participation by pupils was half and half Spanish and Quechua on about half the days. This included stories, riddles, and songs.

Finally, in the case of pupils interacting together in the classroom (mismatched situations), Kinsachata pupils used Quechua in the same way as their Visallani and Pumiti counterparts. However, the use of Spanish as described for the Spanish-only classrooms in insulting or showing off did not seem to occur in the bilingual classroom. The net effect was that Kinsachata pupils appeared to use Quechua even more often than their Visallani and Pumiti counterparts in the area of mismatched situations.

Summarizing the differences between patterns of pupil language use in the two types of instructional settings involves point out that there is a greater quantity of Quechua use in the bilingual instructional setting in the non-ayllu domain and settings. It also involves more than that, however. Whereas in the Spanish-only instructional setting the Quechua utterances were often only short, truncated segments in the midst of lengthy Spanish utterances, in the bilingual instructional setting the Quechua utterances were complete and well-formed thoughts. Since Quechua is a language particularly rich in markers tying discourse to previous and following sentences, this difference is significant. (See Hornberger 1985:414–427 for description of teacher Quechua use as quantitatively more, linguistically more, and communicatively more.)

In sum, patterns of pupil language use in the bilingual instructional setting contrast in both degree and kind with those in the Spanish-only instructional setting most saliently at the following points:

1. Extensive use of Quechua in Content Responses and Reading Responses with their teachers in class.

2. Some use of Quechua in Spontaneous Requests and Spontaneous Comments with their teachers in class.

3. Fewer Spontaneous Comments overall and less interpupil insulting and showing off.

4. More frequent Quechua use in interaction with pupils as well as with the teacher.

5. Both teachers and pupils tend to use a more linguistically complete form of Quechua.

6. Teachers and pupils use Quechua in the exchange of information content that is also in Quechua, while teachers and pupils in the Spanish-only instructional setting use Quechua as a backup in exchanging information that is in Spanish, and that only occasionally.

7. Approximately half of all written language is in Quechua, while in the Spanish-only instructional settings there is no written language in Quechua.

It is evident from the above discussion that pupil language use in the bilingual instructional setting differs in both quality and quantity from the patterns of language use by which the traditional school has fit into the patterns of language use in the community. What are the consequences of these differences for pupil learning?

CONSEQUENCES OF BILINGUAL INSTRUCTION FOR CHILDREN'S LEARNING

The most significant impact of bilingual instruction in the classroom is in the communication of formal education's content: that is, reading, writing, and arithmetic skills. Whereas in the Spanish-only instructional settings there were repeated instances of what I came to think of as form without content or content failure, in the bilingual instructional settings there were indications that the children were taking the content in. These indications consisted of differences in pupil performance in terms of oral participation, reading, and writing.

Oral Participation

One indicator of successful content communication in the bilingual instructional setting was the level of oral participation by the pupils. The key here was the difference in languages being used. The point is that, among the pupils in the bilingual instructional setting, not only was there greater frequency of Quechua use, there was a greater use of language per se in terms of both quantity and complexity. When their tongues were freed to speak their own language, pupils tended to speak more than they would have had they been limited to speaking only in Spanish, as in the Spanish-only instructional settings. Moreover, whereas pupil Spanish language use in both bilingual and Spanish-only instructional settings tended to consist mainly of one-word responses—such as *sí*, *no*, *yo*, number names, or standard SC formulas such as *Ese fulano está fastidiando* (That so-and-so is bothering me), or *Este es mi lápiz* (This is my pencil)—pupil Quechua language use was usually more varied and more grammatically complex. In other words, when pupils were encouraged to speak Quechua, they usually said more, and said it with more variety of expression.

In Kinsachata's third-fourth grade class, when the Spanish monolingual teacher attempted to draw the children out in conversation in Spanish, choosing a topic of interest to the pupils and insisting firmly but kindly in their participation, the conversation was almost painful to listen to because the children responded only with an occasional *sí* or *no*. When the children attempted a longer answer, they struggled for the appropriate words.

When pupils are called on to produce words or sentences in Spanish themselves as part of an assignment, the situation becomes even more critical; and teachers usually give up and start giving the pupils sentences they may copy. After a long lesson on the adjective, with many examples, Sra. Sara of Visallani assigned the class to modify each of a list of nouns with an adjective of their own choice. None of the children even attempted to do so but, rather, were still busily copying the list of nouns when Sra. Sara began to fill in the adjectives herself (10-28-83).

In Visallani's third-fourth grade class, Profesor Gregorio assigned his pupils to write sentences using abbreviations he had just taught them. None of the pupils could do so. It appeared that since the children had no idea what the original words themselves meant, it was impossible for them to attempt to compose sentences with their abbreviations.

The words included: *Señorita* (Miss), *compañía* (company), *avenida* (avenue). One boy put *El* Señorita (using the masculine article for a feminine noun), and two girls composed the sentence *La compañía Ana tiene su hermano* (The Ann company has a brother), in which they confused *compañía*, a word unknown to them, with *compañera* (companion), a standard part of their vocabulary, equivalent to the Quechua *masi* used to refer to their schoolmates.

Gradually, Profesor Gregorio began to put up more examples for the children to copy, but even then he exclaimed: "These kids don't understand" (8-19-83).

In another case, he taught them synonyms in a similar way. The next day after seeing their homework, he said: "Several students did not understand, so I'm going to tell it over again. You must do it again." A frustrating situation for both teacher and pupils.

By the time they reach the fifth and sixth grades, the pupils who are still in school can manage to produce some sentences in Spanish. Profesor Victor of Visallani had his class compose sentences at the board one day (9-21-83). The sentences they produced were all at about the second grade level, usually consisting of three-five words each and using the same verb repeatedly:

> *Juan juega con sus amigos.* (John plays with his friends.)
> *Luis juega con su amigo.* (Louis plays with his friend.)
> *Mi hermana juega con su pelota.* (My sister plays with her ball.)
> *Lucho Jurga [sic] en su casa.* (Louis plays in his house.)
> *Pedro juega con su perro.* (Peter plays with his dog.)

and so on. The problem here was not in writing the sentence but in thinking of it in the first place.

Pupils simply had not acquired enough Spanish to be able to generate their own sentences. They were unsure of both lexicon and grammar. Consider, for example, the following uses of Spanish by pupils: *Voy a cantar un poesía* (I'm going to sing a poem); *La luz nombre le puso con el nombre de día* (The light name he gave it the name of day) (8-13-82). In the first example, the pupil has erred in his lexical choice, and in the second, in his grammatical structure. In both cases, insufficient knowledge of the language is interfering with the pupil's attempt to communicate something he obviously knows and understands.

Yet when teachers encourage oral participation in Quechua, the difference is remarkable. The same pupils who, in Profesor Victor's class, could barely invent a five-word sentence in Spanish, could in Quechua invent complex and varied sentences. These pupils invented a game of making up a sentence in Quechua for me to say back to them in English. In the course of playing this game, many and varied Quechua sentences emerged: *Qullanapi vulita pukllaspanchis wayra hap'iwan* (While we were playing volleyball in Quallana, the wind got me); *Huk paluma urqu puntata halarin* (A dove flew over the top of the hill) V5B 85; *Namay ñachá sinayta mayk'ushanña* (My mother must already be fixing my supper) V7A 450.

On one occasion, Profesor Carlos of Pumiti asked the children to come one by one to the front of the class to tell what they had done over the weekend. As long as he spoke and questioned in Spanish, pupils barely responded at all (two words maximum). After a while, he began to say they could speak Quechua if they wanted, but still got almost no response. Finally, he began to use Quechua himself, and when the pupils were actually convinced that Quechua was in order, they began to tell their experiences in three to four sentences (6-6-83).

In Sr. Sergio's first grade at Kinsachata, where pupils were accustomed to their teacher's using Quechua all the time, lively discussion between teacher and pupils occurred regularly. It was interesting to note that during these discussions, yes–no questions by the teacher tended to be answered by *sí* or *no*, but all other questions were answered in Quechua, sometimes with one word only, but often with complete sentences (10–12–82).

It is often said that Quechua children, and indigenous children in many parts of the world for that matter, are naturally shy and reticent, and that that is why they rarely speak in school; therefore we should not interfere with their cultural patterns by encouraging them to speak out more. In light of observations such as those outlined above, however, I think we should ask ourselves whether at least some of that reticence is due to the fact that the school language in many of these cases is a language entirely foreign to the child.

Of course, more may be involved than language. In some parts of the world, children are shy in school even though the home language and the school language are the same. Philips (1983) has shown that, for the case of the Native American children at Warm Springs, at least, it is the cultural patterns themselves that are precisely the key to the children's participation. Given participation structures that are more congruent with their own cultural patterns, Warm Springs children do participate more in school. Participation structures may also be a factor in the case of Quechua children. Nevertheless, an even more fundamental issue seems to be language. Who, after all, can speak out in a language they do not know?

For example, I had the opportunity to observe one little girl in both classroom and home settings. This little seven-year-old rarely, if ever, spoke in class; yet, at home, she was something of a livewire. She talked nonstop to me (in Quechua), telling me all about the names and ages of her whole family, showing me the decorations on the wall of her home, the blankets woven by her grandmother, borrowing my hat—all this while she jumped on the bed, did somersaults, cared for her two baby brothers, and so on.

Reading

Another indicator of effective communication of content in bilingual instructional settings comes when children read aloud. In a Spanish-only instructional setting, "reading" in the lower grades often consists of repeating aloud what the teacher reads from the board or text. In most cases, pupils are not even looking at the words they are "reading." In one second grade, for example, there were only 8 books for 30 pupils, so most were repeating the words of the "reading" lesson without even seeing them once (5–31–83).

By the time they reach the upper grades, the most successful pupils manage to learn to decipher written Spanish from the printed page or board. In other words, they pronounce the sounds represented there. The Spanish language assists in this by being by and large a phenomically written language: one letter usually represents the same sound. Nevertheless, it becomes apparent over and over again that pupils are pronouncing the words in Spanish with little or no inkling of what they are reading about. Long pauses occur regularly while pupils sound out each word anew each time; they are obviously getting no contextual clues, nor can they "recognize" a word that means nothing to them. The pupils' reading does not respect punctuation marks, or even word boundaries. Sentences and words are split down the middle and rejoined to other words and sentences. Pronunciation is problematic, owing to the conflict between Quechua and Spanish phonological rules. Teachers in the Spanish-only instructional setting rarely even ask summary or review questions when a pupil finishes reading. If they do, they are usually met with a blank or perplexed expression on the pupil's face.

Yet, when children have the opportunity to read in Quechua, the difference is remarkable. In the course of my pupil interviewing in the Spanish-only instructional setting, pupils who had never read Quechua became acquainted with the PEEB textbooks *Kusi* and *Ayllunchis*, as part of the interview. Subsequent to the interviews, pupils in all grades began to ask to borrow the two books.

There would follow a most interesting phenomenon. Children would sit clustered around the books for as long as possible, even up to an hour, taking turns reading aloud. They read fluently, though most of them had never read in Quechua before. Occasionally, they needed explanations of a few letters unfamiliar to them—q, w, h, and the explosives and aspiratives—because they were not found in Spanish; but usually one explanation was enough. They read with understanding, laughing at appropriate moments, commenting on and summarizing to their classmates what they had read. These were the same children who could barely decipher a sentence from their regular Spanish reader, and usually had no idea what they were reading about.

In the interviews, pupils who had stumbled repeatedly while reading in class from their Spanish texts, mistaking every other syllable, read quite well in Quechua, and understood the story they were reading, as shown by their answers to my questions. When they did make a mistake, it usually consisted of substituting a related and sensible word for the one in the text, rather than a nonsensical look-alike substitution as often occurred when they read Spanish. For example, Rufina read *asikunpas* (when he laughed) for *asikuspas* (while laughing), and *halaripuy kaspa* (being pulled) for *halaripuq kasqa* (had pulled) (V7B 4). This sort of mistake indicates that the pupil is reading for meaning, rather than sounds only.

Teachers in the bilingual instructional setting often asked summary and review questions about what the children were reading, and they got appropriate responses. In Kinsachata's first grade, pupils read words from the board, obviously associating pictures above the word with what they were saying, rather than simply memorizing the sounds in order and "reading" them without even looking at the board, as so often happened in Spanish-only instructional settings. They read from their text, after the teacher first read through it with them, with obvious understanding of the words. As in the case of the interviews above, mistakes reflected meaningful use of language: for example, when reading pp. 34-35 in *Kusi*, a few substituted *apakun* (he carries [it] along) for *apan* (he carries [it])—a perfectly sensible substitution of one Quechua word for another. Profesor Victor commented with satisfaction that all the children who started school with him (in the PEEB first grade the previous year) were reading.

Writing

Yet another indicator of effective communication of content in the bilingual instructional setting is in the pupils' writing. Consider first pupil writing in the Spanish-only instructional setting. Pupils are usually asked to copy exercises from the board, and occasionally to write as the teacher dictates. In both cases, in the Spanish-only instructional setting, there is evidence in nearly every child's notebook that he or she has no idea what he is writing. One second grader had copied a sentence from the board, which read *la-casa-tiene-techo-rojo* (the house has a red roof) as *la-casa-tien-et-echo-rojo* (11-41-82), and had repeated her mistake all the way down the page. As a matter of fact, the manner in which most pupils went about copying from the board revealed much about their lack of understanding. Most copied one letter all the way down the page, then went to the next letter and copied it down the page, and so on. The significant point here is that if the child had understood some of the content, she might have copied one word all the way down the page as a time-saving device, but would usually not have copied just one letter at a time. One second grader had copied only as much of each line as fit onto his page, one letter at a time, with the result that he left out large chunks of words:

> *Elsustantivosin*
> *nombraaunasolape*
> *aanimalocasa.*

The model from which he was copying read:

> *El sustantivo singular*
> *nombra a una sola persona*
> *animal o cosa.*

His classmate copied with no spaces: *Elsustantivopluralindica* (10-29-83). A first grader copied *Papá-dame mi pelota* as *papa-me-mi-pe*. All of these examples show that pupils were getting practice at forming the shapes of the letters, but with no understanding of any meaning in the shapes; a perfect example of form without content.

Pupils in the Spanish-only instructional setting learn to be very attentive to form, since they are unable to make sense out of the assignments in any other way. When an assignment is given, the great concern on the pupil's part is usually to know whether it should be written in blue or red ink, or both; on every line; filling one or two sides of the page; and so on (6-1-83).

Cummins (1982) has distinguished between "context-embedded" and "context-reduced" language proficiency, where the former refers to the ability to grasp the content of a linguistic message when it is embedded in a "flow of meaningful context," and the latter refers to the ability to grasp the content of a linguistic message when the context is very much reduced. The significance of the distinction, he writes, is that "acquisition of meaning in context-reduced classroom situations requires more knowledge of the language itself than is typically required in context-embedded face-to-face situations" (1982:5). It is clear that in the situations described above, the pupils' grasp of their second language, Spanish, has not yet reached the level where they can get meaning or content in the context-reduced classroom situation.

The content failure becomes even more noticeable when pupils are asked to write from dictation. In this case, they have no form from which to copy, and are usually at a complete loss. Profesora Hilda once dictated rules of school behavior to her fifth and sixth grade pupils for about an hour, at a pace at which I could barely even get them down. Upon glancing in one pupil's notebook after the hour, I noted that she had managed to get about two to three words out of each 10- to 25-word rule.

Yet when pupils are given the opportunity to write in Quechua, they do so relatively easily. In this case, their knowledge of the language, their first language, is sufficient to supply meaning even in the context-reduced classroom situation. Kinsachata's Profesor Victor dictated sentences in Quechua, which one pupil at a time wrote on the board while the others wrote it simultaneously in their notebooks. This seemed to work fairly well.

After a lesson on the words *usa, ukya, uchu,* and *ukuku,* Kinsachata's Sr. Sergio gave his class the opportunity to come to the board and write the words. Each one in the class did so both eagerly and successfully.

Writing in Quechua comes so naturally to a Quechua-speaking child that once I observed a Kinsachata second grader write even his Spanish assignment in Quechua, labeling his drawings *wasi* and *sach'a* (house and tree) instead of *casa* and *arbol* as the teacher had it on the board; and another time I observed a Visallani second grader write in Quechua, labeling her drawing *sara* (corn) rather than *maíz* as the teacher had labeled it on the board.

Behavior and Discipline

In Visallani's first grade class, there were two pupils who had fairly serious behavior problems in class, but who appeared quite normal and in fact lively and self-confident outside class. There was no way for me to confirm or disconfirm my impression that much of their misbehavior stemmed from the stress of being in an environment they did not understand, the more so because so much happened in a language not entirely familiar to them. It appeared to me that they were used to being in control of a situation and felt very much left out of control in the classroom. One, in particular, seemed particularly anxious to speak Spanish at every opportunity, which I took as a sign that he meant to conquer the "enemy," that is, the foreign element in his world.

Another pupil in the second grade had had to repeat first grade a few times. The teacher reported that this was because of family problems, and that may well be. It may also be that she was unable to do well until she learned some Spanish, which she herself reported to me she had learned only that year.

I noted above that the kind of show-off and put-down behavior observed in the Spanish-only instructional setting did not seem to occur in the bilingual instructional setting. This, too, could be an indication that many discipline and behavior problems may in fact stem from the language gap in the traditional Spanish-only instructional setting.

On the whole, as these instances of increased oral participation, improved and comprehending reading, greater ease of writing, and easier classroom relations exemplify, pupils adapted immediately and wholeheartedly to the expanded use of Quechua in the classroom. Consider the following comments by pupils. Shortly after the new Spanish monolingual teacher arrived to teach the third grade class that had been in the bilingual program up until then, I asked one of the pupils: *Allinchu musuq prufisurniykichis?* (How's your new teacher?) and she replied: *Millay. Mana kichuwata yachanchu* (Terrible. He doesn't know Quechua).

Perhaps the pupils' unequivocal acceptance of the inherent appropriateness of Quechua in all situations in the school is summed up by this humorous response to one teacher's request that the pupils speak to her in Spanish since she didn't understand Quechua: *Yo no sabo hablar canastellano* ([freely] I don't knows how to speak spinach). The humor of the response is in the intentional misconjugation of the first person singular form of *saber* (*sabo* instead of *sé*) and the intentional substitution of a meaningless sound-alike for the word *castellano*, both mistakes designed to fulfill and underline the teacher's opinion (as perceived by the pupil) that pupils who speak Quechua really can't speak properly.

CONCLUSION

The foregoing discussion demonstrates that there is a considerable difference between the bilingual instructional setting where pupils participate in a meaningful way in speaking, reading, and writing and the Spanish-only instructional setting where they by and large do not. The differences are essentially summed up as a more effective transmission of content in the bilingual instructional setting. When content is presented through their own language and culture, the children are able to grasp and respond to the meaning, rather than attend blindly to a form that has no meaning for them.

It remains to be seen whether this difference that appears to be so beneficial for Quechua children can also be fitted into community language use patterns or not. Certainly whether it can or not has implications for Quechua children's future. Elsewhere (Hornberger 1985:435-489, 533-581) I treat that topic in considerable detail, but it cannot be taken up here for reasons of space. Rather, my primary concern here has been to show that bilingual instruction, while departing from the norm for community language use patterns, is yet beneficial for Quechua children as pupils in school. The significance of the pupil's question to the teacher, *Iman chay?* (What's that?), is that it got asked at all.

NOTES

1. The research on which this paper is based was carried out in 1982 and 1983 with the permission and support of the Proyecto Experimental de Educación Bilingüe-Puno (Convenio Perú-República de Alemania) in Puno, Peru; The Dirección Departamental de Educación in Puno, Peru; and the Instituto Nacional de Investigación y Desarrollo de la Educación (INIDE) in Lima, Peru. Financial support came from the Inter-American Foundation and the U.S. Department of Education (Fulbright-Hays). Their assistance is gratefully acknowledged.

2. Citations take the following forms:

- (10-25-83): month, day, and year of an entry in my journal.
- V7A 450: community (V=Visallani; K=Kinsachata), tape number and side, and approximate location on the tape of a quotation from an interview.
- (V, 5-6; 8-22-83): the school (V or K for Visallani or Kinsachata school); grade (1st-2nd, 3rd-4th, or 5th-6th); and date of observed example.

3. The Proyecto Experimental de Educación Bilingüe (Experimental Bilingual Education Project, or PEEB) had been operating in Kinsachata for three years at the time of this study. The first and second grades were at that time bilingual while grades three through six were not.

4. Following local custom, I refer to the directors of the schools as Sr. and Sra., and the teachers as Profesor and Profesora.

REFERENCES

Cummins, Jim (1982). Tests, achievement, and bilingual students *Focus* 9:1-7. Rosslyn, VA: National Clearinghouse for Bilingual Education.
Hornberger, Nancy H. (1985). Bilingual education and Quechua language maintenance in highland Puno, Peru. Ph.D. Dissertation. University of Wisconsin-Madison.
Philips, Susan U. (1983). The Invisible Culture: Communication in Classroom and Community on the Warm Springs Indian Reservation. New York: Longman.

6
Effects of Southeast Asian Refugees on Schools and School Districts
Christine Robinson Finnan

INTRODUCTION

The purpose of this chapter is to illustrate how the local community creates the climate in which education takes place. The implication of this statement for researchers is that outside influences on schools must be assessed when examining schools and schooling. Schools are institutions that can be studied in isolation, but in doing so, we miss the fact that they are part of a larger whole. Schools influence and, in turn, are influenced by their local community. In other words, schools are part of an interdependent social ecology.

The interaction between schools and their community is especially evident when social change is occurring within the schools. Schools are often at the forefront of social change efforts (e.g., civil rights, native language maintenance, access for the handicapped), and the ability to bring about the change depends largely on the reaction of their local community to the change.

This chapter focuses on the integration of Southeast Asian refugee students into local schools (Ellis 1980). It deals specifically with the effects these students have had on schools and districts. We could have limited this examination to areas solely within the domain of schools, such as the students' effects on class size, curriculum, staffing, and programs. This approach, however, would not have explained the varied reactions of schools and districts to this new population. We developed a more accurate framework for our findings by examining the changes in schools as part of a larger social change process occurring in the community. Our findings indicate that when evaluating educational programs designed to achieve social change, we need to ask ourselves if the success or failure of the program is based on the quality of the materials, curriculum, and instruction, or on the willingness of the community to support the social change effort.

Data for this chapter are drawn from a larger study of the effects of refugees on local communities.[1] This chapter provides background information on refugee resettlement, documents the effects of refugee students on schools and school districts, and analyzes these effects in the context of the local communities in which they occurred.

BACKGROUND

Since 1975 schools across the country have absorbed thousands of refugee students from Southeast Asia. These students have been a challenge to teachers, schools, and districts because of their special needs and because their needs are far from uniform. Southeast Asian refugee children come from diverse backgrounds.[2] There are children of well-educated, prominent professional parents; these children need little more than some help learning English. However, there are also children from preliterate tribal families who had never been inside of a school; until recently their native language was unwritten. Schools have also had to accommodate teenagers who had no formal education or whose schooling had been interrupted for several years. In addition to these children, there are some with serious emotional, physical, and medical problems.

It became clear when the first 150,000 refugees arrived in the United States in 1975 that programs for Southeast Asian students had to be established. Most districts, however, found that it was difficult to establish programs. No materials designed for Southeast Asians existed prior to 1975, and there was a severe shortage of trained bilingual staff; in addition, few educators were familiar with the cultures of Southeast Asian refugees. They were also frustrated by the vast differences in educational background and culture represented by the Southeast Asian refugee students.

Refugee families were also unexpectedly mobile. Although federal refugee resettlement policy attempted to scatter refugees across the country, individual families quickly moved to certain localities to join friends and family, find jobs, or escape inclement weather. Large concentrations of refugees formed, particularly in California. It was difficult to predict the number of students from one year to the next and to serve students entering a school midyear.

Many people felt that the Southeast Asian refugee population would be limited to the 150,000 people who fled Vietnam, Cambodia, and Laos in 1975. However, refugees poured out of these countries in the late 1970s, and by 1986 the Southeast Asian refugee population exceeded 800,000. In the late 1970s it had become very difficult for some districts to serve refugee children, and many complaints were directed to state and federal resettlement agencies and to local politicians. The problems most frequently cited by school personnel were:

- Refugee students take too much time from teachers and other students suffer.
- Too few resources are available to help meet the students' special needs.
- Tensions between refugee students and other students exist.

• Federal funds for programs are inadequate and may be available only in the short term, thus creating a financial burden for districts.

These complaints coincided with more general complaints about the impact of refugees on cities and counties. Local government officials and social service providers felt overwhelmed by the influx of refugees. There were concerns at the local level that refugees were taking over all affordable housing and displacing existing populations, and that they were overloading social, educational, and medical services. There were also the somewhat contradictory concerns that, on the one hand, refugees would become welfare-dependent, while, on the other hand, they would take jobs away from Americans. As people became increasingly uneasy about the presence of refugees in their communities, stories about tuberculosis epidemics circulated as did accounts of refugees receiving cars and homes from the federal government. These problems created a negative resettlement atmosphere in many localities, and made the federal government reconsider its refugee resettlement policies.

To examine these effects, we combined field data collection with a review of secondary data sources and an examination of pertinent 1980 census data. Fieldwork was conducted at five sites across the country using modified ethnographic techniques. The sites selected were Orange and San Francisco counties, California; Orleans Parish (New Orleans), Louisiana; Sedgwick County (Wichita), Kansas; and Monroe and Tompkins counties (Rochester and Ithaca), New York.

FINDINGS-EFFECTS OF REFUGEES ON SCHOOLS

"Effects" can be defined as changes, for better or worse, resulting from the resettlement of refugees. These effects change over time and circumstance, and result from activities of refugees, refugee communities, or the refugee resettlement program. The effects of refugees on schools mirror the effects found in the wider community. We found population shifts, changes in programs and staffing, effects on other students (community relations), and costs. These effects are discussed below.

Population Shifts

Population shifts occurred in all school districts studied and, in many cases, refugees merely contributed to a shift in the school population that had begun before refugees arrived. This shift reflects the increasing ethnic diversity of some localities and the movement of white students out of urban and suburban public schools. For example, Tables 6.1 and 6.2 show how the overall ethnic makeup of schools has changed in San Francisco and Orange counties. In fact, in San Francisco, the number of foreign students entering the district from all parts of the world is large enough to necessitate three Newcomers' Centers at

Table 6.1
Ethnic Composition of San Francisco Schools

	1970-71	1974-75	1978-79	1979-80
Total Enrolled	88,757	72,443	60,113	58,122
Percent Enrolled				
All ethnic groups	100%	100%	100%	100%
White	35.1	25.3	20.4	18.9
Black	28.1	29.8	27.6	25.9
Chinese	14.8	16.4	18.8	19.4
Latino	13.6	14.5	15.3	15.6
Filipino	4.1	8.2	8.8	8.8
Japanese	1.8	1.8	1.5	1.4
Korean	0.3	0.6	1.1	1.1
American Indian	0.3	0.4	0.6	0.6
Other Nonwhite*	1.9	3.0	5.8	8.2

*Composed primarily of Vietnamese, Cambodians, Laotians, and Samoans

Source: *San Francisco Examiner*, May 5, 1980

Table 6.2
Change in Proportion of Ethnic Groups in Orange County Schools, 1973-81

Percent Change

Ethnic Group	1973-77	1977-79	1979-81
Hispanic	+4.1%	+6.4%	+5.2%
Asian	+20.7	+21.3	+22.1
Native American	+16.9	+11.5	+6.8
Black	+6.0	+3.4	-0.2
White	-0.6	-2.3	-1.6

Source: Finnan, C., & Cooperstein, R. (1983). Southeast Asian Refugee Resettlement at the Local Level: Role of Ethnic Communication and the Nature of Refugee Migration. Report submitted to the Refugee Resettlement Office.

the elementary level and a Newcomers' High School. These schools are for newly arrived students who speak little or no English.

As part of this overall change in ethnic composition, the number of Southeast Asian students in these two localities has increased dramatically since 1975. In Orange County, Southeast Asian children comprised 1.8 percent of the total county student population in 1979-80, 2.7 percent in 1980-81, and 3.6 percent in 1981-82 (Pierce 1983). In fact, the increase was much more dramatic in certain districts in Orange County. For example, an Orange County district, which I will describe later, considered moving 100 Vietnamese children from one school because of concern that the school had become "too Asian." In San Francisco, the category "Other nonwhite" in Table 6.1 (which includes Cambodians, Vietnamese, Samoans, Laotians, and others) shows the rapid increase in Southeast Asian students.

In some localities, however, such as New Orleans, the ethnic makeup of the school district had not changed greatly (primarily white and black) until the arrival of refugees. Southeast Asians, although only 3 percent of the Orleans Parish school district population, created a visible shift in student population in several affected schools. For example, one elementary school principal said "It was like integration." The school went from 85 percent white and 15 percent black to 15 percent white, 25 percent black, and 60 percent Vietnamese in a very short time.

Population shifts within and between school years also occurred as refugee families moved in and out of the area. These shifts made it difficult for administrators and teachers to carry out educational plans and staff schools. Personnel in Orange County districts cited many examples of student turnover—one district recorded a 105 percent turnover in one year among Hispanic and Southeast Asian students. In 1982 Orange County districts planned for several thousand more Hmong students than were served: The Hmong population in the districts decreased in a short period of time because many families moved to the Central Valley in California.

Changes in Programs and Staffing

The programs most likely to change to meet the needs of Southeast Asian children were bilingual or English as a Second Language (ESL) programs. Most school districts had bilingual programs for limited-English-proficiency (LEP) children when refugees arrived, and LEP program staff were given the responsibility for providing special services for refugees. Refugees have had varying effects on these programs, depending on the structure and size of the program and the populations previously served. Many districts served only Hispanics in their bilingual programs. With only one population to serve, districts could create a bilingual program fairly easily with teachers fluent in English and Spanish, and the curriculum could be taught in both languages. With the influx of the Southeast Asian refugees, however, these districts had to alter their programs because the refugees could not be served in Spanish/English classrooms.

Although a bilingual program designed for Hispanics is not readily adaptable to Southeast Asians, districts with such a program could adapt more quickly to the refugees than districts without any bilingual program. They have experience in working with LEP students, an administrative niche for a refugee program, and familiarity with funding sources for bilingual programs.

Some districts were not familiar with running a bilingual program, and had to adjust to the special needs of refugees and to the programmatic and administrative problems of running a program for LEP students. For example, New Orleans had only a small program serving a few children of 1960 Cuban refugees and a small population of Central Americans. They were not prepared for the influx of refugees. A principal recalled his reaction when a busload of about 60 Vietnamese children (of all ages) arrived at his school in 1975: "We didn't understand each other, period.... We immediately yelled for help from the district." The district could not immediately respond to these requests because it first had to amplify its small existing bilingual program.

Other districts, familiar with serving a multilingual population, were able to adapt their program more easily. San Francisco already had bilingual programs for Hispanic, Chinese, Japanese, Filipino, and Korean students. Three methods of providing services to students are in use, ranging from a true bilingual method to ESL. Southeast Asians, like other students, receive the most appropriate approach that is available to them. The district is also able to single out groups of LEP students in need and serve them in special programs. For example, the Newcomers' Centers and Newcomers' High School provide intensive English instruction in a nonthreatening environment, and a special program was created specifically for preliterate middle school students.

Many districts have chosen to use ESL instead of bilingual programs for refugee children. In some cases, Southeast Asian parents want their children to learn English as soon as possible. They do not feel that native language instruction is the duty of American schools. In most cases, trained, certified Southeast Asian teachers are not easily available. When refugees first arrived, some former Vietnamese teachers were granted emergency temporary certificates but, 11 years later, there is still a shortage of Vietnamese teachers. Lao, Hmong, and Cambodian teachers are next-to-impossible for districts to hire. In addition, all Southeast Asian children cannot be served in the same bilingual classrooms since their native languages differ.

The reaction of most school personnel to serving refugee children has changed over time. At some point, either in 1975 when the first refugees arrived or later when larger numbers of refugees enrolled, school personnel were shocked because they were not prepared for the numbers of children to be served and for the special needs of the students. One district official in Orange County said: "The staff's reaction at first was shock. They came so fast! But once over the shock, the staff have worked hard. Conferences and in-services were well-received." Again, the familiarity of a district with foreign students softened the reaction of teachers and administrators. An elementary school principal in San Francisco said that her staff merely changed the curriculum in response to the influx of refugees. A high school principal in the same district said that refugees were "the subject of a lot of conversation" but that the staff was used to serving "FOBs" (Fresh Off the Boats).

Several changes in teachers' and administrators' roles and activities have resulted from the presence of refugee children. First, coordination systems had to be developed as schools tried to make the best use of the limited number of Southeast Asian instructional aides. Teachers have had to deal with additional personnel in their classrooms or with increased movement of students between their classes and special services. However, most teachers in schools serving low-income, multiethnic populations are used to working with instructional aides and losing children to special pull-out programs. Depending on the level of educational training that Southeast Asian aides have had, teachers have had to know how to orient the aides in order to use them in the most advantageous way (Rubin 1981). Second, principals have had to manage another level of staff, and often have had to work with another district office coordinator. Finally, teachers quickly found that bilingual materials and curricula were not available for Southeast Asians. Rubin (1981) noted that where schools have attempted to provide some bilingual education in the first language of Southeast Asian children, they have been stymied by a lack of materials. Although some materials were developed after 1975, many districts had to make their own, which took teachers' time and districts' money.

Effects on Other Students

Refugees appear to have had little negative effect on the learning opportunities of other children, despite the special needs of refugees and the existence of tension between students in some secondary schools. Potential negative effects have largely been reduced through special services for refugees. ESL classes, special tutoring programs, and bilingual aides reduce the amount of time regular teachers need to spend with refugee children to prepare the refugee children to enter regular classes on a somewhat equal footing with other children.

The degree and nature of the effect of refugees on other children is seen as largely dependent on the ratio of refugee to other students in the school. A school administrator in New Orleans said: "You'd be a liar if you said that an American student would not lose out in a class with 70 percent non-English speakers." Although this is a concern of parents and some administrators (leading some parents to move their children to other schools, and some districts to disperse refugee children), there is little evidence that having a large number of LEP students detracts from the learning of others. For example, another administrator in New Orleans said that white and black students' test scores had not suffered because of the predominance of Vietnamese students in the school.

Often, refugee children stimulate other children or provide good examples for them. Administrators agreed that other students, especially other LEP students, can respond favorably to the example of refugee students. One administrator in Orange County said that when Hispanic students saw the success of Vietnamese students they either "got fired up or dropped out." (As this quote illustrates, the success of refugee students is not always an incentive to others.) An elementary principal in Santa Ana (Orange County) explained why refugee students have not been a burden on his school: "The refugee children's drive has been a light to teachers and other students. Teachers' expectations for all kids have been raised because of the refugee kids. Other children are encouraged by the Southeast Asian youngsters."

To imply that there is not tension between refugee students and other students would be inaccurate. At the elementary level, there is little tension; however, secondary schools often reflect tensions in the community at large, and problems can flare up at the middle and high school levels when they have surfaced in the community. Most high school administrators cited examples of fights between Southeast Asian and other students, but most problems disappeared when school staff worked with the troublesome students. One principal said: "Three years ago the school was a mess. The football team would chase the Vietnamese around. I hired new people who worked together to change the situation. We emphasized responsibility and respect for others and discipline." He added that the potential for problems still exists and reflects relations in the community:

Now [1982] relations are tense. Some fights have racial implications. The refugees haven't assimilated. As an administrator, I wouldn't be surprised if something happened. The potential is there. But I'm also not surprised that no tensions have arisen. Each year gets better. As long as nothing is stirred up in the outside community, it's okay.

COSTS

The potential costs of serving refugee children were quite high, since LEP children are more expensive to serve than other children. To counteract Southeast Asian refugees' language limitations, schools hire aides, bilingual teachers, and translators; develop curriculum; and provide in-service training. Some of these costs are covered by local educational funds, but most costs are met through state and federal funding sources. For example, the Transition Program for Refugee Children (TPRC) earmarks money specifically for refugee children. It is aimed at providing supplementary educational assistance to meet the special educational needs of refugee children and to ease their transition into American society. The program allocates formula grants to state education agencies based on the number of refugee children enrolled in each state, the length of time they have been in the United States, and their age (Jung et al. 1982). This money is especially appreciated by districts because few strings are attached to control how the money is spent; the only requirement is that it must be spent for refugee children.

Other federal and state funding sources are available to LEP refugees. Title VII, a federal funding source for bilingual programs, provides three-year grants for the development and operation of bilingual programs, and districts have sometimes used money from this program to serve refugees. For example, San Francisco Unified School District developed a preliterate program for middle school children with Title VII money. In addition, many states have their own bilingual programs, and they fund local projects.

Some refugees can also qualify for federal programs for children from low-income and migrant families. For example, Migrant Education funds are available to some refugee students because their parents moved to their present home in search of farming or fishing opportunities. In addition, because many refugees have low incomes, their children can make a school eligible for Chapter I funds to provide compensatory education to low-income children. These funds often provide additional tutoring for refugee children.

In addition to funds from federal and state targeted assistance programs, most districts receive some state funding based on the district's average daily attendance (ADA). This is very welcome in districts with declining enrollments because having more students allows them to make better use of their facilities and, in some cases, may prevent the closure of schools.

The balance between money expended on refugee children and money brought into districts to serve them depends on the programs set up for refugees and the grantsmanship of the district. It seems that most districts spend a small amount of their general funds providing special services for refugees. During the late 1970s, some administrators took an advocacy stance for their districts and cited heavy expenses. Some local contributions to programs are the choice of the district. For example, one school district in Orange County contributes 60 percent of the cost of the refugee program. The district chose to provide an exemplary program and had some surplus funds to pay for it.

ANALYSIS

Refugee students affected schools and districts in the above-mentioned ways in all sites studied. However, the nature and degree of these effects varied across the sites. For example, one site reported few negative effects while another had serious problems serving and assimilating refugee students. The other districts reported a few rather transitory problems. To explain the variation, we examined the characteristics of the refugees, government policies, and characteristics of the school districts and of the communities.

We found that the characteristics of the refugees do not explain the variation between sites because the refugee population at all sites is similar. Vietnamese constitute the largest ethnic population in all sites. There are no data available to compare the socioeconomic or educational levels of the refugees prior to their arrival in the United States, and these factors appear to be similar in each site.

All districts found refugee children both a challenge and an inspiration. On the one hand, refugee students everywhere needed special English language instruction, and districts had to create or adapt bilingual or ESL programs rapidly to meet their needs. All districts also had to serve some students with special needs related to preliteracy or poor and interrupted educations in their native country. Districts also had to devise programs for teenagers, for whom language learning was difficult and educational needs pressing because of the limited time left for high school instruction. On the other hand, the students were universally praised for their diligence and respectful behavior, and for their motivation to excel in school.

Government policies also do not explain the differences recorded. The federal refugee program had little effect on schools and districts, other than providing funds through the Transition Program for Refugee Children.[3] In most districts, refugee children brought money into the district because they helped the district qualify for bilingual education or Chapter I funds.

Some characteristics of school districts partially explain the varied reactions to the changes brought about by refugees. Districts that had to adapt to create programs for non-Hispanic LEP students were apt to feel burdened by the needs of refugee students until programs for them were established. The ethnic makeup of the school also influenced perceptions of effects. For example, San Francisco school personnel reported the fewest problems between Southeast Asian and other students. Informants were quick to point out that, given the large Asian population and the large number of new arrivals from foreign countries in San Francisco, Southeast Asians merely added to the existing ethnic heterogeneity of the schools. Only one district, Westminster in Orange County, described serious racial tensions; however, its ethnic makeup was not radically different from other districts in Orange County. These tensions, and an explanation for them, will be described below.

It appears that characteristics of the community have the most important effect on how refugees affect schools, or at least how they are perceived to affect them. The local community creates a climate in which education takes place, and that climate, to a large extent, determines the perceptions people in the schools have of refugees and programs for them. As should be clear from the discussion above, we found little evidence of tangible negative effects, but we did record numerous examples of perceived negative effects. The tensions resulting from the perceived negative effects were as destructive as tangible negative effects would have been.

To illustrate how community reaction to refugees affects the schools, I will present a comparison between the two most extreme cities studied. The cities are San Francisco and Westminster, California. The events described occurred during the late 1970s and early 1980s.

Orange County is a large (population 1.9 million as of 1980), affluent, and politically conservative suburban area adjacent to Los Angeles. While most of it is residential, the county has a substantial service economy in place, complemented by expanding light industry. The local economy has made Orange County appealing to refugees seeking jobs. The county and state welfare systems are widely perceived to be generous, as is California's version of Medicaid, and the educational and employment training opportunities are extensive. Most refugees also acknowledge that the pleasant climate influenced their decision to settle in Orange County.

The population of the county has always been heavily white, but the proportion and diversity of minority groups have been growing at a rapid rate. This change mainly involves Asians and Hispanics. Asians comprised 4.5 percent of the population in 1980, up from only 0.8 percent in 1960. Hispanics made up 14.8 percent of the population in 1980, up from 10.6 percent in 1960 (U.S. Department of Commerce 1960, 1980). The Southeast Asian refugee population was estimated at 55,000 to 77,000 refugees in 1982; of the 44,500 to 62,370 Vietnamese, 10 percent were estimated to be of Chinese ancestry.

The small city of Westminster, in Orange County, is of special importance to this discussion. Historically, Westminster has been a low-income, primarily white area. One of the most visible aspects of the city is a wide boulevard dotted with numerous mini-malls. Prior to the arrival of Southeast Asians, there were high vacancy rates in these malls.

By 1980 the Vietnamese population in Westminster rose dramatically, as did the percentage of Vietnamese students in schools. Prior to 1975 there were no Vietnamese students in schools serving Westminster, but by the 1981–82 school year 12.5 percent of the students in the Westminster elementary school district were Vietnamese (Pierce 1983). Vietnamese not only settled in Westminster, they developed an active business community in the minimalls along Bolsa Avenue. The number of Vietnamese businesses went from a handful of stores in the mid-1970s to more than 200 in less than four years. They were very obvious to everyone in the community because the signs were in Vietnamese only, making other residents feel they were not welcome.

The rapid changes in the character of Westminster brought about a very vocal and angry reaction from its residents. Some of the white residents presented a petition to the Westminster City Council, asking it to suspend all new business permits to Vietnamese businesses. The Council did not act on this recommendation, but citizen pressure and mediation by the City Council led Vietnamese businesses to redesign their signs so that they were written in English and Vietnamese. At the same time, antirefugee feelings were running very high countywide because of a tuberculosis scare that was sensationalized in the press.

Schools were not immune from these problems. Especially in Westminster, some staff, parents, and other students responded negatively to Vietnamese students in their schools. The rapid increase of Vietnamese students did lead to some changes in the schools. Population shifts were especially evident in a few elementary schools in the Westminster elementary school district. In 1979–80, Vietnamese comprised 7 percent of the district, and most of these students were concentrated in a few schools. Pressure from parents and some staff led the district to consider moving 100 Vietnamese children from one of the affected schools because the school was becoming "too Asian." This action resulted in charges of racism and countercharges that the schools "are being invaded." This crisis finally led to a grand jury investigation of the districts' activities.

The elementary and high school districts also had to change their programs and staff rapidly to accommodate the students. Many of the problems described above about lack of bilingual teachers and aides and bilingual materials were felt. The arrival of Vietnamese students had an interesting effect on some teachers at the high school level. The high school principal described problems they had finding qualified teachers to serve the refugee students: "We don't have people credentialed in ESL. There is lots of retraining of PE and history teachers to teach ESL. These retrained teachers get dumped in remedial classes." As the principal implied, many of these teachers did not enter their current specialization with enthusiasm. They felt that they were dumped into the worst classes at the school. Many taught these classes only because they would be unemployed otherwise.

Any negative effects of refugees on other students in the schools was intensified by the negative reaction of the community to the new arrivals. Community pressure led to the threat to move Vietnamese students from one school because white parents felt their children would suffer from the presence of Southeast Asian students. Relations between students at the high school were terrible; there were several incidents of violence involving white and Vietnamese students. A prominent white observer summarized the comments of a number of respondents:

> The concentration of refugees has had an adverse initial impact on the schools. The usual separations among kids in schools existed. There were fights in the school yards, stormy PTA meetings, gray hairs for school staff. It's a two-year problem at best. Kids learn language rapidly; parent don't.... Schools were hard hit initially because of language. It's traumatic especially if school budgets are capped.

At the time of these problems, some school administrators complained that refugee students were too expensive to serve and that funds from TPRC and other state and federal sources were inadequate to serve their special needs. One school official took an advocacy stance and said that the unreimbursed costs of educating refugee students was $1,268 per student.

Tensions had been reduced in Westminster since the late 1970s and early 1980s. However, some observers point out that the potential for problems still exists. The contrast of the reaction of San Francisco and its schools offers some explanation for the tension in Westminster.

Few problems related to refugees surfaced in San Francisco or in its schools. This is in spite of the fact that it too is home to a large Southeast Asian refugee population. The city has a fairly strong economy, primarily in the service industry. Most importantly, though, San Francisco is an ethnically heterogeneous city of immigrants, and it is tolerant of ethnic and cultural differences. Approximately 25 percent of the total population of about 700,000 was Asian at the time of the 1980 U.S. Census; 12.7 percent of the population was black and 12.3 percent Hispanic. The San Francisco Public School District has several Newcomers' Centers and a Newcomers' High School because so many immigrant children enter San Francisco each year.

Refugees live in several pockets across the city, but the largest concentration of Southeast Asians is in the Tenderloin, an area best known for its "street scene"—winos, vagrants, prostitutes, and drug dealers. Residents of this area are primarily poor elderly whites who live in residential hotels and Southeast Asians living in small apartments.

An interesting characteristic of the refugee population in San Francisco (estimated at between 25,000 and 35,000, largely Vietnamese and Sino-

Vietnamese) is the high proportion of Sino-Vietnamese among the Vietnamese population. It is impossible to assess accurately the number of Vietnamese of Chinese ancestry because these refugees sometimes identify as Vietnamese and other times as Chinese. Some people estimate that as many as half of the 19,000 to 22,000 Vietnamese in the city are Sino-Vietnamese.

In the 11 years since refugees have been in San Francisco, only a few isolated problems have occurred; the schools have also been relatively free from complaint and problems. Although few problems have been reported, changes have occurred in the schools. There has been a population shift in several San Francisco schools. For example, the elementary school serving the Tenderloin is now about 60 percent Southeast Asian and Chinese; ten years ago it was largely white. One high school that has historically served many Asian students is now over 70 percent Asian—44 percent are Chinese and 27 percent are Vietnamese. The Filipino Newcomers' Center experienced a dramatic population shift: In 1980 it was 99 percent Filipino and now it is 37 percent Filipino. Most of the remaining population is Southeast Asian.

Problems San Francisco schools have had with their programs and staffing are those shared by all districts. They have had trouble finding bilingual certified and paraprofessional staff. They have also found it necessary to establish new programs. Unlike many districts, San Francisco had well-established bilingual and ESL programs at the high school as well as the elementary level. The only special program they established was one for preliterate middle school students. The staff of San Francisco schools is familiar with the complexity of teaching a multicultural population. One principal said that there were a lot of discussions on how to teach refugee students, but few complaints.

The effects refugees have had on other students has been minor. Students in San Francisco are used to multiethnic, multilingual classes. The dedication and hard work of many refugee students may be an inspiration to some other children. There have been a few problems, such as gang activity and behavioral problems in class, but refugee children have not caused any serious problems.

District officials state that refugees have not cost the district any money. They receive federal funds for the preliterate program and other funds from TPRC for general educational expenses related to serving the refugees. The TPRC funds were especially appreciated because they do not have "a lot of strings" attached. Refugee students also bring in more general funds from the state. San Francisco has been plagued by declining enrollments, and refugees help raise the average daily attendance. In California, schools are funded by the state on the basis of ADA.

As the two examples illustrate, San Francisco and Westminster reacted very differently to the influx of refugees. Characteristics of the refugees and federal and state policies offered no explanations for the different reactions to the arrival of refugee children in these two cities. Westminster and San Francisco serve similar refugee populations; Vietnamese comprise the majority of their Southeast Asian populations, although San Francisco's Vietnamese population is probably more heavily Sino-Vietnamese than Westminster's. The populations are large in both cases and are probably similar in terms of the occupational and educational backgrounds of the adults. There appears to be little difference in the characteristics of the refugees to account for the different reactions.

Federal and state policies regarding placement of refugees and funding of refugee and school programs are the same in Westminster and San Francisco. Both cities have large refugee populations due largely to secondary migration. They also receive funds for public assistance, refugee programs, and school programs based on the same formulas. Again, characteristics of federal and state policies have little effect on the reactions in these two cities.

There are some critical differences between characteristics of San Francisco and Westminster. The most important difference is the visibility of Southeast Asians and the general receptivity toward change. In San Francisco, Asians are everpresent. Few people could distinguish between refugees and other Asians. In Westminster, Asians were a novelty prior to the settlement of Vietnamese there. The Southeast Asian population in San Francisco could not easily be singled out and accused of negatively affecting the city, which was easily done in Westminster. Although refugees opened businesses in both cities, San Franciscans were used to store signs in foreign languages and were happy to have legitimate businesses functioning in the Tenderloin. In Westminster, stores that were obviously owned by Asians were strange and somewhat threatening, even though the Vietnamese stores revitalized failed business areas.

The different reactions within the schools is also primarily a result of visibility. It is true that San Francisco had an elaborate program in place, designed to serve a multicultural and multilingual population, but that program is really more of a product of a city that immigrants enter invisibly. Racially different immigrants from anywhere in the world would probably be viewed with suspicion in Westminster because of their visibility.

The two cities also differ greatly in their acceptance of change. San Francisco has historically been a liberal city, priding itself on being at the forefront of social change. Westminster, in contrast, is a conservative city and is slow, in fact resistant, to change. Both the visibility of refugees and the character of the two communities offer the best explanation for their differing response to refugee resettlement.

CONCLUSION

Southeast Asian refugee children have affected the schools they entered. They have changed the ethnic composition of the schools, challenged staff and other students, and sometimes required services that were paid out of district funds. Most districts, however, responded to these changes with little complaint. This chapter shows that factors influencing the perceptions of how refugees affect schools lie outside the schools. The wider community shapes a resettlement climate that is felt in the schools and largely determines whether refugee children are seen as a burden or a challenge.

This study illustrates how people react to social change driven by public policy decisions. Public policies are made in response to global and national concerns, often without a complete understanding of their ramifications at the local level. Average citizens, not policy makers, live with the changes brought about by public policy. Their reactions to these changes vary depending upon the following four factors:

1. *The nature and degree of the change.* If the change is dramatic, either because it involves large numbers of people or the target population is unusual, people may respond unfavorably. To remain in the sphere of refugee resettlement, as an example, it was not surprising that people were threatened and responded negatively to the resettlement program when thousands of refugees entered their communities. Large numbers are not the only influential factor, though. Local communities responded very negatively to the resettlement of the Marielito entrants from Cuba. The number of Marielito refugees was not large, but the nature of the population—many former prisoners—was threatening.

2. *The amount of preparation for the change.* If people are warned in advance, understand the change proposed, and if the nature and degree of the change are controlled, negative reactions can be reduced. However, it is often difficult to prepare people for social change because the change often occurs unpredictably and without sufficient warning.

3. *The general receptivity to change.* Some communities are more receptive to any kind of social change than others. In fact, some communities pioneer social change while others resist it. San Francisco and Westminster are prime examples of the two extremes. San Francisco is very liberal and accepting of social and cultural differences and change, while Westminster is conservative and slow to change. The same differences in receptivity to social change accounted for the varied reactions to the civil rights movement in the 1960s. Some communities needed little persuasion to accept the reality of equal rights, while other communities continue to resist it.

4. *The visibility of social change.* Resettlement of Southeast Asian refugees into American communities was a highly visible form of social change (except in communities such as San Francisco) because the refugees are Asian. Resistance to resettlement probably would have been much milder if the refugees had been from Poland, Russia, or another European country. Unfortunately, most federally initiated social change involves moving people who are visibly different (e.g., blacks, language minorities, handicapped, and women) into mainstream institutions and activities. If the federal government retains its role as a force for equality, its policy makers must recognize the tendency to resist visible change.

Refugees did affect schools, just as they affected communities at large. The reaction of people within schools to the changes brought about by refugees reflects a more generalized reaction to social change. A broader base of explanation for these reactions is available when schools are examined within their wider community setting. Reactions that otherwise might appear extreme or unusual can often be explained by tracing these reactions into the community surrounding the schools. This was true for the Southeast Asian refugee resettlement program and for the civil rights movement, and it will likely apply to future social change efforts.

NOTES

This study was conducted while I was at SRI International, Menlo Park, California. I wish to acknowledge the contribution of the Deputy Project Director, Rhonda Ann Cooperstein, as well as the other project staff: Michael Knapp, Anne Wright, and Margaret Needles. This chapter is taken from an SRI report entitled "Southeast Asian Refugee Resettlement at the Local Level," SRI International, Menlo Park, November 1983.

1. This study was prepared by SRI International, Menlo Park, California, under Contract No. 600-82-0283 for the Office of Refugee Resettlement (ORR), Social Security Administration, Department of Health and Human Services. The contents of this chapter do not reflect the position or policy of ORR.

2. The Southeast Asian refugee population in the United States is composed primarily of the following ethnic groups: Vietnamese, Sino-Vietnamese, Cambodians, Laotians, and Hmong. There are also small populations of tribal peoples from Laos and Vietnam.

3. The Office of Refugee Resettlement transfers funds to the Department of Education for the Transition Program for Refugee Children.

REFERENCES

Ellis, Arthur. 1980 The Assimilation and Acculturation of Indochinese Children into American Culture. Sacramento: Department of Social Services, State of California, August.

Jung, Steven, Linda Phillips-Jones, Dorothy Reynolds, and Marian Eaton. 1982. Evaluability Assessment of the Transition Program for Refugee Children. Palo Alto, CA: American Institutes for Research in the Behavioral Sciences, September.

Pierce, David C. 1983. A country of immigrants: Effects of and responses to the second wave of Indo-Chinese refugees into Orange County, 1979-1982. Unpublished doctoral dissertation, George Washington University, Washington, DC.

Rubin, Joan. 1986. Meeting the educational needs of Indochinese refugee children. Draft paper. National Center for Bilingual Research, August 1.

San Francisco Examiner. 1980. Faces are changing in San Francisco schools. May 5.

U.S. Department of Commerce. 1961. The 1960 U.S. Census of Population. Washington, DC: Government Printing Office.

U.S. Department of Commerce. 1981. The 1980 U.S. Census of Population. Washington, DC: Government Printing Office.

7
Cooperation and Conflict between Parents and Teachers: A Comparative Study of Three Elementary Schools

Richard L. Warren

INTRODUCTION

Relationships between teachers and parents, school and community inform us about the nature of schooling and teaching. The comparative roles that schools and teachers, parents and community play in cultural affirmation and transmission are part of the data through which we determine continuity of belief and behavior among individuals, groups, institutions, and the cultural system in its totality.

This chapter presents a comparative description and analysis of parent-teacher relations in three elementary schools. The data are drawn from case studies carried out over a period of 15 years. The first study was of a school in Rebhausen,[1] a rural German village. The second study was of Calhoun, a school located in Dennison, a northern California suburban-industrial city of 100,000. The third and most recent study was of Campbell, a California school with a bilingual program and a predominantly Hispanic pupil population, located in Westland, a community of 45,000 close to the Mexican border.

We are accustomed to attribute to schooling and teaching powerful socialization and enculturation influences reflecting dominant cultural norms and values. Data on cross-national school studies reported here have led this author to conjecture that structural characteristics these school have in common may at significant points override cultural differences. Hence in this chapter the central question addressed is: What is the comparative influence of organization and unique cultural setting in explaining commonalities and differences in parent-teacher relations among the three schools? Related questions include: For what reasons do parents and teachers interact and on what occasions? How accessible are the two groups to each other? What schooling issues are regularly addressed in the interaction?

RESEARCH ON SCHOOL-COMMUNITY CONTINUITY

Continuity between school and community is, we find now, more problematic than earlier research on schools indicated. In the seminal studies of the 1940s (West 1945; Warner 1949; Hollingshead 1949) schooling was in general found to be a benign and placid reflection of the broader social system. But in an increasing amount of subsequent research with diverse theoretical perspectives (Becker 1953; Coleman 1962; G. Spindler 1963; Henry 1963; Nordstrom et al. 1967), a correction to that view began to accumulate. The separatist, disjunctive characteristics of life in schools became more visible.

More recent case studies are not sanguine on the question of continuity between school and community. To an increasing degree schools in modern and modernizing societies are found to have a tenuous relationship to their cultural contexts, especially where the research focus is on the schooling experience of racial and ethnic groups (Gay and Cole 1967; Wolcott 1967; Grindal 1972; King 1967; Rosenfeld 1971; Ward 1971; Hostetler and Huntington 1971; Collier 1973; Ogbu 1974; Wax 1980). Schools, it is increasingly argued, are not sensitive to cultural differences and serve mainly the interests of Anglo, middle-class, achievement-oriented populations. The notion of schools as socializing institutions isolated from and impervious to cultural, community, and parental contexts is a familiar theme in the social sciences of education. In an early study of Chicago teachers, Becker (1953) conceptualizes the school as a "self-contained system of social control." In Clausen's work on socialization theory, Lippitt (1968:342) observes:

Very few [socialization] agencies and agents define their socialization functions in terms of its [sic] complimentarity to the parental function, or in terms of collaboration with parents.... Parents perceive school personnel as wanting and expecting them to keep their distance from the program. And interviews with teachers typically indicate their perception of parents as unqualified amateurs who are likely to create problems in the carrying out of an effective school curriculum.

G. Spindler (1974:81) makes the following somber observation: "The educational bureaucracy in a complex urban system functions in some ways like an alien cultural system in relation to the local community, the children in school, and their parents, whether these parents are members of minority or majority groups."

More recently the concept of "teaching culture" or "cultures of teaching" is being employed to examine teaching and its professional, organizational, or cultural context (see, for example, Feiman-Nemser and Floden 1986). In Anderson-Levitt's (1987) review of cross-national research reported by Spindler and Spindler (1987) and Ben-Peretz and Halkes (1987) she raises the question of a transnational teaching culture.

In this chapter the problematic relationship across cultures between schooling and its context will be examined through a focus on parents and teachers, surrogates, respectively, for the community context and the school.

OVERVIEW OF CASE STUDIES

Each of the case studies discussed here holds a general view of schools as (1) academic organizations with internally generated social norms, role expectations, and patterned behavior, and (2) instruments of cultural transmission and socialization for the parental constituency and the broader culture/community. Each study also has a particular research interest. The first study of the Rebhausen School (Warren 1967) focused on the stabilizing and mediating role of the school and teachers in a German village undergoing cultural change as a result of industrialization. The second study of Calhoun Elementary School (Warren 1969, 1973a, 1973b, 1974, 1975) focused on the teaching experience. That research was organized to examine teaching within four major contexts— classroom, school, parental constituency, and school district. It described the operating relationships between teachers and the key roles and organizational arrangements at various contextual levels. The third study of Campbell Elementary School (Warren 1981, 1982) focused on a bilingual–bicultural program—a program that represented a major federal/state mandated intervention directed at affecting significant changes in classroom and school practice.

The comparison developed here is cross-cultural, involving a school in West Germany and two in California, with pronounced differences in pupil ethnicity. Strictures about cross-cultural comparison typically include unit of analysis, comparability of data, equivalence in meaning and function, quality and quantity of data available, and control of the data by the writer (Lewis 1961). In this comparison the concepts of school, teacher, and parent are equivalent at the three sites. Second, the studies described and analyzed here were all carried out by this author. Finally, because there is a research interest common to the three studies, the nature and quantity of data are acceptably similar.

Differences in site and population characteristics are identified as the comparison proceeds. Rebhausen, Dennison, and Westland range in population from 3,000 to 100,000 and in date of "incorporation" from approximately 769 A.D. to 1956. The German village is located in a rural farm area; the California communities belong to the sprawling urban-residential landscape of that state. Most significantly, the three schools serve parental populations whose median occupational profile centers on semiskilled vocations. Each of the schools has an enrollment of close to 400 pupils, grades 1–8 in Rebhausen and grades K–6 in Calhoun and Campbell.

Rebhausen teachers and parents are experiencing a profound social-economic change in the character of the community and the pace of community life— change that is accelerated by regional and national developments, but change that was with some reluctance initiated by the community itself. Campbell teachers and parents are actors in quite different social change, one sanctioned by federal and state governments, one that focuses on a change in status and power of a long-neglected ethnic minority. Change that affects Calhoun teachers and parents is less perceptible, but it is present in the accelerated mobility that characterizes the population.

PROLOGUE: CONTEXTUAL VARIABLES

In this chapter pertinent data from case studies of school and neighborhood are extracted to develop a cross-cultural comparison of parent–teacher relations. Such relations are embedded in a context that can be developed only selectively here. Among contextual variables important to understanding the agenda of parent–teacher interaction, instructional process and organization are paramount.

Instructional Process

In describing instructional process I will compress and summarize extensive observational data on classroom life.

Rebhausen. Instructional processes in Rebhausen reflect a pedagogical point of view in which the mastery of factual knowledge is basic. Elementary school children are considered too young to evolve meaningful opinions and ideas about the more controversial aspects of political and social developments. The evolution of personal opinions and ideas is to be preceded by a mastery of relevant facts, a process that necessarily continues into later adolescence. Consequently, the primary obligation of the teacher is to present the facts and carefully organize learning procedures to insure their mastery. The tradition of a teacher's staying with a class for two or three years gives the process of mastery a longitudinal quality. Facts students learn or poems they memorize are not to be forgotten from one year to the next. Review and reinforcement are therefore important teaching techniques.

The teacher overwhelmingly dominates the instructional process. Teacher–pupil exchanges establish and reinforce an unbending relationship in which the pupil learns to find the important cues to successful behavior and general school performance in the teacher's words and actions. The content of the student's learning experiences is almost always rigidly controlled by the teacher. Opportunities for manifesting and expressing individualistic renditions of this content are constrained within narrow limits. The recitation process is, in this respect, particularly significant. Lines of communication run almost exclusively between individual students and the teacher, with the latter controlling and directing the content of the communication. Only in a few instances does any meaningful exchange occur, in which students examine each other's ideas. In one sense students are, in the classroom, isolated from each other intellectually and therefore more vulnerable to and dependent on the dictates of the teacher. The pattern of discipline reflects a markedly authoritarian implementation of teaching responsibilities. The use of physical punishment, shame, public denunciation, and peer censorship to affect acceptable behavior and academic performance in the classroom are widely shared instructional and disciplinary devices. The prevailing teaching style is one that maintains the teacher in the center of classroom activity—directing, telling, correcting, judging.[2] As agents of cultural maintenance, teachers perform both a unifying and an isolating function. Because they share and impose rigorous standards of memorization and subject-matter mastery, they are as a group and as individuals important instruments of sociocultural unity. Because they share and impose unilaterally rigorous standards of behavior, they are instruments of social isolation.

Campbell. In contrast to prevailing instructional processes in the Rebhausen classrooms, the bilingual-bicultural model at Campbell emphasizes developmental placement and individualized instruction. The latter is implemented through the use of curriculum management systems. These are essential systems of terminal objectives (lengthy lists) and criterion-referenced tests to be used with each student, primarily in the areas of reading and math. The demand these systems place on teachers' time is formidable. Their widespread use determines to a great extent the kinds of socializing experiences pupils are, in fact, having. In brief, curriculum management systems are, like state and federal mandates, a kind of intervention in the life of the school—and quite literally an intervention between teacher and pupil.

Teachers observe rightly that these systems—and the help of an instructional aide—free them for more individualized instruction. At the same time, the systems (by definition and in operation) provide not only the content of learning experience but also the structure and sequence of behaviors required to reach a learning goal. In the process they foster the formation and maintenance of small groups of pupils who function as a part of the system but who also evolve adaptation to curriculum systems. Now and then pupils engage in cooperative behavior—give spelling tests, hear each other read, answer questions, correct mistakes. Most of the time they proceed independently through each phase of the system—from one exercise to another, from one unit to another, from one color code to another. Their progress is evaluated by the teacher who then assigns the next learning increment to be undertaken. But the isolating influence of a curriculum system is muted by the dynamics of small groups and this effect is enhanced by the absence of continuous direct adult supervision. Generally, then, across all Campbell classes small group and individualized instruction processes dominate, and within these instructional modes social as well as academic transactions are a continuing part of the daily life of classrooms.

Achievement is an instructional value shared by the faculties of the two schools. Rebhausen teachers place comparatively greater emphasis on continuity in the acquisition of knowledge and on the social as well as the intellectual authority of the teacher. Campbell teachers place greater emphasis on independence and the influence of peer groups.

Calhoun. Instructional processes in Calhoun classrooms may be fairly characterized as traditional. Small group and individualized instruction are the exception and the furnishings and arrangements that accompany such instruction are absent. Desk chairs in orderly rows are typical. The teacher is at the front of the classroom teaching children through lesson recitation in social studies, helping them work math problems at the blackboard, demonstrating a science principle. Or the teacher is moving through the rows inspecting work-book assignments being completed, helping individual pupils, nudging a child into the task at hand. The assessment of pupil progress by Calhoun teachers is a familiar routine. Homework, tests, workbook exercises, and the like provide data that can be transferred to a grade book. To such quantitative data a Calhoun teacher, like her Rebhausen and Campbell colleagues, may add, at least in moments of indecision, a factor based on less systematic and more impressionistic observations of a pupil's social behavior: attentiveness, partici-pation, and cooperation. But the grade book and the report card provide the essential profile of pupil progress.

In all three schools the production of a functioning academic unit—one that proceeds through the year at an acceptable pace unencumbered either by con-tinuing internal disruptions or by embarrassingly low achievement record—is the most compelling obligation a teacher faces. It is in the organization of instruction that the schools differentiate themselves and transmit values derived from the school's community context and the teacher's professional context.

Organization

Because Rebhausen, Calhoun, and Campbell are elementary schools, there are structural equivalencies with regard to curriculum sequence and the daily schedule. There are also structural differences. Calhoun and Campbell teachers are, in an organizational sense, closer to parents and more vulnerable to them because the teachers are employees of school districts, screened, hired, and assigned by local school officials and elected local school boards. Rebhausen teachers are employees of the state and at the outset of their careers are assigned teaching positions through the state Ministry of Education. Although the three faculties share a middle range occupational status, there are differ-ences that presumably affect parent–teacher relations. Rebhausen teachers occupy a social position of prestige in the rural community and are accorded patterned deferences in social intercourse. Calhoun teachers experience no such social advantage. Campbell teachers derive added status from the respectful attitude Mexican parents bring to the school—and from the strong reputation of the bilingual program. In structural terms Rebhausen parents and teachers are most distant from each other; Campbell parents and teachers, the closest.

PARENT–TEACHER INTERACTION

Turning now to parent–teacher interaction I will begin with data on Reb-hausen and will use that study as a baseline for comparison with the two California schools. To keep the text tied closely to site and time I will employ the ethnographic present, the mode in which observations and findings were first presented. I will draw extensively on unpublished reports as well as pub-lished articles to make the comparisons as explicit as possible and to evoke for the reader the context in which parent–teacher relations unfolded. The studies were carried out in the following periods: Rebhausen, 1964–65; Calhoun, 1967–70; Campbell, 1977–80.

Rebhausen

Village and School. Rebhausen is located at the edge of a hilly region in Southwest Germany. For centuries agriculture, in particular *Weinbau* (the cultivation of grapes and the production of wines) has been the dominant economic activity in Rebhausen. Land—its ownership, distribution, and use—is still a fundamental concern of village natives. But a chemical factory is irrevocably changing village life. In March 1955 there was a net population increase of 1. Ten years later, in March 1965, there was a net population increase of 53. Those moving in included a large number of foreign workers. The predominant vocational categories of those moving in were skilled labor and administrative personnel. Of those moving out the majority were unskilled labor. The factory is not only affecting changes in economic activities but also creating in the life of the village new and alien communities. It now employs over 900 workers, only half of whom are residents of Rebhausen. With the factory working three shifts at full capacity, it is expected that within a few years the work force will increase to about 1,200.

Education for the natives, approximately 70 percent of the population, typically has consisted of eight years of elementary school and three years of part-time or full-time vocational school. The pattern is much the same for factory workers. It is different, however, for management personnel and the small number of professionals living in the village. For them, education extended either through a middle school (seven years beyond the first four years of elementary school) or through a Gymnasium (nine years of a college preparatory education beyond the first four years of elementary school) and a university (four years).

The Rebhausen School has an enrollment of 410 and a faculty of six men and five women. Their average age is approximately 33 and average number of years teaching experience approximately seven. They are not natives. Most of the teachers began their teaching experience in other elementary schools in the region, came to Rebhausen for the second teaching position, and aspire to teaching positions in more urban areas. Teaching assignments are generally made with the women in the lower grades and men in the upper grades. Since it is also traditional that teachers stay with the same class two, three, or even four years, the distribution of teachers by sex among the grades varies.

Parents and Teachers. The State Constitution affirms the right of parents to a cooperative role in school affairs. The Ministry of Education implements this provision by making mandatory the organization of parent councils. Consequently, within a month after the opening of school at Rebhausen meetings are scheduled by all teachers. I attended the one for parents of first graders in Frau Boettcher's class.

The meetings are held at the school in early evening. Frau Boettcher's classroom has 20 parents present, 5 men and 15 women, representing 50 percent of the children in the class. The teacher has opening remarks prepared and a list of suggestions she hopes the parents will follow. She talks about her hopes for the year, that the children will learn and will enjoy school, that they will be good citizens, and that parents will be pleased with the progress their children make. She suggests school supplies they will need and then asks for questions. A parent is concerned about grades.

Q. Why don't you give 1's (the equivalent of A's)?
A. They don't belong at this level. If children become accustomed to 1's now, the grade won't mean as much to them in the upper grades. Anyway, you shouldn't put too much pressure on them about grades.

The talk about grades goes on. Then Frau Boettcher reminds them they are there to elect two individuals to serve as chairman and cochairman of their own first grade group and as representatives of the group to the parents' council. Herr Kranz, a middle-aged businessman, native, and a member of the village council, is elected chairman. Frau Doering, wife of the principal, is elected cochairman. The meeting breaks up and parents start home, talking about their children and homework, the teachers, their own school experiences. When the first meetings and elections are completed, the principal calls a meeting of the council to elect officers and to consider the role of the council and the needs of the school. Herr Bergmann, the bank president, is reelected president and Herr Schroder, the town clerk, reelected vice-president. No vote is taken; by informal acclamation the group is happy to have to two men continue their offices.

Herr Bergmann, representing the council to the principal, reiterates his statement of graduation night that the function of the council is to intervene in the affairs of the school when a problem requiring outside mediation arises between parents and school personnel. He considers the leadership of the school to be in excellent hands and the faculty to be competent. There is, therefore, no need for the council to be active. The principal acquiesces and suggests that members of the council can help the school by bringing parental complaints to him.

The narrow interpretation of the council's interests reflects certain historical and social developments. The council itself is new to the life of the village, a product of a constitutional promulgation following World War II. Second, the traditional social structure of the village has dictated a distinct social distance between teachers and parents. Teachers and principal, along with the mayor and clergy, have occupied the apex in village society. They are *Respektpersonen*, a classification that assigns to them the whole catalog of social amenities the traditional culture has created for ranking members. Also, since the determination of educational policies and directives is the domain of the state, the operating space of such a council is narrowly constrained.

Third, parents are also generally satisfied with the relationships between teachers and pupils. Most parents experienced a more severe discipline in their school days than that to which their children are exposed. What they observe now is a more comradely relationship, a development they welcome, at least as it manifests itself in the immediate, daily life of the school. However, the trend is also suggestive of a weakening of the discipline and order of the traditional folk life. When parents observe that the children no longer always give teachers their due respect (such as crossing the street to greet them), they feel regret. They want their children to be *anständig*, (respectful and well behaved).

A final factor affecting the work of the council is the attitude of the faculty. They view the council with mixed emotions. A friendly cooperative relationship with parents is considered desirable. At the same time, the whole matrix of relationships is, teachers know, relatively unexplored and therefore unpredictable. They suspect that the council, as an institution, might lead to a habit of parental intervention that, unrestrained, could challenge the professional and personal authority of the teacher. The only control device available to them is a kind of cautious indifference. They prefer to organize the one parent meeting required of them and call additional meetings only when parents are needed to act on a problem the teachers want to solve.

The uncertainty of the teachers about the council is aggravated by the growing presence of a constituency over which they exercise less influence. Factory parents are not integrated into the life of the community and are not, therefore, subject to the traditional constraints the folk culture imposes. For them, in this setting at least, teachers are not necessarily Respektpersonen. Frau Borner, a second grade teacher, expresses a view common among the faculty: "I like parents in rural areas. In the city when the child isn't doing well it is considered to be the teacher's fault. Here they tend to leave the teacher alone and to accept the teacher's evaluation of the child."

Confronting the centers of power and prestige in the community, of which the school is one, is for the average Rebhausen native an unwieldly experience. Consequently, when an excited parent shows up at the school to lodge a complaint or submit the same in writing, the whole process is characterized by an awkward, brittle, unpredictable quality. By general understanding, parents are to seek out the teacher during the school day, at the recess. There are no conference periods set up after school, when a parent can talk privately. Sometimes this kind of exchange takes place, but it is generally accidental and does not usually involve a redress of grievances. Parents locate a teacher and have five minutes to reach an understanding, while they stand outside the classroom with students milling about as the recess begins and ends. Whatever sense of urgency the parent comes with is usually compounded by conditions forcing a hurried, excited exchange.

The possible threat of legal action is often present in parent–teacher conflict. Teachers are conscious enough of their legal vulnerability to feel, with some seriousness, that *Ein Lehrer steht mit einen Fuss in einem Gefängnis* (a teacher stands with one foot in prison).

Legal cases involving corporal punishment have had such disastrous results for the teachers involved that much has been published by educational organizations to remind teachers of the precautions they should take. The norms for the use of corporal punishment that teachers are expected to follow and that reflect state policy can be summarized as follows:

1. Corporal punishment of girls and children in the first and second grades is forbidden.
2. In the education of boys, corporal punishment is to be eliminated. It is permitted to be used only in very rare cases.
3. Teachers still on probation are absolutely forbidden to use corporal punishment.

The policy of the state is in conflict with the practice of corporal punishment in the Rebhausen school. It is clear that, despite the power the Ministry of Education exercises over the professional advancement of teachers, the latter do not accept the policy as binding, and state authorities do not choose to enforce the policy. They appear willing to wait until legal action, instituted by a parent, forces state intervention. This ambiguity leaves Rebhausen teachers uncertain as to the course such intervention will take. Consequently they are beginning to be more cautious in their use of physical punishment. They agree that native parents consider a teacher weak if he or she does not use force when appropriate, but the factory parents will be more likely to intervene on behalf of the child when force is used. They conclude it behooves a teacher to know the parent whose child he or she is about to punish.

In Rebhausen, and we shall see in the other studies, the quality of the principal's leadership is also a key factor in fostering cooperation and in mediating conflict between parents and teachers. Herr Doering, for five years a teacher in the school, began his principalship with the advantages of elite status. He also began with an unusual vote of confidence. He is Catholic in a predominantly Protestant village. (By tradition the principal is a member of the dominant faith.) The selection of the principal is made by the mayor and village council—from a list of three names approved and forwarded by the County Office of the State Ministry of Education. Herr Doering applied and his name was among the three. His appointment is a measure of respect and affection he commands in the village—and from his faculty.

The prescriptions Frau Boettcher presented at her parents' meeting are a compendium of cultural and organizational messages for parents. Clean fingernails (and clean handkerchiefs) are measures of cleanliness, a value inherent in family and village life and accepted as the perogative and obligation of teachers to reinforce. Instructions and precautions to parents concerning their limited role in teaching children to write protect and reinforce professional judgments of the teacher but also maintain the values of obedience and respect required of the children. Although most of the teachers are not natives and are oriented toward a more urban, cosmopolitan life, they share and reinforce other cultural values inherent in village life. They romanticize and reinforce love of nature and hard work, values to which natives are firmly committed. The teachers are old enough to have experienced war and poverty, themes the natives use to evoke the past. Most parents perceive faculty mode of discipline and punishment as consistent with their own. Furthermore, the faculty under the leadership of Herr Doering are sensitive to the role the school might play in helping children—and their parents—adapt to changes the chemical factory is bringing to village life. Hence there is impressive continuity between school and community. But Frau Boettcher has first of all to run a classroom. Her prescriptions are directed at parental behavior that serves the organizational needs and interests of schooling and teaching in Rebhausen.

As a subject of inquiry the problematic nature of parent-teacher relations emerged as a question in this first study of a German village and school. Parents are viewed by Rebhausen teachers as a potential threat to their authority and professional role, even when the system in its totality is very protective. Factors that lead to a feeling of vulnerability among teachers include the attitude of factory management parents toward the teachers' traditional status, the inexperience of the faculty with organized parent groups, and the threat of legal action. But there remains an impressive list of allies: a strong tradition of classroom autonomy, an elite status with village natives, the fact that teachers are employees of the state rather than a local school board, their tenure rights as civil servants, the general attitude of parents toward the role of the parent council, and parental aspirations for children consistent with teacher expectations. It is not enough. Teachers still desire more insulation from parental intrusions on their classroom autonomy.

The next two sections will present data on neighborhood and school, parents and teachers, at Calhoun and Campbell. Data on Calhoun are selected to illustrate the diversity of parent-teacher interaction at that school, interaction not found at Calhoun or Rebhausen. We will begin with Calhoun, the school with the most problematic parent-teacher relations.

Calhoun

Neighborhood and School. Calhoun School is located in the most rural part of Dennison and its attendance area is geographically the largest in the district, including both farmland (primarily truck farming and nurseries) and new housing tracts. Nineteen percent of Calhoun's families live in houses on relatively unimproved streets that connect with the main thoroughfare and offer access to the farmlands. About 25 percent of the families in this area are engaged in farming. Included in this number are farm owners, supervising personnel, and migrant workers. The other families are engaged in a wide range of professional, semiskilled, and unskilled occupations. Over 80 percent of Calhoun's families live in a five-year-old development of modest homes. Most of the residents of the tract have lower-middle-class jobs—they are skilled or semi-skilled factory workers, building trades workers, and the like.

The typical family is young and mobile. About 34 percent of the parents are under 30 years of age. At least 75 percent of the families have lived in the community less than three years. Over 80 percent of the families have moved at least twice since their oldest child was born; 25 percent have moved more than five times. Approximately 33 percent of both fathers and mothers did not complete high school. High school graduation marked the termination of formal education for 48 percent of mothers and 32 percent of fathers. Only 7 percent of the fathers completed college and/or graduate studies. However, 60 percent of parents aspire to a four-year college education for their children, and another 10 percent to at least a junior college education.

The faculty is young and inexperienced. The average age of the 14 teachers (3 male, 11 female) is 29. Nine of the teachers are under 30. The principal is 39 with one year of experience as principal. The average length of teaching experience is three years. Like the parents, the teachers are mobile. Half of them have been residents of the state less than three years. At the end of the year, six teachers left the school. Five of them have been at Calhoun only the one year; the sixth, two years.

Parents and Teachers. Parent–teacher interaction at Calhoun is measurably more frequent than at Rebhausen. The interaction is an admixture of written communications, phone calls, prearranged conferences, unannounced visits, and chance encounters. Most interaction is initiated by the school. In only a few instances is the interaction highly structured, that is, the location, purpose, and procedure of the interaction are known and accepted by both parents and teachers.

The one formalized, carefully planned interaction between parents and teachers during the year is the grade conference during the first two days of Thanksgiving week. There is no school, but these two days are part of the teacher's work year. Letters go out, schedules are juggled, phone calls are made, and teachers, responsible for setting up the times, persist until amost all parents show up (92 percent; in four out of five instances the mother came alone). Preparations also involve instructions by the principal. He reminds the teachers to have report cards ready and to limit each conference to 20 minutes. He tells them to start out with something positive and to make sure parents receive adequate information about the basis for the grades. He reminds them that he wants, before the conference, a copy of any report card with a profusion of D's or F's—in case a parent wants to see him too. The district affirms these conferences as "valuable for teachers and parents to know each other and share the insights that each has regarding the interest and capabilities of the student." Both teachers and parents express satisfaction with the conferences.

Celebrations, such as Halloween and Christmas, are also occasions for encounters between parents and teachers. But most interaction initiated by the faculty is designed to inform parents concerning the progress of their children and to provide general information about school and class programs. Indeed, if there is a measurable decline in a child's performance, the teacher wants to make sure the parent knows about it. A frequently used device of requiring parents to sign worksheets, tests, and other examples of a child's assigned or completed work is a quasi-legalistic strategy that serves one of several purposes. It co-opts the parent into the teaching process. If a parent sees work a pupil has done or has to do, presumably the interaction will facilitate a better performance—although in general teachers feel parents are not able to provide very much useful help with homework. It also protects a teacher from accusations of malfeasance in office, such as failure to inform the parent of a child's academic or behavioral problem. Indeed, if it is probable a pupil will receive an F on the next report card, the teacher understands she or he is obligated to send home a "cinch" note—a formal letter apprising parents of the problem, one therefore that presumably makes official or "cinches" whatever more informal warnings the teacher may already have conveyed.

The practice of having parents sign homework is also followed by Rebhausen teachers, so that parents "won't have any excuse later on when the grades come home." Fraulein Wollner reported that some parents refuse to sign because they think their signature indicates approval of the work. One obstinate parent refused to sign the report card as well. He was obliged thereafter to go to the school if he wanted to see the report card. State law requires a parental signature if the card is to be sent home each time.

The frequency of interaction between Calhoun teachers and parents varies from month to month. During a month devoid of special events (report cards, plays, etc.) that might have generated additional conditions leading to interaction, teachers logged their "contacts" with parents and reported 88, almost half of which were initiated by teachers. The contacts for individual teachers ranged from 1 to 11. The teacher who had only one contact was one with seven years' experience, and she offered the explanation that the class was a particularly good one and she organized classroom work so that routine assignments are completed in school. The teacher who had 11 contacts was in his first year and observed that he was somewhat uncertain how to "handle" parents—as uncertain as Rebhausen teachers were with factory parents.

Efforts by parents to right a perceived wrong or to "take things in their own hands" are infrequent but significant because teachers tend to view them as intimidating. Each Calhoun teacher had stressful encounters with parents during the past year; several had more than their share, more often than not because one particular parent kept the pressure on all year. These experiences are invariably recounted in the faculty room, and up-to-date communiques issues if resolution is slow in coming. As in Rebhausen the experience of one becomes the experience of all, and among colleagues those forces that divide pale before the sense of loyalty to a united front in face of a parental confrontation.

The parent-teachers organization is the mechanism through which parents and teachers are expected jointly to structure and to experience mutually useful and supportive interaction. We have seen that Rebhausen's parent council is a very limited forum for parent-teacher interaction, and we shall find that Campbell's PTA has been largely displaced by Advisory Committees. Calhoun has a Parent-Teachers Association that is less than successful in building the kind of cooperative relations the district hopes for. Attendance at meetings is poor. Some 40 percent of the parents report they seldom attend the meetings, 30 percent not at all. Their feelings about the meetings vary: "They promote better parent-teacher relationships," "The only good thing I can see in them is a method of gathering to raise money for extra school equipment," "I feel it is a good way to waste an evening." Most teachers are more emphatic than parents in their disenchantment with the meetings: "At the last meeting there were more teachers than parents," "It's not very active—the same ineffectual 'blah' body most of them are."

The principal is not a forceful mediator in parent-teacher relations, but there is a mixed reaction to his leadership. When observations were begun in the spring of 1967, Larry Vincent was completing his first semester as a full-time principal at Calhoun. He had come to the school and was appointed a teaching principal the first year. He is on probation as principal and anxious about how the district administration views his performance. He is a cautious and diffident individual. The teachers are fond of Larry, and they say social relations within the faculty are very friendly. Calhoun is always compared favorably with other schools the teachers have known. They attribute this not only to the fortuitous circumstances that brought the faculty together, but also to Larry's respect for them as individuals and his unobtrusive administration of the school. They wish he were more decisive in matters in which the efficiency of their work is involved. They wish he were more capable of helping them on pedagogical questions, but they prize the freedom that accrues from the nature of his leadership.

A shift in research site from a village in southwest Germany to a metropolitan community in northern California resulted in data that reinforce earlier findings, though the organizational and cultural context of parent-teacher relations at Calhoun is different from that of Rebhausen—and more complex. Calhoun teachers are employees of the local school district, governed by a polity, the school board, which is the agent of parents and other residents in the community. Parental involvement in the life of the school through formal parent groups and informal interaction with teachers and administrators is a long-standing expectation. Evaluation of teaching competence is accomplished at the school level, by the principal on behalf of the school district. Calhoun teachers do not experience the degree of professional autonomy that Rebhausen teachers do. Their relations with parents are not as stable. In retrospect the choice of Calhoun as a site led fortuitously to a plethora of data on conflict in parent-teacher relations. The principal's inexperience and diffident style of leadership, the teachers' inexperience, and the newness of residential areas are factors influencing the tentativeness of parent–teacher relations.

With data from two schools we can begin to answer the questions posed at the outset of the chapter. The answers need to be viewed within the context of cultural factors that differentiate the two schools and their neighborhood/ community settings. Rebhausen is a small, homogeneous community in the early stages of significant socioeconomic change. However, in spite of the new factory and the new residents it attracted, there persists in the dominant native population the legacy of a folk culture—values that affirm and reinforce traditional rural life, a social structure differentiated horizontally along a model personality continuum, carefully monitored behavior and interpersonal relations, and, overall, a long-standing belief that the village is essentially self-sufficient and can provide spouse, education, and work. Calhoun's "community" is largely a new and impersonal residential area. Families in the same block know each other by name, but extended contacts are as yet infrequent. Residents were attracted to Dennison because of job opportunities, better housing, and, for most of them, the promise of a more homogeneous community than the urban areas they had left.

The parental constituencies in the two schools differ in socialization values. Rebhausen parents focus on obedience and conformity; Calhoun parents, on competitive skills and independence. They differ on educational expectations. Rebhausen parents expect the school to reinforce the legitimacy of the village culture and social structure. They want their children to accept parental vocations as their own. Calhoun parents expect the school to teach skills instrumental to socioeconomic mobility.

Thus far we have seen that across these two different cultural settings the vulnerability of the teaching role is a common denominator. Social custom and the organization of schooling and teacher employment are factors that insulate Rebhausen teachers from parents, but the teachers are not assured. The same factors operate in the Calhoun setting to render teachers more accessible to parents than they wish to be. A central fact of the relationship is that teachers manage a group process but parental critique of success focuses on an individual.

We found that the object of interaction between parents and teachers is usually the assessment of individual pupil progress and the appropriate use of organizational resources and arrangements to facilitate the instructional process. In general the interaction is not a forum for affirming cultural and socialization values, particularly those that are manifest in instructional processes. However, data on school and family life point to an underlying harmony of adult expectations about the social behavior and development of children.[3] Hence, continuity of school and community—as measured by shared socialization values—is accomplished not because parents and teachers interact effectively but simply because they are members of the same cultural system.

Campbell

Neighborhood and School. Westland is located in the southwest corner of southern California. Mexico is a 20-minute drive south; Los Angeles, a two-and one-half hour drive to the north. The city's population of 45,000 is part of a metropolitan area of over 1.5 million people. Westland's 6.6 square miles form almost a square, bounded on the west by the ocean and on the north, east, and south by communities that are part of the metropolitan area. Like so many California coastal communities, Westland's boundaries are "redefined" by freeways that disrupt old neighborhoods and give birth to new subdivisions. The two north-south freeways that run through Westland divide the city into a large middle section, commercial and residential, and two outer sections. To the west of the main coastal freeway are light industry, the marine terminal, and a small neighborhood that is Campbell's attendance area.

Campbell families typically live in small frame houses set on small lots fronting wide paved streets. Street-corner lots are generally occupied by gas stations, warehouses, and the like. Small businesses are interspersed among the houses as are vacant lots, some with aging rundown boats hoisted on scaffolding. There is a worn but clear appearance to the groups of houses—with colorful flower beds dispersed intermittently in yards along with bicycles and toys.

In education and occupation Campbell parents are by traditional criteria below middle-class status. Seventy-five percent have completed no more than the eighth grade. Many stopped after six years in Mexican schools. Occupation of husband is typically semiskilled or unskilled—cannery worker, construction, dishwasher, gardener, pipe fitter, dock worker, truck driver, painter. In responding to a home language survey most Campbell parents check the "Spanish origin" category. They have close ties to Mexico. Typically all but one member of the immediate family—husband, wife, and both sets of grandparents—were born in Mexico. Slightly more husbands than wives were born in the United States. Almost half of the families maintain continuing contacts with Mexico through weekly or bimonthly trips across the border to shop or visit relatives. Among the small number of parents who checked the "white" category are several who were born and raised in Mexico and whose children are Spanish dominant.

The Campbell faculty is composed of relatively young individuals (average age in the early 30s) with diverse social and ethnic backgrounds. There are 14 teachers excluding the preschool and learning disability classes; 13 females and 1 male. Among the 13 female teachers seven are Mexican American and bilingual. Three of them were born in Mexico and attended Mexican schools in the early grades. One of the six female Anglo teachers is also bilingual. The male teacher is black and bilingual.

In September 1977, 405 pupils were enrolled at Campbell: 87 percent were of Spanish origin, 10 percent were Anglo, 1 percent was black, and 1 percent Filipino. The school has always had a high proportion of Hispanic children.

Over the past decade that proportion had been steadily increasing from 81 percent in 1967 to 91 percent in 1979.

Parents and Teachers. Campbell School has virtually ideal conditions for cooperative relations between parents and teachers. The two groups are participants in an innovative program that is both instrument and symbol of the renaissance of the school and the affirmation of the worth of the dominant neighborhood ethnicity. The program itself, a language-maintenance bilingual-bicultural model, embodies as a self-conscious goal cultural continuity between school and neighborhood. The teachers are experienced and competent and the bilingual program is for them an instrument of recognized professional achievement. Administrative leadership is also a positive factor. Campbell's principal, Fred Whitman, is not a stranger to the neighborhood. He taught fourth grade at the school for four years and achieved a reputation as a skillful teacher. He is perceived by teachers and parents as a competent, understanding, and fair administrator. Because he is bilingual and Mexican American his office (with the help of the community aide) functions as a mediator between school and parents, especially parents who are non- or limited-English speaking. Another factor that increases parental interest in the school is job opportunity. Among mothers there is a pattern of increased involvement in school activities, which leads to a paid position, that is, from attendance at advisory committee meetings, to being a classroom volunteer, to serving as an advisory committee officer, and finally to obtaining a part-time position as an instructional aide. In brief, Campbell is inundated with parents—noon supervisors, advisory committee officers, volunteers, aides, parents on errands, parents preparing a Mexican luncheon, and such. It is a condition we affirm as much to be desired in the cause of good public education, but it exists alongside a professional and social distance that at Campbell as at Rebhausen and Calhoun separates parent and teacher roles and persists in the face of ameliorative circumstances.

Campbell has a community aide and two program advisory committees—roles that are not part of school organization at Rebhausen or Calhoun. At Campbell they lead to a dramatic increase in parent involvement in school life. However, their influence on parent-teacher interaction is ambiguous because they intrude on traditional alignments of authority and interaction between parents and teachers. The consequences are not predictable. Community aides in Westland are the responsibility of a district administrator in charge of special programs, but each aide is directly supervised by the school principal who influences the aide's implementation of the role. According to the program administrator, most aides are "kept on a tight rein" and effectively restricted to what are essentially clerical and minor administrative duties. The performance of Martha Cuneo, Campbell's community aide, represents a more ideal realization of the expectations for the role. She recruits parents for membership and offices in advisory committees and the PTA, helps plan meeting times and programs, sends out notifications, prepares newsletters, assigns committee responsibility for meeting activities, and sends out evaluation questionnaires.

For the classroom volunteer program she recruits participants, orients and places them in classrooms based on teacher requests, keeps records of participation, and organizes a ceremony to honor the volunteers. She also makes home visits. In her role as community aide Martha Cuneo serves as an organizational broker among the school's adult constituencies. In carrying out her activities, in particular those involving advisory committees and classroom volunteers, she is variously an agent of the district, the principal, parents, and teachers. On balance she spends more time representing parental interests but her immediate superior is Fred Whitman, the principal. Her duties are organizational and clerical but he does not keep her on a "tight rein." Because she is respected by parents and teachers for her careful and friendly organizing skills, her work is not constrained by prevailing sensitivity to maintaining role boundaries.

It is within the context of her work with parent groups that parental interests and her role as community aide come together and are legitimated by state and federal mandate. Campbell[4] has three organized parent groups: the Parent Teachers Association and two advisory committees, the Bilingual Education Committee and the Compensatory Education Committee. The advisory committees derive essentially from state and federal program funding requirements. Proposals for funding or the renewal of funding under Title I and Title VII of the Elementary and Secondary Education Act and subsequent amendments include provisions for the establishment of parent advisory groups and for their integration into planning, implementation, and review of program proposals.

Among the three groups the traditional PTA is the weakest—because of the existence of advisory committees and the opportunities for part-time work at the school. By definition and mandate the advisory groups have more entrée to involvement in issues that require action by the central administration.[5] Hence there is opportunity for the accretion of power by these groups to a degree not typical of the PTA.[6] It is an incipient power that is advanced in small increments as parents become more practiced in examining how the system and separate schools are proceeding on various matters—and in exerting public pressure to affect a particular outcome.

It is in the monthly meetings of advisory committee officers that the quality of parental involvement is shaped and given direction. In these meetings the officers organize programs for the general meetings and arrange for parental help with special school assemblies and money-raising activities. They also organize parental involvement in the preparation and evaluation of Campbell's School Improvement Plan. Since the plan addresses in detail the main components of the school program, including parent participation and parent education, committee members, in their review role, acquire a large agenda of school-centered topics with which they become familiar and about which they are asked to make a judgment. The monthly meetings are not constrained by any preconceived notion of committee boundaries.

The Campbell faculty selects a representative to the monthly meetings of advisory committee officers—but that person attends only when the meetings are held every other month at the school. Parents are not represented at faculty meetings. Many of the topics discussed at advisory committee meetings—and faculty meetings—concern administrative aspects of schooling and are resolved without cooperative parent–teacher interaction. Topics in which both groups play a fundamental role are not always addressed collaboratively.

One such topic was a student attitude survey. The survey on ethnic identity was proposed and developed because in their school improvement program filed with the state, the faculty had committed themselves to measuring improvement in student understanding and acceptance of multiethnic backgrounds. The proposed survey asked direct questions about a pupil's feeling of ethnic identity ("I think of myself as American, Mexican, Chicano"). Parents heard of the proposal and opposition formed to what they felt was an unwarranted intrusion on personal beliefs.[7] The survey was discussed at an advisory committee officers' meeting and at a faculty meeting, but only the principal was a participant at both meetings. The survey was not carried out.

It was not the only instance of conflict—between parents and teachers or among teachers—that centered on minority status and ethnicity. The issue of whether children with language problems (at Campbell almost all Hispanic) should leave the classroom for special instruction (as technically required by state law) split the faculty. The position an individual teacher or aide took on the issue came to be a measure of commitment to the bilingual program in general. Conflict also erupted between parents and one teacher who advocated a transitional rather than a language maintenance bilingual program. In a long letter to the School Board supporting her position the teacher stated that Campbell pupils were "being directed toward being 'Mexican' more than 'American.'" Parents protested her stand and at the next School Board meeting a petition with over 100 signatures was presented asking for her transfer. The protests led to an extensive review of Campbell's program and, at the end of the year, to the transfer of the teacher.

Parental influence displayed in the transfer of a teacher is in stark contrast to the influence of parents in Rebhausen—and Calhoun as well. The incident further confirms the significance of advisory committees and the community aide as instruments of parent training and involvement in school life. It also demonstrates the validity of faculty concern for the consequences of such roles. Perhaps most significantly, the incident reminds one how politicized the cultural role of ethnicity in an American school and community has become.

Campbell's bilingual-bicultural program—and ethnic values inextricably bound up in it—present parents and teachers with fundamental questions of cultural affirmation and transmission. The questions are within a context of historic and changing accommodations between dominant culture and minority ethnicity. The questions are not resolved in the broader society but are nevertheless projected into the school to be mediated within a maze of judicial, legislative, administrative, organizational, and curricular factors. For parents and teachers, responding cooperatively to such questions is difficult. Teachers do not find it easy to discuss them in faculty meetings, while parents approach them with increasing skill and aggressiveness. There is no orderly, collaborative exchange of ideas and attitudes between them. Hence those factors that bring parents and teachers into closer and more frequent contact do not significantly mediate those factors that separate them.

SUMMARY

The absence of an effective bond between parents and teachers is a striking commonality among the three schools in their distinctive neighborhood/ community settings. This phenomenon prevails across different and complex combinations of school-community characteristics. No single variable— whether conceived broadly as continuity in school and family socialization values are more narrowly as the employment conditions of teachers—furnishes a satisfactory explanation.

The quality of parent-teacher relations at Calhoun is the most predictable. A reticent inexperienced principal, an inexperienced faculty, a new neighborhood, the ineptness of the teacher evaluation process—these and related factors work against an effective bond between parent and teacher even though the two groups agree on a common core of socialization values.

Rebhausen's profile of pertinent cultural and organizational characteristics is different. Among the three schools it is the most unambiguous example of continuity in schooling and cultural context. In spite of socioeconomic changes that the factory is beginning to bring to village life, there persists a core system of norms and values manifest in home and school. In general teachers are not natives, and they do not aspire to integrate themselves into village life; but they perform as functional socialization agents. They accept and reinforce parental expectations that the school will prepare children to move into a highly strati-fied social structure and into social-occupational niches the parents themselves occupy. In the village social structure the teachers are elites, and conditions of employment further insulate them from parental intervention. But they are apprehensive that with urbanization and industrialization will come new client populations and a gradual erosion of their authority.

We have already seen that at Campbell the bilingual program with its ethnic connections is both a powerful unifying force in parent-teacher relations and a source of tension and conflict. For parents ethnic affirmation is a secondary goal of the program. Like Calhoun parents, they view the school as an instrument of social mobility for their children. The socialization values parents and teachers share are a unifying factor as is their common interest and pride in the success of the bilingual program. But for parents the primary goal of the program is the social and economic advancement of their children. For teachers the program offers first of all a more challenging and prestigious setting for the practice and display of their professional competence. Hence the two groups adapt to each other within the context of roles that the schooling process organizes.

At the outset of this chapter the question was asked, What is the comparative influence of institution and unique cultural setting in explaining commonalities and differences in parent-teacher relations? We have found a good fit between teacher and parent socialization norms and values in three schools with distinctively different characteristics or settings: a village in rural, southwest Germany; an Anglo middle-class neighborhood in a northern California metropolis; and a lower-middle-class Mexican American neighborhood in a southern California metropolis. But in all three schools relations between parents and teachers are complex, tentative, and stressful. Continuity in socialization value does not ameliorate differences. The institution cannot resolve the basic conflict between parental interest in the progress and life chances of a single child and teacher interest in the successful management of a group enterprise.

Parents and teachers are key socialization agents in the lives of children. They are cultural carriers and transmitters of norms and values they have learned and they deem important to their role. In a time of intense concern for effective schooling we try to diminish the separative effects of organization on the two roles and achieve an open exchange. As we seek such accommodation, we need to recognize those enduring realities that characterize parent-teacher relations.

NOTES

1. Pseudonyms employed in the original research reports will be used.

2. I wish to emphasize that this characterization of classroom life in Rebhausen derives from research carried out in 1964–65. Schools, like other institutions in West Germany, have in decades experienced waves of intense interest change. It may be that instructional modes among present Rebhausen faculty vary observably from the profile I am presenting.

3. When, for example, parents at Calhoun are asked, "What personal traits do you want most of all for your children to develop?" they answer: "honesty," "have moral principles," "self-confidence," "leadership ability," "be friendly." Rebhausen parents put *anstandig* (respectful and well behaved) first and then *gehorsam* (obedient), *ehrlich* (honest), *ein guter Schuler* (a good learner), and finally an awareness of life's seriousness (*Das Leben hat Aufgaben*). English-speaking parents at Campbell reply: "respect for elders," "respect for other's rights, privileges, and property," "good behavior," "being a good student," "honest." Spanish-speaking parents answered: *respecto, buena conducta, serio, educado, disciplinado*. Parental responses are consistent with socialization values that faculties in the two schools profess. These values are to be sure not always consistent with socialization that proceeds within instructional processes.

4. An evaluation report of Campbell's bilingual program includes this statement: "Although this does not pertain directly to the program, there was concern expressed by staff members regarding parents being in the teachers' lounge. Teachers do not have a place in which they can express themselves freely. There is no staff privacy and they feel uncomfortable."

Faculties of the three schools share a sensitivity to parental surveillance. Rebhausen teachers acknowledge the social constraints on their public behavior, and when they want as a group to enjoy an evening of partying, they remove themselves to another village where "they have their privacy." Calhoun teachers are not subject to the same intensive surveillance, but they do not feel free of it. Encounters with parents in extra-school settings are awkward. Several of them chose note to live in Dennison in order to avoid such constraints.

5. In contrast, the contractual agreement between the Westland School Board and the Westland Elementary Teachers Association seeks to delimit parent-teacher inter-action. In the section on hours of employment it stipulates that with regard to staff-parent meetings, parent-teacher conferences, open house, faculty meetings, and the like, "in no event will a unit member be required to serve more than 20 hours per work year in these capacities." By tacit agreement between principal and teachers the 20-hour limit is ignored. Calhoun teachers work under a similar type contract. The condi-tions of employment for Rebhausen teachers are part of the state civil service code.

6. See Rodriguez (1980–81), Cruz (1979) and Matute-Bianchi (1979) for research on the role of advisory committees in school affairs. They report that in general the work of such committees is ineffectual. I did not find that to be the case at Campbell, but recent federal legislation and funding procedures have resulted in a diminished role for advisory committees.

7. Not all teachers approved the survey. Those who did not felt, like the parents, that it was too personal and too heavily weighted toward the Spanish minority.

REFERENCES

Anderson-Levitt, Kathryn M.
  1987   National culture and teaching culture. *Anthropology and Education Quarterly* 18:33–38.
Becker, H.
  1953   The Teacher in the authority system of the public schools. *Journal of Educa-tional Sociology* 27:128–144.
Ben-Peretz, Miriam and Rob Halkes
  1987   How teachers know their classrooms: A cross-cultural study of teachers' understanding of classroom situations. *Anthropology and Education Quar-terly* 18:17–32.
Coleman, J. S.
  1962   The Adolescent Society. Glencoe: The Free Press.
Collier, J.
  1973   Alaskan Eskimo Education: A Film Analysis of Cultural Confrontation in the Schools. New York: Holt, Rinehart and Winston.
Cruz, N.
  1979   Parent advisory councils serving Spanish-English bilingual projects funded under ESEA Title VII. In Working with the Bilingual Community. Rosslyn, VA: National Clearinghouse for Bilingual Education.
Feiman-Nemser, Sharon and Robert E. Floden
  1986   The cultures of teaching. In M. Wittrock (ed.), Handbook of Research on Teaching, pp. 505–526. New York: Macmillan.
Gay, J. and M. Cole
  1967   The New Mathematics and an Old Culture: A Study of Learning Among the Kpelle of Liberia. New York: Holt, Rinehart and Winston.

Grindal, B.
 1972   Growing up in Two Worlds: Education and Transition among the Sisala of
         Northern Ghana. New York: Holt, Rinehart, and Winston.
Henry, J.
 1963   Culture Against Man. New York: Random House.
Hollingshead, A. B.
 1949   Elmtown's Youth. New York: John Wiley.
Hostetler, J. A. and G. E. Huntington
 1971   Children in Amish Society: Socialization and Community Education. New
         York: Holt, Rinehart and Winston.
King, A. R.
 1967   The School at Mopass: A Problem of Identity. New York: Holt, Rinehart and
         Winston.
Lewis, O.
 1961   Comparisons in Cultural Anthropology. In F. W. Moore (Ed.), Readings in
         Cross-Cultural Methodology. New Haven, CT: HRAF Press.
Lippitt, R.
 1968   Improving the Socialization Process. In Clausen, J. A. (ed.) Socialization and
         Society. Boston: Little, Brown.
Matute-Bianchi, M. E.
 1979   Parent and community participation in federally funded bilingual education:
         A view from the bottom up. Unpublished dissertation. Stanford University.
Nordstrom, C. E., E. Z. Friedenberg, and H. A. Gold
 1967   Society's Children: A study of Ressentiment in the Secondary School. New
         York: Random House.
Ogbu, J.
 1974   The Next Generation: An Ethnography of Education in an Urban Neighbor-
         hood. New York: Academic Press.
Rodriguez, G.
 1980-   Citizen Participation in selected bilingual education advisory committees. In
 81   NABE, The Journal of the National Association for Bilingual Education.
         4(2):1-21.
Rosenfeld, C.
 1971   "Shut Those Thick Lips!": A Study of Slum School Failure. New York: Holt,
         Rinehart and Winston.
Spindler, G. D.
 1963   Education in a transforming American culture. In G. Spindler (ed.), Educa-
         tional and Culture: Anthropological Approaches. New York: Holt, Rinehart
         and Winston.
 1987   Why Have Minority Groups in North America Been Disadvantaged by Their
         Schools? In Education and cultural process: Anthropological approaches, 2nd
         ed. George Spindler (ed.). Prospect Heights, IL: Waveland Press, pp. 160-172.
Spindler, George and Louise Spindler
 1987   Cultural dialogue and schooling in Schoenhausen and Roseville: A compara-
         tive analysis. Anthropology and Education Quarterly 18:3-16.
Ward, M. C.
 1971   Them Children: A Study in Language Learning. New York: Holt, Rinehart
         and Winston.

Warner, W. L.
1949   Democracy in Jonesville. New York: Harper and Brothers.
Warren, R. L.
1967   Education in Rebhausen: A German Village. New York: Holt, Rinehart and Winston.
1969   Teacher encounters: A typology for ethnographic research on the teaching experience. Stanford Center for Research and Development in Teaching (now Institute for Research on Educational Finance and Governance). Research and Development Memorandum No. 45.
1973a   The teaching experience in an elementary school: A case study. Stanford University: Stanford Center for Research and Development in Teaching, Technical Report No. 35.
1973b   The classroom as a sanctuary for teachers: Discontinuities in social control. *American Anthropologist* 75:280-291.
1974   Parents and teachers: Uneasy negotiations between socialization agents. In Donald E. Edgar (ed.), The Competent Teacher: Studies in the Socialization of Teachers. Melbourne, Australia: Angus and Robertson.
1975   Context and isolation: The teaching experience in an elementary school. *Human Organization* 34(2):139-148.
1981   Bilingual Education at Campbell School: A Case Study. Report to the National Institute of Education, Washington, DC.
1982   Schooling, biculturalism, and ethnic identity: A case study. In Spindler, G. (ed.), Doing the Ethnography of Schooling: Educational Anthropology in Action. New York: Holt, Rinehart and Winston.
Wax, M.
1980   Desegregated Schools: An Intimate Portrait Based on Five Ethnographic Studies. New Brunswick, NJ: Transaction Books.
West, J.
1945   Plainville, U.S.A. New York: Columbia University Press.
Wolcott, H.
1967   A Kwakiute Village and School. New York: Holt, Rinehart and Winston.

PART III
SOCIALIZATION OF
YOUNG ADULTS:
CULTURAL CONFLICTS
ACROSS CULTURES

8
Cross-Cultural Adaptation and Learning: Iranians and Americans at School
Diane M. Hoffman

The anthropological study of education is based upon the notion that the transmission of culture is a fundamental educational process, and that this process cannot be understood without reference to the cultural context and outcomes of learning at both the individual and group levels of analysis. Given the significance of culture as both a frame and a primary source of content in the educational process broadly defined, when two or more cultures interact a primary educational question thus becomes one related to learning of culture itself in such cross-cultural situations.

Most ethnographic studies of cross-cultural interaction in the classroom have focused upon the ways cultural differences contribute to ethnic conflict, providing rich documentation of how different communication styles and underlying assumptions and values contribute to minority failure. Ethnic conflict resulting from cultural discontinuities is assumed to lie at the root of difficulties experienced by some minority students in achieving school success. As noted by Ogbu and Matute-Bianchi (1986), however, micro-level studies of the interaction process in classrooms neglect the more important question as to why some minorities fail while others are successful in meeting the academic demands of the school. A focus on cultural differences/conflict per se does not afford an adequate conceptual framework for understanding cultural and societal factors operating at the macro level of analysis.

Anthropological studies of education in culturally plural settings have often been based on this implicit model of cultural conflict. By placing the issue of cultural difference at the core of analysis of classroom learning and teaching, such models present a view of culture as something that determines the way people interact as well as the outcomes of their interaction, neglecting the fluid and dynamic aspects of culture as interpretation and meaning negotiation.

When seen from a conflict perspective, cultures are basically incompatible entities that one either adopts or rejects. As Judith Kleinfeld (1983:182) writes, "Anthropology has become associated with a cultural conflict model of education that poses 'either/or' choices between a minority culture and a western culture rather than a 'both/and' approach that encourages children to achieve competency in both a local and a national culture." In the ethnographic literature, models of culture conflict in which majority and minority are discrete and incompatible modes of cultural identity have obscured or even precluded focus on the ultimately more interesting theoretical questions that concern what, why, and how cultural idioms and meanings are acquired in the process of cross-cultural interactions, and how such acquisition may affect cultural identity.

This chapter considers cultural differences in Iranian and American interaction patterns in the context of underlying assumptions and values governing the process of education as implicitly conceptualized by the two cultural groups. Though differences superficially resulted in culture conflicts at the school where this research was conducted, culture learning, rather than conflict, was the primary issue underlying Iranian and American interaction at the school. Strategies of culture acquisition as well as the nature of Iranian cultural identity enabled these students to engage in a form of adaptation to the institutional environment of the school that could overcome what were perceived by Americans as fundamental impediments to academic success.

IRANIANS—A "SOMEWHAT" MINORITY

It should be noted at the outset that the use of the term "ethnic minority" to describe the Iranian population in the United States is problematic. The term connotes social, political, and economic disadvantage—characteristics that may not, in fact, be shared by all those cultural groups that may conceivably be called minorities. Indeed, we have few concepts to describe cultural groups within U.S. society that do not more or less explicitly evoke concepts of inequality or disadvantage. This may be a primary reason why most anthropological studies of education in culturally plural settings have dealt with groups such as Asians, blacks, Hispanics, or Native Americans—groups whose status relative to U.S. society as a whole is commonly characterized as "disadvantaged." The notion of cultural difference in itself has come to be associated with notions of economic disadvantage, social inequity, and political oppression.

Iranians in the United States are a major—perhaps *the* major—cultural minority group that does not fit this image of the ethnic minority. They have not acquired recognition as an ethnic group by the mainstream; nor do they consider themselves an ethnic component of U.S. society. Despite the media attention focused on Iran in recent years, Iranians in the United States remain a hidden, unrecognized, and poorly researched group. The *Harvard Encyclopaedia of American Ethnic Groups* describes Iranians as the least-well-known of all American minorities (Lorenz and Wertime 1980).

The Iranian group does not fit the typical ethnic minority image for a number of reasons: in general, Iranians are highly educated, economically successful professionals of relatively privileged social class, many of whom might be classified as unwilling exiles rather than immigrants (Sabagh and Bozorg-Mehr 1987). They have not established well-defined ethnic neighborhoods or obvious ethnic occupational niches, and they display a strong cultural preference for remaining in the background. Indeed, when asked why there are so few studies of Iranians in the United States, one Iranian responded, "Perhaps it is because they do not want to be studied."

Though no exact statistics are currently available as to the number of Iranians in the United States, it is believed that the largest population resides in Los Angeles. According to *Time* magazine (1983:22), Iranians are the second largest minority group in Los Angeles after the Mexicans, numbering about 200,000. Estimates given by the 1980 U.S. Census (1983: Table 195) report 25,510 Iranians in Los Angeles, but this figure does not account for the very large number of Iranians who are present illegally, and those who register themselves under other ethnic categories such as Armenian, Jewish, or Assyrian.

The majority of Iranians arrived in the United States during and after the Iranian revolution of 1978–79, escaping the turmoil and economic hardships occasioned by the fall of the Pahlavi regime and the establishment of the Islamic Republic of Iran. These Iranians joined the approximately 60,000 Iranian university students who were already here and who constituted the largest group of foreign students on U.S. campuses.

The economic position of Iranian immigrants arriving in the United States following the revolution is much lower than that of prerevolution arrivals (Sabagh and Bozorg-Mehr 1987), though Iranians remain overall a relatively successful and well-educated group. They are, however, an extremely heterogeneous population in terms of religion and ethnicity, including Sunni as well as Shi'a Muslims, Bahais, Jews, Assyrians, Armenians, and Zoroastrians. Political factionalism is a noted feature of the population as well. Though such heterogeneity is often cited as a reason for a lack of group cohesion among Iranians, it appears that cultural factors such as strong family and in-group orientation, an informal and highly flexible political style, as well as a preference for individualistic action have also contributed to lack of ethnic group cohesion.

Another significant aspect of Iranian adaptation in the United States that may contribute to a lack of strong community or cohesion is the lack of what might be called a minority or an immigrant mentality. Those Iranians who arrived during or after the revolution preserve a strong desire to return to Iran, and they regard life in the United States as a temporary—and in many ways unsatisfying—alternative to the lives they left in Iran. Even among those Iranians who have decided to remain in the States to pursue a career (often those who arrived before the revolution as students), most say they would return to Iran if the government were to change. Among this professional group there is a strong ambivalence about remaining in the States. Many say that although they have gotten used to American life and would find living in Iran very difficult, there is a strong attachment to Iran that precludes full identification with American values and life-style. Though the majority of Iranians presently view the United States as a better alternative to Iran, they do not share the common immigrant mentality in which the United States is seen as a land of opportunity, one whose values and meanings are freely and positively embraced. For many, although the United States is thought to offer economic and career advantages, it is a step down rather than a step up in life-style and the realization of life's aims. This is reflected in the resistance Iranians maintain toward classification as an immigrant or minority group: In the words of Iranian professionals, "We are a quiet minority, a successful minority, unlike other minorities." "We don't want to be thought of as just another bunch of immigrants." "We are a somewhat minority."

Since the Iranian revolution, however, there have been a number of developments among Iranians in the United States that point toward the development of greater community cohesiveness and the possible emergence of an immigrant community. Various Iranian organizations have been established (though few of these have succeeded, due, ostensibly, to constant conflicts of interest and what Iranians themselves call the Iranian inability to work together toward common goals). Iranian media have expanded to included numerous television and radio stations that broadcast regularly in Persian. Farsi-language schools have been set up for Iranian children; cultural programs, including performances of Iranian classical music and poetry, have found dedicated audiences. Large-scale community social activities have also become more frequent since the revolution, including popular music concerts featuring famous singers, arts exhibitions, and film showings.

Yet Iranians remain a relatively unrecognized group within the fabric of American pluralism, displaying a desire to remain somewhat apart from the mainstream as well as from other ethnic groups. There is a recognized sense of cultural superiority among Iranians vis-a-vis non-Iranians (Ansari 1974), which does not, however, mitigate the Iranian desire to become successful and to enjoy the material benefits that life in America is thought capable of providing.

THE NOTION OF CULTURE LEARNING
IN AN ANTHROPOLOGICAL CONTEXT

Before turning to an analysis of Iranian patterns of culture acquisition within the school setting, it is helpful to consider the notion of culture learning itself, particularly within the context of an anthropology of education. Some of the significant issues involved in the culture learning process appear to be the role played by the symbolic expression of intercultural meanings in the environment, institutional and individual responses to cross-cultural differences, individual as well as group-level processes of adoption or rejection of cultural meaning complexes, and creation of cultural mediating identities that serve to bridge differing cultural meaning systems. The extent to which a minority cultural group adopts or rejects the underlying cultural meaning system of the school depends ultimately upon the ways perceived cultural discontinuities can facilitate or hinder the acquisition of the second culture at a deep or self-impacting level.

As distinct from enculturation (the term used by anthropologists to describe the primary learning of a first or native culture), culture learning is taken to refer to the learning of a second or different culture. This concept has more in common with notions of cross-cultural or intercultural learning, since it places primary emphasis on the learning that takes place across cultural boundaries. Acculturation (a term applied to the gradual adoption of a foreign culture by a group as a result of residing in that culture for an extensive period of time) and cultural adaptation (a term having a similar meaning but perhaps focusing more on social and cultural adjustments or changes that are made in response to life in a foreign culture) can be regarded as fundamentally based on culture learning, though they are not typically studied from such a perspective. The choice of the term "culture" learning—as opposed to "cultural" learning—reflects more of an emphasis on the acquisition of culture at a deep or affective level rather than in a purely cognitive fashion (as in learning about a culture), emphasizing the nonformal aspects of the process as opposed to formal study or learning.

Though it would seem that anthropology—and particularly the anthropology of education—would have a major interest in the conceptualization and documentation of processes of culture learning, to date there has been little substantive research addressing this issue. As noted by Wolcott (1982), the anthropology of learning has been preoccupied with consideration of the process of culture transmission rather than culture learning. Although some anthropologists have considered the notion of culture learning, particularly in the context of discussions of enculturation or fieldwork experience (see Burnett-Hill 1974; DuBois 1955; Hansen 1982; Kimball 1972; Neville 1984), as a concept culture learning has been used more frequently in social psychological research on intercultural relations. This research has focused on evaluating the behavioral and cognitive manifestations of the process rather than upon dimensions of affect and cultural identity outcomes. Much attention has been given to the conscious acquisition of rules of cultural behavior, patterns of social interaction, and cognitive categories (See Detweiler 1980; Furnham and Bochner 1982; Guthrie 1975; Watson 1977). In the majority of cases behavioral adaptation has been taken as the unstated goal of all cross-cultural learning, the assumption being that persons already enculturated into a first culture cannot in fact do more than adapt on a surface or rule-governed level to the demands of another cultural setting. In other words, the process of culture learning has been implicitly conceptualized as one of behavioral management, in which the learner attempts consciously to match his or her actions with what has been learned about the proper ways for acting in the second culture. Such behavioral adjustment may involve to some degree attitudinal acceptance of the alternative pattern, but such acceptance is in itself not viewed as significant; it is only the means to an end characterizable by adequate performance in the alternative cultural setting. Moreover, behavioral adjustment refers to a process of conscious change toward a known goal (the desired pattern of behavior) and rarely to processes of behavioral change over which the learning has no control or toward which no conscious learning effort has been made. Inadvertent imitation or absorption of a cultural pattern has not been considered in the literature as a relevant dimension of culture learning except by Kimball (1972). Kimball suggests that the subconscious learning of psychological and behavioral patterns be more closely examined as a truer index of cross-cultural adjustment than conscious adaptive strategies.

The notion of culture learning developed in this chapter has more in common with a model based on the acquisition of psychological and behavioral patterns based on deep affective identification with the new cultural system than with a simple behavior skills model. A second important characteristic of the present approach is the stress that is placed upon the symbolic dimensions of learning cross-culturally. Recent studies of enculturation and cultural transmission have pointed to the role of symbol as the key to the analysis of learning process: "The study of cultural texts, symbols, and discursive formations has hardly begun in the educational world. Its promise is that it will provide descriptions and theories of the processes of cultural acquisition and transmission, of the processes by which children learn institutionalized identities..." (Funnell and Smith 1981:294).

Such an approach seems to point the way to a consideration of how culture learning can be conceptualized as a process of identity creation and reformation through the communication and acquisition of nonexplicit cultural meanings embedded in the constructed institutional environment. As Gwen Kennedy Neville (1984:160) writes in an analysis of culture learning through ritual:

Through identifying the ritual events that form the symbolic center of a culture (whether of the classroom, school, ethnic group, town, or national state), and then discerning the internal order and pattern of these events and the cultural messages they carry in their symbolic content, one can discover a significant locus for cultural teaching and cultural learning.

Learning the implicit meaning of what is explicitly taught in school, for example, involves learning how to learn—to "read" the context, or to interpret it. Thus acquiring or learning culture occurs through a process of cultural interpretation of the environment. As Judith Hansen (1979:145) has remarked, learning in school is highly dependent upon learning the knowledge and skills that enable "reading" the context, or upon acquiring an ability to learn that is essentially interpretive.

Moreover, in cross-cultural situations, as noted by Cora DuBois (1955), Hanvey (1979), Spiro (1984) and others, the acquisition of intercultural understanding inevitably involves more than mere cognitive learning about the new culture: It involves affective identification with new patterns of belief, action, and value. Thus the fundamental issue underlying a symbolic view of the culture acquisition process appears to be the way in which cultural interpretations carry affective impact for the individual—that is, in the extent to which they can be perceived and valued as self-relevant and capable of being integrated within a revised vision of self. Ultimately the effects of cross-cultural learning must be evaluated in terms of cultural identity and commitment. Consideration of the role of symbol, interpretation, and affect in the acquisition of a second culture has yet to receive much attention in the anthropology of education. Yet, as will be seen, accounting for such affective dimensions of learning is crucial to the development of frameworks capable of providing theoretical insight into basic questions of minority education, as well as issues surrounding all instances of cross-cultural adaptation and adjustment.

IRANIANS AT AN AMERICAN SECONDARY SCHOOL

Although Iranians are not often considered to be a major ethnic minority in American secondary schools, in such cities as Los Angeles schools in certain areas of the city have substantial Iranian student populations. At the time this study was completed (April 1986), as much as 25 percent of the student body at one school was reported to be Iranian; at other schools, the percentage was between 10 and 12 percent. Exact counts, however, were not available since neither "Iranian" nor "Middle Eastern" was listed as an ethnic category in school enrollment statistics. To a certain extent there was reluctance to draw any attention to Iranians within the schools because of incidents involving Iranian and American students that had received negative publicity in the media.

This pattern of avoidance in consideration of aspects of Iranian students' experience and presence in the schools was reflected in what might be called a relatively consistent pattern of institutional blindness toward Iranians as a group. Iranian holidays were not celebrated in these public schools as were those of other ethnic groups. School district seminars ostensibly dealing with the multicultural character of the constituent student population did not mention Iranians. School language days devoted to celebrating linguistic diversity paid little or no attention to Farsi. Iranian staff and teachers, when interviewed, admitted that one could insult Iranians with impunity, though not members of other ethnic groups.

As a cultural minority at one American secondary school in Los Angeles, Iranians posed somewhat of an enigma: On the one hand, they were definitely considered to be foreign; yet they did not fit into any of the established ethnic categories at the school such as Anglo, black, Asian, Hispanic, or Native

American. Lack of familiarity with the culture as well as lack of a convenient ethnic categorization led many American faculty to consider Iranians as "the most foreign" of all cultural groups at the school. Although individual teachers did not personally express any negative attitudes toward Iranians, they assessed the general attitudinal environment of the school toward Iranians as negative. Iranian students were frequently characterized as "obnoxious," "arrogant," "dishonest," "macho," and "difficult." Teachers called Iranians "the most difficult culture" to deal with; Iranians were thought to be much "harder to teach and to get along with" than any other group at the school, including blacks and Hispanics. Iranians were often labeled as "cheaters," though they were also praised for their ambition and desire to succeed.

Indeed, though teachers and administrators tended to view Iranian students as a problem, the nature of this problem was certainly not underachievement or school failure, for Iranians were recognized as among the most academically successful students in the school. They were frequently praised for "saving American education" and for being "even better than the Americans" as far as academic performance was concerned. When teachers and administrators were asked to describe what they thought the major problem with Iranians at the school was, most focused on aspects of behavior that seemed to imply lack of respect for the rules of the school, such as cheating. Others thought discipline in general was the problem. Some said Iranians "have no moral sense." Some felt that not a few of the problems they experienced with Iranians could be attributed to differences in the educational systems of the two countries. The most common belief was that "school must be terrible over there" and that students do not learn to think, but only to do rote work. Most faculty felt that the education Iranian students receive in the United States was far better than what they received in Iran. Iranians, however, tended to feel that Iranian education was superior. Such comments as, "I'm doing in 12th grade here what I did in 8th grade in Iran" were very common. In Iran, according to the Iranians, school was much more serious, requirements tougher, and the general level of curricular material much higher.

Most of these students had been in the United States for periods ranging from a few months to six years. Nearly all had been enrolled at some point in English as a Second Language classes; although the earlier arrivals tended to enroll in higher-level classes from the beginning, therefore spending less time in the ESL track. More recent arrivals (students in the States less than two years) tended to be enrolled in more ESL classes for longer periods of time. Nearly all Iranian students were highly critical of ESL and desired to get out as soon as possible, since ESL was viewed as an impediment rather than an aid to academic progress.

Though Iranians were generally recognized as an academically successful group, there were variations among them in academic performance. Some students received failing grades, particularly those in the ESL track. Differences in relative academic performance must be evaluated in light of specific patterns of Iranian adaptation to the cultural meaning environment of the school.

GENERAL PATTERNS OF IRANIAN
CULTURAL ADAPTATION TO THE SCHOOL

Although on the surface the school appeared to encourage and value cultural diversity (indeed the multicultural character of the student body was something of which teachers and administrators were expressly proud), the underlying structure and commitment of the system was toward inculcation of fairly rigid patterns of moral and social action based largely on the observance and maintenance of rules and regulations. The fundamental assumption was that not only the functioning of the institution itself but the functioning of interpersonal relations within the institution must be governed by the observance of regulations, and that the learning of regulations as well as the desire to follow them is both possible and to be expected of all cultural groups at the school. In a deep sense, the purpose of the school was to cultivate acceptance of and commitment to an American world view based on the supremacy of legalism. Although it can be argued that every institution has rules and regulations that demand conformity, the extent to which the institution expects deep cultural commitment rather than simple surface-level conformity on the part of outsiders to that system is variable. It may be the case that a particular characteristic of American (secondary) education is the unusual degree of commitment that it believes is possible and necessary in individuals who are outsiders to the American culture; or, in other words, the extent to which it maintains an enculturative and incorporative view of itself in relation to cultural outsiders.

This orientation poses particular problems for members of cultural groups that do not see themselves as American and that do not experience any pressing need for deep cultural commitment to the American system. This was particularly true for Iranians, who, on the contrary, tended to maintain a deep affiliation with Iranian culture, and rejected attempts to change that affiliation. In fact, the fundamental problem (from the perspective of teachers and administrators) with Iranian students at the school was their refusal to accept, at the appropriate level of commitment, the fundamental moral orientation of the school as it was embodied in concepts of rule and legality. As one Iranian teacher told his American faculty audience,

Iranians...do not accept American laws, and therefore, they are not part of the environment....[But] the school policy is this: as long as a student is here, he or she is American, with the same privileges and same responsibilities...we expect them to be like Americans. Some resent that, but in the end they all give in.

In effect, Iranians were not accepting or learning American culture at the level demanded of them by the school.

Primary characteristics of Iranian rejection of the implicit educational mission of the school were social separatism, defiance of expectations (sometimes overt, most often covert), and instrumental orientation toward academic achievement/success, combined with symbolic forms of nonacceptance of institutional power as expressed in language and social behavior. This resistance was frequently mentioned in administrators' and teachers' comments to the effect that Iranians were "constantly trying to get around or to bend the rules."

Iranians perceived the school environment as being overly concerned with insignificant rules rather than with the real issues. Often, this rule preoccupation was thought to impede true education, as is reflected in the statement written in large, carefully formed block letters by one Iranian student on a classroom blackboard: "Don't let school get in the way of your education!" Indeed, this statement expresses a fundamental reaction of Iranian students to the American school: learn and become educated—that is, acquire the best of what education has to offer, but do not allow yourself to become mired in the values and assumptions of the cultural institution. It thus reflects a strong orientation toward instrumental adaptation, but not at the expense of fundamental cultural values and identity. It thereby conflicted with fundamental American assumptions about the nature and role of the school as an educational institution, since Iranians did not develop any sort of commitment to the system at the level of broader cultural meanings and values. In the words of one teacher,

Iranians seem to want to learn a lot about American culture. But they're not going to be part of it. They seem very removed from it. I don't see them trying to be Americanized. I haven't seen any outright defiance, but there's not total acceptance either.

For American faculty at the school, not wanting to become American and being very successful within the system at the same time posed a paradox. It went against the assumption that success in the American system demands some degree of inner commitment to that system, to its values and methods. Iranians were not, in sum, acquiring the moral rule of law upon which the school as enculturative agent was based; yet they were learning enough in other domains to become successful within the rules of that system. Thus they did not fulfill the American faculty's expectations of cultural minority behavior, which deemed that academic success comes only with acceptance of or assimilation to a basic Americanized identity, or at least one whose values do not conflict with the fundamental moral basis of the institution.

Another instance of Iranian resistance to the perceived values of the school culture is illustrated in a comment made by one Iranian student to his peers during lunch break: "This is America—Speak Persian!" This statement demonstrates Iranian awareness of fundamental American expectations governing the roles of cultural and linguistic minorities (that they should "speak English" and become a part of American life as much as possible), but it also shows Iranian refusal to accept those premises.

Iranian resistance on a symbolic level to the culture of the school was also expressed in what American faculty considered to be the widespread practice of cheating. Iranians themselves admitted to cheating, but most did not take the dim moral view of it that was held by the school. For some, it was a game of skill; for others, merely an amusing pastime. In the words of one Iranian, "Just because someone cheats doesn't mean he's a bad person inside." However, for Americans at the school, cheating was morally reprehensible, a symbol of personal corruption. Iranians acknowledged that Americans viewed cheating as an immoral act, yet they did not share a similar moral perspective.

At the level of social behavior, Iranian resistance to certain tacit expectations regarding social interaction within the school was pronounced, with Iranian students in classrooms consistently seating themselves apart from both Americans and other ethnic groups. In some cases this meant occupying one half of a classroom, or one entire row of desks, leaving the others to be occupied by students from other ethnic groups. At the conclusion of the lunch period, all students except the Iranians would begin to proceed to the next class; the Iranian students, however, would remain at their tables until everyone else had left and would leave only after being admonished by an administrator.

When viewed from a perspective emphasizing cultural conflict, such fundamental differences in values can be seen only as causes of school failure and maladaptation. However, we have seen that despite such conflicts, Iranians have developed patterns of learning and adjustment that do not lead to typical minority-group maladaptation and low academic performance. We must therefore consider in more detail the differential impacts of cultural conflict for Americans and Iranians, and the nature of the role of cultural identity in mediating cross-cultural communication difficulties.

COMMUNICATION AND CULTURAL ADAPTATION: PATTERNS IN THE CLASSROOM

At the heart of all learning there is a cultural meaning that is perceived, evaluated, and acted upon. Meanings particularly salient in Iranian–American patterns of communication concerned the perceived locus of responsibility for student learning, the communication of interpersonal caring from teacher to student, the role of questioning, cognitive differences in assigned tasks, the perception of rules and their significance, and the communication of authority. In the case of Iranian–American classroom interaction, conflicts in communication were perceived differently by Iranian students and American teachers, and had different impacts on mutual cultural learning and adjustment.

A significant difference in Iranian and American communication and behavior was related to the perceived locus of responsibility for student learning. For American teachers, students were responsible for their own success as well as for their own failure. The extent of their learning was entirely their own responsibility. They chould choose to do their homework and study or not, but the consequences were borne by them alone. If a student failed, it was his or her own fault for not doing the assigned work.

This was very different from the Iranian view, however, where *teachers* were perceived as responsible for student learning. When American teachers did not communicate this sense of responsibility, Iranian students felt that the teacher was uncaring and neglecting his or her primary educational role. Nearly all Iranian students, regardless of academic level or number of years in the school, felt that American teachers "did not care." Students said: "In the U.S. teachers don't make you study. They don't really care if you study or not." "In Iran, teachers *have* to teach the students. They explain something four or five times. Here, it's two times. American teachers say, 'You just have to listen.' " "American teachers don't care. Teachers were different in Iran. They took more time to explain and answer questions. It was harder, but better." "In Iran, teachers are like your parents. You have to do what they say, like be on time. Here they say you should be on time, but they don't really care. Mrs. X. doesn't care if I do my homework or not. They don't care about the students here. That's why students go all over the place." For Iranian students at this school, simply writing a homework assignment on the blackboard was symbolic of a teacher's not caring whether the assignment was done or not, since the teacher did not bother to communicate in a direct, personalized fashion the significance of the assignment. For Iranians,· the communication of caring could be achieved only through individualized and personal transmission of information. The tendency of American teachers was to use more impersonal channels or modes of communication such as writing on the board. American teachers also addressed the class as a whole rather than particular individuals, especially when giving directions or instructions. For Iranians this style of address was lacking in necessary personalization. Since it was felt that teachers were not addressing anyone in particular, the message did not carry an implicit command to pay attention.

Students also felt that teachers did not care because of their perceived lack of tolerance for repeated requests for explanation. The students quoted above emphasized that teachers "would explain something four or five times"—but that here "it's only twice" and that they "just tell you to listen." Tolerance for repeated explanation was, for Iranians, an indication that the teacher cares that the student understand.

Further evidence for the notion that Iranian communication styles emphasized personal over impersonal modes of information transmission was found in a strong Iranian preference for receiving information from peers rather than from an impersonal source such as a book or blackboard. This was especially true when the desired information was not available directly from the teacher, either because he or she would not answer the student's question individually or because the information was already available elsewhere. Iranian students in ESL classes rarely copied anything from blackboards; they preferred to copy from their friends or to ask their friends to explain something verbally.

Closely related to the role of caring in communication was that of questioning. Iranian students in general questioned the teacher more than any other non-Anglo group, and they also asked more substantive or content-related questions than other students in ESL or remedial classes. Some teachers found that this constant questioning was annoying, and it doubtless contributed to the image of Iranians as demanding and aggressive. For American teachers, questions were simply requests for information. For Iranians, however, their main significance, over and above the informational, was the establishment and maintenance of individualized, interpersonal communication channels whose maintenance was regarded as an indication of interpersonal respect. In one class, the teacher inadvertently and consistently interrupted his exchanges with Iranian students, so that the fundamental character of the question/answer exchange as an opportunity to open lines of communication was undermined. It was not so much the information communicated that was important as the general character of the exchange and the perceived willingness of the teacher to recognize the student's appeal for personal attention. One student said: "Teachers just don't like Iranians. You can see by their expression, by the way they explain a question. It's like you're hassling them. They don't respond to Iranian students' questions as well as they do to other students' questions." It was clear to the Iranian student that teachers were not willing to respond to Iranian students' questions in an appropriate way—that is, in a way that expressed tolerance, patience, and recognition of the interpersonal value of the question in the context of the student/teacher relationship.

Differences in Iranian and American approaches to cognitive tasks also became evident in the course of classroom interaction. In general, teachers stressed an analytical perspective, while Iranian students preferred a holistic approach to subject material. This difference in cognitive style was responsible for what some teachers interpreted as an inability to think among Iranian students. Frequently, the sorts of exercises that teachers asked students to do required labeling, defining, or manipulating certain elements apart from a context. Iranian students, however, consistently preferred to write entire sentences or paragraphs, for example, rather than simply words, even though the task required them to write only words. Such tasks as outlining according to a model or selecting certain types of sentences from a paragraph obscured what for Iranians was the more significant meaning of the whole. Furthermore, teachers were often more concerned with whether or not the instructions were being followed properly than with the meaning of what was being done. When it was discovered that students were not following instructions, teachers logically attributed this to some sort of cognitive deficiency, rather than to what were in fact perceived by Iranians as misplaced priorities.

CULTURAL CONFLICT, ADAPTATION, AND IDENTITY

As discussed previously, the culture learning process impacts the self at the level of cultural identity through a process of interpretation or learning to learn, which allows the deep acquisition of alternative forms of affect and self-conceptualization. The role of cultural differences in affecting this learning process is a crucial yet neglected area of investigation. Differences have largely been conceptualized as impediments to learning and cross-cultural adjustment of cultural minority groups. In the Iranian case, however, cultural differences in communication and values did not hinder school learning. We must, therefore, consider that the crucial issue may be the type of response to conflict that a group adopts, and the ways cultural identities may be restructured through various cultural learning strategies to overcome the presumed learning impediments of cultural conflict. Indeed, the very experience of cultural conflict may vary interculturally as well as intraculturally.

In the school, Iranians and Americans had different perceptions of as well as responses to cultural conflict. For Americans, conflict—and, by extension, cultural identity—was an "either-or" proposition—one either became American or remained Iranian. When conflict arose, it precluded learning by locking the individual on one side of the cultural fence. Behavior, value, and commitment were linked; inner commitment and values were necessarily tied to one's social behavior and action.

For Iranians, however, the nature of cultural identity was different. Inner values and commitment did not necessarily have to be consistent with social behavior and action. One could thereby "act American" in some situations, and yet remain fundamentally Iranian in cultural commitment. Conflict, as a situational event, was not experienced as a significant impediment to adjustment since it did not fundamentally involve the self or demand an internal value reorientation. Iranian cultural identity was thus not a linear, either-or proposition, but an incorporative, integrative one.

It thus appears that the major factor in school adjustment among Iranian students was a sort of cultural identity that facilitated acquisition of alternative behavioral, cognitive, and affective frameworks, thereby successfully mediating culturally different meaning systems. Such a cultural mediation process went on despite cultural differences and conflicts that arose in interaction between Iranians and Americans. For Iranians the relative independence of social and inner selves gave the individual much situational adaptive flexibility that could be expressed in both cultural resistance (at the inner level of values and commitment) as well as the successful adaptation (at the level of social self). Variations among Iranians in relative academic success were in fact related to the extent to which the individual could assume an incorporative identity focused upon acquiring selected behaviors and orientations from American culture, while maintaining a firm sense of Iranian identity.

These highly successful Iranians relied upon a culture acquisition strategy best characterized as "cultural eclecticism." This strategy involved selecting the behaviors thought to represent the best of both cultures and creating a blended social self having characteristics of both cultures. The cultural eclectics emphasized their appreciation for some aspects of American culture and their desire to adopt "the good things," while rejecting the bad. At the same time they desired to maintain the good traits of Iranian culture. They tended to be quite flexible in their adaptation, yet to remain in basic cultural orientation firmly Iranian. As one said, "I have adapted to this culture more than any of the Iranians, yet I never try to say I'm not Iranian. I will definitely be Iranian always." On the surface, these Iranians appeared to be the most well-adjusted, getting along with everyone at the school and generally being model students. Although they seemed to be learning American culture to the greatest degree, they were in fact learning *about* the culture rather than becoming American.

A second group were those Iranians who experienced what might be called spiritual alienation. Their fundamental learning style was not focused upon acquisition of perceived positive cultural traits, but upon situational behavioral adaptation combined with maintenance of fundamentally Iranian values. Many of these students were enrolled in ESL classes and were less academically successful than the first group, although they did not lack the desire to succeed. They tended to criticize what they perceived as a lack of human warmth in American culture and were often considered to be the most difficult students because of their sometimes outright resistance to rules, regulations, and expected patterns of behavior. They also were firmly committed to Iranian culture, and did not have as much appreciation for aspects of American culture as the eclectics; indeed, many felt spiritually isolated from American culture. Though they wanted to succeed in the United States, they wished to do so with a minimum of compromise of Iranian values, ideals, and patterns of behavior.

A third group of Iranians were those who were becoming superficially acculturated while at the same time rejecting American culture at the deep identity-impacting level. The majority of these students had been in the States from five to six years, and were above-average students. This group appeared to be the most Americanized in terms of speech and social behavior (students mixed Persian and English and had American-style social lives, including some dating and occasional drug use), but in many ways they were also the most adamant in asserting their identity as Iranians and in the somewhat disdainful attitude they had toward American culture. Typical comments were: "I love being Iranian. I will never give up my identity." "I don't ever want to be American, not a bit." This group tended to have less interest in academics or professional occupations and more interest in business; females often had no goals other than to get married. These students were paradoxically the most traditional in asserting cultural values and ideals, but the most willing to experiment with the superficial aspects of being American. Their basic learning strategy was focused upon outer self-transformation in accordance with the demands of a new social and cultural situation. This group also experienced the most intense conflict between the material seduction of American life and ideal notions regarding Iranian identity and behavior.

The type of adaptative response most conducive to success in the school appeared to be eclecticism. Those Iranians who fundamentally rejected American culture while becoming superficially acculturated were moderately successful, and those who felt spiritually isolated experienced the most difficulty in their personal encounters with faculty and administration at the school as well as in achieving high levels of academic performance. This indicates that for members of cultural minority groups, success in school seems to hinge on the existence of a certain type of cultural identity that will allow situational adaptive flexibility and incorporative cross-cultural learning, without, however, allowing cultural conflict to threaten cultural self-definition.

To a great extent Iranian students' patterns of culture learning were not identity-impacting in the deep sense of the term, for Iranians were not becoming American so much as participating in patterns of instrumental and situational behavior directed toward the pursuit of particular, limited goals. They adopted cross-cultural learning strategies that allowed them to preserve a sense of being Iranian despite superficial acculturation to the values and ideals of the institution. Cultural conflict was thus not generally an impediment to learning or cultural adjustment. For the majority of Iranian students the acquisition of American cultural values as embodied in concepts of morality and rule was not intrinsic to the achievement of academic success.

Yet success from the mainstream point of view was necessarily tied to more than superficial coping with school life; it also meant reforming one's cultural orientation toward value acceptance of the basic premises of the institution. Thus, Iranian students' desire to maintain an Iranian cultural identity rather than to restructure it in terms amenable to the adoption of fundamental American cultural perspectives posed a problem for the institution. Iranians were engaged in a process of learning about the institutional culture, but they were not in fact learning to adopt it as their own. They constituted a separate society at the school that, though superficially open to learning and contact with institutional culture, did not radically reinvent its cultural orientation.

CONCLUSION

To a great extent the cultural conflict model of intercultural relations, particularly in the anthropology of education, has drawn attention away from the examination of the nature and process of cross-cultural learning in interaction situations. Though cultural differences play a significant role in interaction, the cultural decision to accept, adopt, reject, or reformulate a cultural orientation as a result of cross-cultural contact is a central educational issue that needs to be examined from a perspective emphasizing learning rather than conflict. If individuals and groups engaged in a process of cross-cultural interaction are primarily involved in inventing and acquiring symbolic structures that act as intercultures or bridges toward the acquisition of a different system of cultural meanings, the sort of cultural identity that results may in fact be the essential yet unexplored dimension in our conceptualization of learning processes. It remains for the anthropology of education to forge new ground in the ways we conceptualize this learning in the fabric of a culturally plural society.

REFERENCES

Ansari, Abdolmaboud
1974   A community in process and in the dual marginal situation: The first genera-
        tion of the Iranian professional middle class immigrants in the U.S. Unpub-
        lished Doctoral Dissertation, The New School for Social Research.
Burnett, Jacquetta Hill
1974   On the analog between culture acquisition and the ethnograhic method.
        Anthropology and Education Quarterly 5:25-29.
Detweiler, R.
1980   Intercultural interaction and the categorization process: A conceptual analy-
        sis and behavioral outcome. *International Journal of Intercultural Relations*
        4:275-293.
DuBois, Cora
1955   Some notions on learning intercultural understanding. In George D. Spindler,
        ed., Education and Anthropology. Palo Alto, CA: Stanford University Press.
Funnell, Robert and Richard Smith
1981   Search for a theory of cultural transmission in an anthropology of education:
        Notes on Spindler and Gearing. *Anthropology and Education Quarterly*
        12:275-295.
Furnham, A. and Stephen Bochner
1982   Social difficulty in a foreign culture: An empirical analysis of culture shock.
        In Stephen Bochner, ed., Cultures in Contact: Studies in Cross-Cultural
        Interaction. New York: Pergamon.
Guthrie, George M.
1975   A Behavioral Analysis of Culture Learning. In R. Brislin et al., eds., Cross-
        Cultural Perspectives on Learning. New York: John Wiley.
Hansen, Judith Freedman
1979   Sociocultural Perspectives on Human Learning. Englewood Cliffs, NJ:
        Prentice-Hall.
1982   From background to foregound: Toward an anthropology of learning.
        Anthropology and Education Quarterly 13(2):189-202.
Hanvey, Robert G.
1979   Cross-cultural awareness. In E. C. Smith and L. F. Luce, eds., Toward Inter-
        nationalism: Readings in Cross-Cultural Communication. Rowley, MA:
        Newbury House.
Kimball, Solon T.
1972   Learning a new culture. In S. T. Kimball and J. B. Watson, eds., *Crossing
        Cultural Boundaries*. San Francisco: Chandler.
Kleinfeld, Judith
1983   First do no harm: A reply to Courtney Cazden. *Anthropology and Education
        Quarterly* 14(4):282-287.
Lorenz, J. H. and J. T. Wertime
1980   Iranians. In S. Thernstrom, ed., Harvard Encyclopaedia of American Ethnic
        Groups, pp. 521-524. Cambridge, MA: Harvard University Press.
Neville, Gwen Kennedy
1984   Learning culture through ritual: The family reunion. *Anthropology and Edu-
        cation Quarterly* 15(2):151-166.

Ogbu, John and Maria Matute-Bianchi
  1986   Understanding sociocultural factors: Knowledge, identity, and school ad-
          justment. In Beyond Language: Social and Cultural Factors in Schooling
          Language Minority Students. Los Angeles: Evaluation, Dissemination and
          Assessment Center, California State University.
Sabagh, Georges and Mehdi Bozorgmehr
  1987   Are the characteristics of exiles different from immigrants? The case of
          Iranians in Los Angeles. *Sociology and Social Research* 71(2):77–84.
Spiro, Melford E.
  1984   Reflections on cultural determinism and relativism with special reference to
          emotion and reason. In Richard A. Shweder and Robert A. LeVine, eds.,
          Culture Theory: Essays on Mind, Self, and Emotion. Cambridge: Cambridge
          University Press.
Time
  1983.   "The New Ellis Island." June 13:18–25.
U.S. Bureau of the Census
  1983   1980 Census of Population, Detailed Population Characteristics: California.
          Series PC–80–1–D6. Section 1. Washington, DC: U.S. Government Printing
          Office.
Watson, Karen Ann
  1977   Understanding human interaction: The study of everyday life and ordinary
          talk. In R. W. Brislin, ed., Culture Learning. Honolulu: East-West Center.
Wolcott, Harry
  1982   The anthropology of learning. *Anthropology and Education Quarterly*
          13(2):83–108.

9

The Winter of Their Discontent: Cultural Compression and Decompression in the Life Cycle of the Kibbutz Adolescent

Steven Borish

INTRODUCTION

One of the primary tasks of educational anthropology is to make explicit some of the many ways in which cultural processes influence classroom interaction. An approach that takes these cultural processes into account can give teachers, psychologists, administrators, parents, and students themselves a much greater depth of understanding about what it is that actually goes on inside classrooms.

Neither the formal goals of the curriculum nor the teacher's daily lesson plan will be effectively realized if there is active or passive resistance to the learning process by sufficient numbers of students. In trying to understand the reasons for such an orientation on the part of students, we must remember that the school classroom is only in appearance a self-contained unit, separated from other contexts. Each of its social actors is located in a variety of contexts, and events occurring in these other contexts may be of crucial importance for understanding attitudes and behaviors that appear in the little world of the classroom. Life-cycle events, for instance (Erikson 1950, 1968; Sullivan 1953; Evans 1970; Munroe, Munroe, and Whiting 1981) may be providing specific kinds of stresses that manifest themselves in behaviors seen in the classroom. Sociolinguistic factors and the nature of the speech community (Heath 1983; Labov 1969; Giglioli 1972) are often relevant as well.

The work of George Spindler (1959, 1973, 1974a, 1982), and of George and Louise Spindler together (1982, 1987), has contributed significantly to our understanding of how cultural perspectives and processes influence classroom interactions. One of George Spindler's most provocative notions is his distinction between periods of compression and decompression in the life cycle (G. Spindler 1970, 1974b). Compression phases are marked by increased cultural stress, often accompanied by tightened role definitions, a circumscribing of previously permitted behaviors, and the taking on of new responsibilities and obligations. Severe puberty initiation rites (as described in Herdt 1982; Young 1965) accompanied by physical hazing and various forms of tissue mutilation (e.g., nose-bleeding, male circumcision, female clitoridectomy) provide a clear example of what is meant by "cultural compression." Phases of cultural decompression are characterized by a relative relaxation of stress; the individual has the time and opportunity to unwind from an earlier compression state if previously subjected to one, and to be socially present without the special pressures of the compression frame (for a discussion of frames and meta-communication see Bateson 1972).

One of the challenges in the comparative analysis of cultures that Spindler has bequeathed us is to delineate the relationship between phases of compression and decompression in the individual life cycle. In what follows, I report on data from an Israeli kibbutz, dealing with the situation of those in the developmental stage of early (12–14) and late (15–18) adolescence, with particular emphasis on the latter. I will show that a set of behaviors frequently observed in the school setting cannot be understood without a closer look at how the young people in question are being affected by the exigencies of the total life cycle. The method here is similar to that employed by Bateson (1972), who prior to formulating the double-bind hypothesis asked himself the following question: To what kind of early socialization in the home would the forms of communication observed in schizophrenic patients provide a response that was (in their own eyes, at least) an adaptive and meaningful one?

What are the forms of communication that I observed among kibbutz adolescents? A 16-year-old boy is sent home from school for minor disciplinary infractions; in his own eyes he is a heroic rebel against what he sees as the stifling conformity represented by the school world. The school is "a factory for learning," says another boy, who hates every minute that he must sit in a classroom. Waking up late in order to miss the bus, laughing and dismissing schoolwork as "stupid," ridiculing the school and its teachers, making a relatively poor performance on tests and exams—the foregoing is a small list of some of the attitudes and behaviors I frequently encountered among them. These behaviors were the cause for a considerable degree of concern on the part of many members of the older generation, who were observed on numerous occasions to be disturbed and more than a little anxious about the syndrome of withdrawal and what it might or might not imply. For reasons equally grounded in the cultural context of these life-cycle events, they appeared to me in the main to be both helpless and ineffectual in countering this mood and its many manifestations among their adolescent children.

I shall argue that a significant proportion of those in late adolescence are subject to a form of cultural compression in which anticipation of events in the life-cycle phase immediately to follow interferes with their ability to immerse themselves totally in one aspect of their present experience, namely academic learning. Their response to this cultural compression is to express withdrawal through various forms of what Goffman (1961b) called role distance. This distance and its stylized presentation is displayed not against all aspects of their institutionalized socialization, but most notably and significantly to the sphere represented by the school and the classroom. The process is one that can be called *compensatory disequilibrium*.

Two important points are implied. First, the unique life-cycle pressures of kibbutz adolescence must be clearly understood before the classroom behavior of adolescents makes good sense. Second, and at a more general level, this analysis strongly implies that the life cycle as a whole must be taken into account in order to explain any one part of it. A major advantage of Spindler's cultural compression model is that it requires us to look at the events in the life cycle from this larger, more integrated perspective.

SOCIOLINGUISTIC FACTORS: "THE LITTLE ENGLISH VILLAGE"

The primary research site for this study, Kibbutz Gan HaEmek ("garden of the valley"), is a 39-year-old Anglo-Saxon kibbutz in the Upper Galilee region of Israel. Settled primarily by Jews from England and the British Isles (and possessing highly vocal minorities from continental Europe, the United States, Australia, and South Africa), it belongs to the decentralized and ideologically pluralistic Ichud federation. My fieldwork included four visits over a period of 20 years, the longest being a period of residence of 18 months (1978–79), the most recent a one-month visit in the summer of 1984. While doing fieldwork in 1978–79, I served for nearly a year as a kibbutz plumber, and was for seven months in charge of the plumbing workshop, a situation that gave me unparalleled access to the world of kibbutz adults as well as to the subworld of meaning inhabited by their adolescent children.

In addition to systematic observations recorded daily in a field notebook, my research methods included the recording of firsthand oral material obtained through taped interviews made in members' homes. Fifty-nine such ethnographic interviews were conducted with members, children, and several long-term volunteers. A wide cross-section of kibbutz society was represented, and I cite from the resulting transcriptions frequently in this chapter. This procedure not only enables kibbutz members to speak and be heard in their own words, but enables the reader to encounter directly some of the material from which my conclusions have been drawn.

A word or two about the sociolinguistic status of Kibbutz Gan HaEmek is required. Gumperz (1972:219) has defined a speech community as "any human aggregate characterized by regular and frequent interaction by means of a shared body of verbal signs and set off from similar aggregates by significant differences in language usage." The linguistic peculiarities of such groups set them apart from their immediate neighbors; their verbal behavior can be analyzed as a system, with its own finite set of rules and codifications. Judged by these criteria, Kibbutz Gan HaEmek constitutes, beyond any faint shadow of a doubt, a true speech community. Membership in this particular speech community is one factor influencing how the kibbutz adolescents are perceived by teachers and age-peers in the regional high school.

The speech community at Gan HaEmek is characterized by a mixed bilingualism, in which Hebrew and English pay co-dominant roles. It is not that Hebrew is not spoken. One hears a great deal of Hebrew everywhere on the kibbutz. It is rather that so much English is spoken along with, beside, and even in between the Hebrew words. One hears as well occasional lapses into German, French, sometimes Yiddish, and here and there a phrase in Afrikaans, but these are all muted undertones in a linguistic symphony (or cacophony) that is carried on using variants of current British English, mixed with Hebrew.

As a speech community, the kibbutz is absolutely unique. Consequently, when its children go out into the greater Galilee they may be subjected to friendly ribbing by teachers, fellow students, and passersby. In my judgment this situation does not reflect an inability to use either Hebrew or English as effective instruments of communication, but rather more scholastic criteria: their relative insufficiency in "High Hebrew," their use of idiosyncratic grammatical constructions, and the presence of minor phonetic variation in their speech (for reasons of space I cannot describe their speech patterns in greater detail in this Chapter).

I mention these sociolinguistic factors because they are unquestionably one factor behind the role distance often observed in late adolescent kibbutz youth to the classroom setting in the regional high school. Yet in my opinion they are secondary rather than primary causes of the mood of alienation I so often encountered. If they were really important to Gan HaEmek's adolescents, one would probably have observed at least some serious attempts to master the standard patterns and conform to the "normal" dialect. Instead, those with whom I talked seemed to be at home with and stubbornly accepting of their linguistic departures from the ideal norm. They viewed these departures not as moral failings but as causes for laughter, and for rueful, nonserious self-criticism.

PRIVATIZATION AND THE BAR MITZVAH RITE

Childhood on an Israeli kibbutz is a time of cultural decompression. Regardless of the particular kibbutz or kibbutz movement, the childhood years are the subject of intense ideological focus and concern. The aim of this focus is to permit children the maximum possible opportunity for the growth of personal freedom in all of its many dimensions. This includes the capacity for unhindered self-expression, the experience of spontaneous enjoyment, and the development of useful skills in all areas of life. Behind this cultural view of childhood is a special vision of "the Jewish identity" and how best to realize it within the institutional context of the kibbutz (for a more detailed discussion of these and related issues see Gonen 1975; Spiro 1979; Borish 1982).

Parenthetically, Gan HaEmek is one of the growing number of kibbutzim that have made a transition from the traditional communal sleeping (Spiro 1956) to another pattern that has been called "familistic" sleeping (Shepher 1969). The most important single difference between the two systems is that in the former the children sleep at night in a communal house with age-mates; in the latter they sleep in the home of their parents. If one asks a child on a kibbutz with familistic housing (*lina mishpaktit*) where "home" is, the reply will almost certainly be that "home" is the parents' residence. If the same question is asked on a kibbutz with the traditional communal housing (*lina meshutefet*), the child will probably answer that home is the children's house, where he or she not only lives during most of the day (as do the children in familistic housing) but also sleeps at night together with age-mates.

The difference in the two responses indicates a significant shift in self-reference. Familistic housing, with its greater emphasis on the nuclear family, is a weaker variant of collective child rearing. Yet the young child continues to spend the entire day together with his or her peers in a supervised round of activity on the kibbutz. The *kita*,[1] or age-class, continues to exist as a social unit. Where such continuity in communal socialization persists, it is not true to say that communal education has been done away with. It is probably more accurate to distinguish between a strong and a weak variant of communal education. The change in children's sleeping patterns is only one manifestation of an increasing tendency to withdraw energy from the collective structures and invest it instead in the individual, the nuclear family, and the "quasi-family-like groups" that dominate informal social networks. This *trend toward privatization* is fundamental in understanding the dynamic of culture change on the kibbutz.

No matter how sweet and protected the years of childhood, powerful biological and cultural programs interact to bring about a transition to adolescence. The passage into puberty is marked with appropriate ritual: the Bar Mitzvah is a traditional Jewish rite of passage that is performed—on Gan HaEmek—once a year, for all those who are 13 years of age. With the Bar Mitzvah begins a process of cultural compression that will gradually intensify as it leads through the adolescent years, reaching the highest degree of compression during the time of army service. An analysis of the Bar Mitzvah rite will help in making clear some important features of adolescent social environment on the kibbutz, in particular the privatizing trends that influence both adolescent and adult development.

It is a commonplace of anthropological theory that the public ceremonials of a society tell us a great deal about its social life: They reinforce what Goffman (1961a) has called "the public order," and constitute in themselves an element of social organization. In the case of large public mental hospitals, such institutional ceremony (exemplified by skits, group meetings, and sports events) may function to give some cohesiveness to a society otherwise dangerously split between staff and inmates. On Kibbutz Gan HaEmek, tensions between the public and the private world reflect the increasing emphasis placed on the latter.

Under such conditions the public ceremonials are both an occasion for celebration and an opportunity for individuals to merge their public and private worlds in a spirit of spontaneous involvement (Goffman 1961b:37). "Public ceremonials" may be defined as those occasions where large segments of the kibbutz community, or even the entire community, are invited to come together in order to perform a specific ritual function. Friday night programs, religious festivals, and the collective Bar Mitzvah are examples of public ceremonials. The term "celebration" would do as well.

Compared with the Bar Mitzvah ceremony as I have seen it in England or the United States, a kibbutz Bar Mitzvah has a special flavor and intensity. It must be seen and at least vicariously participated in before one can appreciate what it means for all who are involved. Prior to the day itself, each boy and girl who is to take part must keep a "Bar Mitzvah book." This book records 13 tasks or "blessings" (*mesimot*) that must be accomplished before the day of the Bar Mitzvah. A boy will do a day's work in one of the branches, stand guard duty one night along with the adult guards, make a trip to one of the big cities and report on it. He will do a "good deed," such as cleaning up a soldier's room during the week so that it is clean for the soldier's return on Friday evening.

These and the other "missions" confer a flesh-and-blood meaning on a ritual whose meaning is all too easily lost. The year of the Bar Mitzvah is an intense experience for the group of boys and girls about to undergo the collective ceremony. The doing of the Bar Mitzvah deeds puts great pressure on them because these tasks must all be accomplished outside of, and in addition to, regular school work. The keeping of the Bar Mitzvah book requires both considerable effort and a large investment of time. Some Bar Mitzvah books, it is said, are thicker than others, and not all of those who are to be in the ceremony view it with the same air of warm, nostalgic satisfaction shown by their parents or by visiting anthropologists. To them it definitely has something of the character of an ordeal.

The ordeal culminates at last on the day of the Bar Mitzvah. When that day finally comes, visitors descend on the kibbutz from abroad as well as from Israel. They come bearing both gifts and smiles, for it is a happy occasion. In the morning there is a Torah reading, carried out with a snappy precision that is not surprising considering that the Bar Mitzvah candidates are reading in their native language. When the reading has been completed, there is time for socializing. Parents show off the kibbutz and their children to old friends and visitors. A grand feast is held in the afternoon on the lawn outside the dining room. In the evening the Bar Mitzvah group stages a theatrical, and a very good one, out in the same place under spotlights on an outdoor stage. The atmosphere is an emotional one for all participants, and is comparable perhaps only to a wedding in the intensity of its dramatic realization. It moves smoothly from beginning to end, with none of the truncated or anomic quality that I observed in many other public ceremonials.

Yet even in the ritual of the collective Bar Mitzvah a trend toward privatiza-tion can be discerned. It does not appear in the details of the formal ritual as I have described it, but in subsequent activity that takes place behind the scenes. In particular, it manifests itself in the way that the gifts brought by family and visitors are divided up among the group of 13 year olds in the Bar Mitzvah group. In order to make clear the nature of this change, it is necessary to trace the three stages of development in the area of socialization relating to the giving of Bar Mitzvah gifts.

The first stage was characteristic of the early years of the kibbutz (founded in 1948) when there were very few gifts, very few children, and an extremely low material standard of living. At that time, whatever gifts there were, were kept privately by the recipients. After a number of years, however, a system appar-ently developed in which those who shared the rite of the collective Bar Mitzvah also began to share the gifts they received at that time. Bicycles and books were the usual extent of the largesse, with an occasional watch or transistor radio. Fountain pens were another item not in short supply. Of course the kibbutz itself at this stage was a little more prosperous, and there were more children.

As this second-stage system evolved, it became the custom to put most of what money was kept by the individual boy or girl into a common kitty. A certain amount was kept by the original recipient, enough to buy something that he or she "really wanted." The rest was donated to the common fund. Money in this fund could be used to buy something for the group as a whole. It could also be used to equalize the inequality in gifts received by the group, something that typically occurred because some children had more (and wealthier) outside family than others. Pooling the resources had other advantages besides ensuring a rough equality: a boy or girl who had received three fountain pens didn't need two of them, and such redundancies could profitably be corrected through trade. It was natural, under these circumstances, to divide up and exchange gifts; the custom had both a moral and practical basis.

The practice of redistributive sharing of Bar Mitzvah gifts had been practiced for many years until the time of my last full year of fieldwork (1979), at which point, for reasons about which no one is clear, it simply ceased to function. It is interesting to explore the responses of kibbutz members to the sudden demise of this custom of gift redistribution. A young woman who worked as a *metepelet* (caretaker) commented:

There was, every year until this year, a kitty. The kids put all their money together and divided it up equally among them. This year *the parents, and the children, refused to do it*. They wanted to keep everything. This is the first year ... this year they decided that they didn't want to have the kitty any more: whatever a child gets, they keep (italics added).

From her we learn that the children and the parents acted together; there was no rebellion by the Bar Mitzvah group acting alone. On the contrary, what seems to have happened is a sudden crystallization of beliefs, a true value shift, instigated as much by the parents as by their children.

I quote from another young woman whose brother was a member of the Bar Mitzvah group:

Kids get a lot of money, and usually they get together with their parents and make an agreement. Everyone buys something they really want, the rest gets put into a fund and they can do what they want with it, *buy something for the group*. The children decide, with the consultation of the parents. This year it was very unorganized, they didn't come to any agreement like this, everybody just kept their money. *It came to very big amounts. They bought something with it or kept it in the bank.* This was the first time it happened like this (italics added).

From her comments we learn two things: first, that the old custom of buying something for the group has been replaced by a pattern of individual consumption; and second, in marked contrast to the past, quite large sums of money were involved. She went on to predict that the action of this year's group would set a precedent for next year, those in next year's group being members of the same class (kita): "It's not fair if half the class gives the money to the group, and half keeps it all for themselves."

The kibbutz secretary, when asked about these developments, simply replied, "I would say there *was* a policy on Bar Mitzvah gifts. I would say it doesn't exist any more." Another kibbutz member, a father with two late adolescent children, made the following insightful comment:

It's an attempt, and formally it sounds good. The kids give in the money they get, a sum is taken out to cover, say, a tape recorder, and the rest will theoretically be divided among the rest of the children, especially the children who didn't get. It was highly mathematical, but in practice, those kids who had to give in their money expected to get presents. Today this whole area is largely ignored. *It's something the family is getting, it's to the family, ultimately* [he imitates a family member speaking] "It's for our Bar Mitzvah and we want to keep it." It's a very natural feeling. What is a present if you don't get to keep it? (italics added)

His comment provides an additional perceptive insight. The gift is regarded as belonging not so much to the individual Bar Mitzvah boy or girl as to the family. Taken together these comments and observations point to a critical feature of the trend toward privatization: the reemergence of the nuclear family as the psychologically important unit of consumption within the otherwise collectivized kibbutz economy.

A single member of the Bar Mitzvah contingent may now be presented with gifts worth more in currency than an entire kibbutz family's allowance for a whole year. And, at least partially as a consequence of this, the standard of living of adolescents in Gan HaEmek has risen even faster than that of their parents. This observation is equally true for those in early and late adolescence.

"I was always struck by the fact that in the kids' rooms, you look around, and they've got electronic clocks, cassettes, and the cassette radios, scattered all over the room, and their parents bring in their old tattered transistor radio sets to repair," said a kibbutz electrician, who has repaired the appliances of both members and their children for many years.

Other evidence of the trend toward privatization among adolescents and young adults can be found. In addition to the apparent demise of the custom of redistributing Bar Mitzvah gifts, there is weakened participation in the "Children's Society" (chevrat yeladim). This institution represents a parallel structure organized by and for those between the ages of 14 and 18 with the goal of giving them experience in democratic self-government (as well as organizing lively parties and planning trips around the country). Nir, an earnest, hardworking and reliable 17-year-old then serving as secretary for this society, often expressed a high degree of satisfaction with the performance participation of many of his peers.

I had a conversation with Nir about chevrat yeladim. They had a meeting last week, and only 23 of the 49 members came. Such half-hearted participation seems to be not at all infrequent, though it is especially severe now near the end of the school year. Those in the senior class (Kita Yud Bet) had the "excuse" of the finishing exam (Bagrut) and the senior project (Avodat Gemer), but Nir feels that they use this, and that it isn't right. Some people do all the work. Those who do not come to the meetings will go on all the trips and come to all the parties, but won't do any of the organizational work necessary to set everything up [from field notes].

The decision to end the custom of pooling Bar Mitzvah gifts is only one of a series of recent decisions that increasingly emphasize private consumption within the context of the family. These include changes in the areas of trips abroad, the introduction of a comprehensive budget (Taktsiv Kulul), and the acquisition of color TV in members' homes. The threat that ties all these developments together is the change in material standard of living that the kibbutz has experienced in the last decade and a half. The choice has been made to funnel the new wealth increasingly into private rather than collective consumption, so that it can be enjoyed within the ever more comfortable confines of the family and the limited friendship group.

Thus the degree of privatization seen in the younger generation reflects a pattern of overall developments within the community. "Today you don't see a kid of 13 or 14 without a stereo," said one disgruntled young member with more than a hint of bitterness, who went on to remark:

It's a natural continuation of the situation generally. People get married, they get a lot of money and presents. New members who come, come with a lot of stuff. Kids after the army now don't have to give the money in, so, if you think about it, why should the kids? With the kids it just hurts more, for some reason. You expect them to stay out of it. Why should they? Nobody else does, so you can't expect the kids to be better. If anything they'll be worse.

The communal Bar Mitzvah does more than symbolize the passage from childhood into adolescence. It marks the beginning of a long and intense period of cultural compression. For those who have undergone the rite, this compression is manifested in (1) the strains and tensions of the rite itself, particularly the doing of the deeds or missions and the keeping of a Bar Mitzvah book; (2) the movement from the elementary school, located on the kibbutz itself, to the regional high school (from being big fish in a small pond, they suddenly find themselves demoted to lesser status, that of small fish in a much bigger pond); (3) the necessity of coming to grips with the changes of puberty and the complex working out of one's sexual identity; (4) the anticipated move out of the parental quarters into the young people's housing (*bet neerim*); and (5) the introduction to the adult work world and the obligation to perform well in the sphere of work.

If one themes ties all of these developments together, it is that of the peer group coming to replace the parents as the primary locus of the self and its values. Outright rejection of parents is rare by adolescents on Gan HaEmek and, for the most part, they tolerate the inconsistencies and foolishness of their parents with good-natured amusement and affection. Nevertheless, they have embarked on a different phase of the life cycle, and relationships with parents are fundamentally altered, never again to be the same. One of their most serious tasks at this juncture is to develop ways of coping with cultural compression. Slowly building in its intensity, this compression will characterize most of the next decade of their lives.

THE WORLD OF THE LATE ADOLESCENT

To understand what is happening with those in this age grouping (15–18) on Kibbutz Gan HaEmek, it is helpful to begin with a small tour of their living quarters. As the kibbutz plumber, I often let my roving eye slide over the artifacts in their rooms when my work brought me there. The signs of their subculture, a little universe all its own, were many and varied. On the wall of a 15-year-old's room there is a poster with a picture of Snoopy, remarking sagely that "work is the crabgrass in the lawn of life." In an adjoining room a Blaupunkt speaker hangs loosely on the inside of the bathroom door. In the shower stalls themselves one can see double shower heads, installed by the occupants and not by kibbutz officialdom. (I will let the slow reader figure out exactly what they are intended for.)

As these images imply, to be in the late years of adolescence on Gan HaEmek is to live in a subculture that is tolerant of experimentation. It is one that also is more than a little detached from the world and expectations of its elders. In one area, however, the expectations of the adolescent subculture and those of the older generation usually coincide. This tendency toward agreement is found neither in the sphere of the classroom and its obligations, nor in that of informal social life (in these two domains strain, conflict, and uneasy cooperation are often seen). These sphere in which it is not unusual to find agreement is that defined by the work roles.

Beginning at the age of 13, each kibbutz youngster is "required" to do a *yom avoda* (day of work) in the kibbutz economy. Starting with just a few hours at age 13, the officially mandated number of hours rises until by about age 17 they are expected to do a full eight-hour work day, one day a week. Many, however, ignore from the beginning the legal limits of the requirement and insist on working an eight-hour day from the beginning. The more strenuous, exhausting, and potentially dangerous the work, the better. As Esther remarked one day of her 18-year-old son, late for tea because he was working a 12-hour day driving a tractor in the cotton fields, "I think some of these kids have an overdeveloped sense of responsibility." Although she may have been annoyed at him for not being home in time for tea, it was not too hard to detect the note of pride in her voice. Early and positive adjustment to the world of work is one of the distinctive achievements of kibbutz socialization.

This intense drive to succeed and excel in work assignments is part of a wider cultural pattern, one that is summed up in the term *gibush* (from the Hebrew verb *l'hitgabesh*: to crystalize out, or to consolidate in a group). Learned early as a part of kibbutz socialization, it enables a group of kibbutz adolescents on a work detail to organize themselves, in the words of one member, "without words, almost telepathically."

In order to understand this unusual ability to crystallize out, to form into groups for the purpose of accomplishing particular tasks, a related concept, that of *hevra*, must be described. It has in essence a double meaning: the first refers to an abstract notion of community, togetherness, and sociability. Thus one can say of a particular group that "its hevra [accent on the second syllable] is excellent." The second refers to a particular small group, either a work group or one gathered together for purposes of sociability. In this case it is often used as a term of address.

Thus a work supervisor may say, "Okay, hevra [accent on the first syllable], let's get back to work." It has the connotation of harmonious group relationships in both instances, whether for social or work-related goals. The term is subject to occasional misuse in Israeli society by wheedling advocates of pseudogemeinschaft: perhaps the outstanding example of this I saw was the falafel vendor in Jerusalem who kept calling out loudly to all those who walked past his shop, "Come on, hevra, come and have some falafel."

The concept of hevra, and the related notion of gibush, are not easily translated, for there are no comparable terms in the English language that carry the same precise connotations. These terms nevertheless must be understood as carrying a special meaning for those who have experienced the very real, indeed sometimes all too intense, togetherness of collective child rearing (whether in family or communal sleeping). The capacity to crystallize out quickly into groups, and to successfully lead such groups, is one of the strong by-products of kibbutz socialization, and I believe that it does much to explain the still superior record of kibbutz-born men as soldiers and officers in the Israeli army (Amir 1969).

The extent to which gibush, or group crystallization occurs can be illustrated by the use of what might be called "restricted implication pronouns" within a group. Thus when Udi, a soldier in sick bay, was visited by a member of the same class the following quick interchange took place:

Udi: Who's here now? [meaning: Who's on the kibbutz now?]

Opher: No one. They're all in the army. Yonatan's coming for Shabat.

The "who" of Udi's question contained, although it did not have to specify it, a restricted implication: who *among our class* is here? Speech forms like this imply a tightly knit social group that has lived, worked, and played together over an extended period of time. The speech patterns of these two soldiers mirror basic features of a world they share with the kibbutz adolescent, who is soon to become a soldier like them.

In the context of this kind of group membership, it is not difficult to understand how a fierce drive to do well in work often develops. Indeed, the drive is not just to do well, but to work to the fullest extent of one's capacity, to work to exhaustion and even beyond it, as shown in the following paragraph taken from my field notes:

I see Giora [18 at the time] walking down the steps of the dining room, looking fit as a fiddle after breakfast. "You're looking okay," I say. "I worked the chickens last night, I'm doing a few hours in the factory this morning," he answers matter-of-factly. "If it were me, I'd be totally exhausted, walking around in a fog," I say quite truthfully. "Oh, it's not so bad. You just hold yourself together and then you feel all right," he says, giving me, 15 years his senior, a little lesson in work discipline. It is during his summer vacation, he has worked from eleven at night until three in the morning loading chickens in cages, and will work a full eight-hour day in the factory.

Perhaps the area in which expectations of late adolescents and those of their elders are least likely to coincide is that implied by what might euphemistically be called "social relations." What double shower heads imply is even more strongly implied by the presence of double beds, makeshift or otherwise, in the room of many a precocious 15-year-old. It is well known by everyone that girl friends from nearby kibbutzim occasionally (or more than occasionally) occupy them. Matters of the flesh, then, constitute one bone of contention. Whether cigarette smoking should be allowed in the young people's clubroom (*moadon*) is another.

A second area in which their expectations and those of the older generation often do not coincide is that demarcated by their relationship with the regional high school. Here, as stated before, one encounters in them a frequent mood of detachment and withdrawal from the demands of formal education. In spite of the fact that it is a modern high school, with highly trained teachers who often go out of their way to be responsive and sympathetic to their students' needs and problems, many find it "boring" and disconnect themselves as much as possible from its sphere of influence.

I will return to their disillusionment and alienation from formal education, but before doing so wish to sketch in some further details the ethos of this group. Peter Berger (1963:118) defined a reference group as "the collectivity whose opinions, convictions and courses of action are decisive for the formation of our own convictions and courses of action. The reference group provides us with a model with which we can continually compare ourselves." One can, in the processes of identity formation, be very much influenced by groups of which one is not a member; the reference group falls into this category.

I was continually struck by the extent to which the reference group for a good number of kibbutz adolescents seemed to be the hedonistic youth culture of the United States and Western Europe. Thus Giora came to me one day after work and proudly announced, in the tone of voice of one who has mastered an mportant piece of information, "Hey, did you know that Joni Mitchell wrote the Woodstock song that Crosby, Stills, and Nash recorded?" The same day a new album by someone like Neil Young appears on the streets of Los Angeles, it will be flown, sent, or even hand-delivered to someone, most probably someone Giora's age, on Kibbutz Gan HaEmek. This efficiency in cultural transmission is understandably not a great joy to senior kibbutz members, whose model of "pioneering" and of Hebrew culture may come as a consequence to seem at times both to themselves and to their adolescent children something that is just a little quaint, if not actually outdated.

During the same time of my fieldwork, Margolit, one of the most respected members of the senior class, continually referred to herself and other members of her age group as "freaks." They were about five or ten years behind Berkeley and Los Angeles in their slang and fashions. "We freaks," she used to say, laughingly, taking her idiom from (although she did not know it) an America that by then had all but vanished. Although she and her peers are fond of the kibbutz, it is to them a known world, one whose thousand small moments of boredom and ennui endlessly repeat themselves, as illustrated in the following interchange:

S.B.: The boys that you grew up with are usually just too much like friends that you've known all your life, right?

Margolit: Like brothers. I know them so much! It's so boring to come to a table where I know where everybody sits, and how everybody is going to act, and what every-body's eating... every day it's the same [she expresses disgust], the same [repeats].

Within Israeli society the Kibbutzim have undergone a "withdrawal of status respect" (Hagen 1962). No longer universally looked up to as it was during the early pioneering days, it is now, in the eyes of many of the emerging power groups in Israel, a landed aristocracy, a part of the upper middle class. This consummate irony of the historical process is well-exemplified in an epithet I saw often repeated in the popular press, which described kibbutz youngsters as the "WASPS" of Israel. In this context the acronym referred not to White Anglo-Saxon Protestants, but to its alleged Israeli counterpart: White Ashkenazi Sabras with *Protekzia*. (The Ashkenazi are the European Jews; a sabra is a native born Israeli, and protektzia means influence or power.)

In their travels around Israel, kibbutz adolescents learn that the kibbutz is no longer looked up to as it once was. They must struggle with a dual image. The educational institutions of the kibbutz teach them that they are the elite of Israel. From earliest childhood, they have learned that they are the superior kibbutz children, and part of a special and select group. They may yet be both amazed and impressed when they visit the house of a wealthy friend in Tel-Aviv. *Totzeret chutz laaretz—hakol!* (everything is from abroad) remarked one boy after such an experience. They may sometimes even envy the easy sophistication of the city kids from North Tel-Aviv, and in the process develop an ambivalence about who they are, and who they are becoming. "What would it be like to have an apartment and live in Tel-Aviv?" many of them wonder, and look forward to finding out once their army service is finished.

Contact with foreign volunteers, exposure to the music and styles of the Western youth subculture, and the ambivalence of their own cultural heritage as children of the kibbutz are some of the important factors influencing their attitudes and behavior. Tel-Aviv and Jerusalem have become magnets, drawing them out of what many see as their circumscribed, little world.

COMPENSATORY DISEQUILIBRIUM AND THE HIGH SCHOOL BLUES: A MODEL OF COMPRESSION AND DECOMPRESSION IN THE LIFE CYCLE

In spite of the fact that they attend a modern high school, with a sophisticated variety of course offerings (including such things as photography and tractor mechanics), many late adolescents show a mood of detachment and withdrawal from formal education. The mood is partly attributable to factors within the school itself. As a woman with ten years' experience on the staff there remarked, the attitude of the teachers varies from an easy permissiveness to belief in a strict disciplinarian regime. The resulting lack of consistency is one factor behind their dissatisfaction with school routines.

An additional factor intrinsic to the school itself is the sudden necessity, when the final year approaches, for them to abandon whatever permissiveness they have previously experienced and apply themselves strenuously to the task of doing well on the high school finishing examination (Bagrut). This sudden expectation that they will switch into a high-performance mode startles and upsets many of them. As Giora said unhappily, "It's not a school any more: it's a factory for remembering." Most do not take the frenzied demands of teachers and parents very seriously. What sustains them is their knowledge that it is all really just a game, that their lives haven't yet become serious:

S.B.: Is there a lazy atmosphere in school because of the Bagrut?

Margolit: No, I think because of the Bagrut we are staying in school. Really!! [laughter] Because if you don't do Bagrut, so everybody tells you, you can't do anything after, so you must do it. And that's what's keeping us in school. But [she thinks a minute] it's funny. We have to be in, really in—to try to make it good for the Bagrut, but we never do it...just give it up, I don't know. It's bad because the teachers are bothering you. No *mishmaat*, what do you call mishmaat? [discipline, order]. You know, when they tell you what to do and you listen to them. There's nothing like this, you never listen to the teachers, it's like a friend of yours.

S.B.: You never listen to the teachers? [amazed surprise]

Margolit: Not really, *b'etzem* [in fact], because you know, we now understand that when we'll get out, it will be harder. Now we have a big holiday, and we meet our friends every day. It's only a big holiday. We know when we'll get out, we'll have to be *achrai'i* [responsible].

During this holiday in the last years of school, they are allowed a basic freedom that in American culture is found only among children from so-called disadvantaged groups: they have "permission," in transactional terms (Berne 1972), to get thrown out of school. When this happens there is much head-shaking and verbal disapproval (communication at the social level: "bad, bad"). But they are neither punished nor sanctioned in any effective manner, and what one sees on the faces of offenders is most often a sheepish and fairly unconcerned grin (communication at the psychological level to them by the community: "bad, bad, but okay").

Although some of their elders—and perhaps even a few peers—may attempt to subject them to verbal sanctions, these too are usually ineffectual. After one has, in a small way, established both one's independence and one's character by getting thrown out of school, the disapproval of the insensitive is a small price to pay for a drink of such heady delights. One boy who was thrown out refused to go back, and worked excessive hours in an agricultural branch until he hurt his back and could no longer drive a tractor; at that point he went to work in the factory.

I should point out that not all kibbutz adolescents experience the dissonance and dissatisfaction that I have been describing. Some do manage the passage through these years without the withdrawal from school learning that many of their peers manifest. What is important for the purposes of this chapter is to connect the observations of the dissonance and role distance that do occur with an overall analysis of the relationship between stages of compression and decompression in the life cycle (for related case studies dealing with problems of learning in adolescence, see Hart 1974; McDermott 1987).

The period of cultural compression that began with the Bar Mitzvah ceremony continues even through the apparently successful adaptations of the high
school years. They learn the strategies they need to get along in the subculture
of the regional high school, and succeed in acquiring friends from other kibbutzim along the way. They develop ways of coping, both with the academic
demands and those of the kibbutz work world. Yet by the time their last year of
high school approaches, and graduation is imminent, all share a common
knowledge that what they have been through is truly child's play compared to
what is about to come.

The real rite of passage is not the Bar Mitzvah that took place when they
were 13, but the army duty that is now imminent. After the year of service (*snat
sherut*) that most elect to perform in the year following high school graduation,[2]
it is to the army that they must go. There they will receive the mishmaat that
they managed to escape in the regional high school. From the big fish that they
have now managed to become in the regional high school, they will once again
be demoted to small fish who must swim not just in a larger pond, but out in the
open sea. Up to that time, the little kibbutz has been the setting for their world.
They face now the prospect of a "matrix shift" (Pearce 1986) out of this safe
and limited world to the dangerous duties of a larger world and its uncertain
future.

Though they have been educated to live a kibbutz way of life, the pattern of
their life cycle allows for virtually no free choice until they are well into their
early twenties, and have finished their years of army service (three-four years
for boys, one year for girls). Until then nearly every decision is made for them,
and almost everything they do takes place within the context of the group. The
pattern of cultural compression that began with the Bar Mitzvah rite continues,
gradually intensifying, until they are well into their early twenties. It is not until
after their army service is finished that they will be allowed a phase of cultural
decompression.

Continuing formal education and career decisions are further postponed
during these postarmy decompression years. It is only now that they are allowed
to realize their long-deferred dreams of world travel. It is only now that they
can take advantage of the long lists of former kibbutz volunteers, visitors, and
fellow-travelers who have written down their names in the little black address
books, and leave Israel to explore leisurely the possibilities of life in London,
Los Angeles, perhaps even Kathmandu. The anticipation of this additional
postponement of formal education beyond even the army years introduces a
peculiar discontinuity into their perception of the relevance of schooling to
them at the present time. To an 18-year-old kibbutz adolescent contemplating
the immediate future, the concerns of formal education and practical career
decision making must appear to be inconsequential matters light years away
from the priorities of the present.

Yet even in the midst of prearmy cultural compression, they find that they are
granted an odd de facto reprieve. The kibbutz adolescent is not really punished

for deviations from the norm, whether these relate to schoolwork or to extra-curricular social life. He or she faces instead everywhere a warm, concerned community of adults. His "mistakes" cause committees to be formed. Her "problem" is debated and discussed by anxious parents in a spirit of calm and rational inquiry. Persuasion and not discipline is the major mode of attack. Knowing well what their adolescent children will soon be facing, it is under-standably difficult for kibbutz parents to bring the full weight of authority to bear on the typically small misbehaviors and infractions, the indifference to established custom, that 16- and 17-year-olds happily permit themselves.

As a perceptive kibbutz member pointed out to me, no kibbutz young person is allowed to fail. Yet when the boundaries between success and failure are collapsed, it is difficult to be a person whose acts have real consequences. In the meantime, they swim in a sticky sea of cotton candy, or as many of them refer to it, their *hamama* (greenhouse). It is a cocoon from which they know they must escape, at least for a time, to find out who they really are.

For the mood of detachment, dissonance, and role distance from academic learning that characterizes many (though not all) of them at this time, I have chosen the term "compensatory disequilibrium." What exactly does the term imply? It is closely related to what Berne (1972:260) calls "reach-back": that period of time during which an impending event begins to have an independent influence on an individual's behavior. It is meant to suggest an interference with one frame or domain of life-cycle events in a given phase of the life cycle, brought about by the sensed anticipation of events in the life-cycle phase (or phases) immediately to follow. The model implies that "feedforward" processes (Pribram 1971) connected with anticipation of future events may be as impor-tant as feedback from actual past events in shaping the patterns of continuity and discontinuity at each stage of the human life cycle.

SUMMARY AND CONCLUSION

This chapter has focused on the relationship between alternating stages of cultural compression and decompression in the individual life history of kibbutz adolescents. It has provided an illustration of how these concepts, derived from the work of George Spindler, can contribute to a sharpened, clarified under-standing of frequently observed role distance in the sphere of the school and academic learning. One of the major contributions of the compression/decompression model is that it provides a powerful analytic tool, integrative in nature, demonstrating how the life cycle process as a whole can potentially influence any one of the successive stages.

Adolescence on Kibbutz Gan HaEmek is the winter of their discontent; it is soon followed by the year of service and then by the army. It was only a few years ago that a youth was cleaning up a soldier's room as one of his Bar Mitzvah deeds. Now it is his turn to be the soldier. As Margolit said a little poignantly of her impending departure for the year of service, "we won't see all the class again." What she meant by this was not that she would never see them, but that their relationship would never again be the same. Perhaps more than most places in the world the high school years in Israel are laced with the bitter nearness of war, and in its omnipresent shadow these years are granted to them by the community almost in the spirit of a moratorium. It is one in which they play at playing, but are unable to conceal even from themselves the terrible seriousness of the years that lie immediately ahead.

NOTES

1. The kita is a social age-grade; it is not to be identified with a class in school. Thus a single kita may contain those who are in (to give an example) both the seventh and eighth grade.
2. The shnat sherut is a voluntary "year of service" given by most kibbutz adolescents between their last year of high school and the beginning of army duty. Voluntary work on a young kibbutz, or among immigrants in a development town, are examples of the type of involvements usually taken on during this year.

REFERENCES

Amir, Y. 1969. The effectiveness of the kibbutz-born soldier in the Israel Defense Forces. *Human Relations* 22(4):333-344.
Bateson, G. 1972. Steps to an Ecology of Mind. New York: Ballantine.
Berger, P. 1963. Invitation to Sociology: A Humanistic Perspective. New York: Anchor.
Berne, E. 1972. What Do You Say after You Say Hello?: The Psychology of Human Destiny. New York: Bantam.
Borish, S. 1982. Stones of the Galilee: A Study of Culture Change on an Israeli Kibbutz. Stanford University, Department of Anthropology.
Erikson, E. H. 1950. Childhood and Society. New York: W.W. Norton.
_____. 1968 Identity: Youth and Crises. New York: W.W. Norton.
Evans, E. D. 1970. Adolescence: Readings in Behavior and Development. Hinsdale, IL: Dryden Press.
Giglioli, P. P. (ed.). 1972. Language and Social Context. Harmondsworth: Penguin.
Goffman, E. 1961a. Asylums. New York: Anchor.
_____. 1961b. Encounters. Indianapolis: Bobbs-Merrill.
Gonen, J. 1975. A Psychohistory of Zionism. New York: Meridian.
Gumperz, J. 1972. The speech community. In Giglioli (ed.) 1972.
Hagen, E. 1962. On The Theory of Social Change. Cambridge, MA: MIT Press.
Hart, C. W. M. 1974. Contrasts between prepubertal and postpubertal education. In G. Spindler (ed.) 1974a.
Heath, S. B. 1983. Ways with Words: Language, Life and Work in Communities and Classrooms. Cambridge: Cambridge University Press.
Herdt, G., 1982. Rituals of Manhood: Male Initiation in Papua New Guinea. Berkeley: University of California Press.
Labov, W. 1970. The logic of non-standard English. In F. Williams (ed.), Language and Poverty. Chicago: Rand McNally 1970.

McDermott, R. P. 1987. Achieving school failure: An anthropological approach to illiteracy and social stratification. In G. Spindler (ed.) 1987, pp. 173–209.

Munroe, R. L., R. H. Munroe, and B. B. Whiting (eds.). 1981. Handbook of Cross-Cultural Human Development. New York: Garland.

Pearce, J. C. 1986. Magical Child Matures. New York: Bantam.

Pribam, K. 1971. Languages of the Brain. Englewood Cliffs, NJ: Prentice-Hall.

Shepher, J. 1969. Familism and social structure: The case of the kibbutz. *Journal of Marriage and the Family* 31.

Spindler, G. 1959. The Transmission of American Culture. Cambridge, MA: Harvard University Press.

————. 1970. The education of adolescents: An anthropological perspective in E. Evans (ed.), Adolescents: Readings in Behavior and Development. Hinsdale, IL: Dryden Press.

————. 1973. Cultural Transmission. In Alan R. Beals with G. and L. Spindler, Culture in Process. New York: Holt, Rinehart and Winston.

————. 1974. From omnibus to linkages: Models of the study of cultural transmission. *Council of Anthropology of Education* 1:2–6.

————. 1982. Doing the Ethnography of Schooling. New York: Holt, Rinehart and Winston.

————. 1987. The transmission of culture. In G. Spindler (ed)., Education and cultural process: Toward an anthropology of education. 2nd ed, Prospect Heights, IL.: Waveland Press. pp 303–334.

Spindler, G. and L. Spindler. 1982. From Familiar to strange and back again: Roger Harker and Schonhausen. In G. Spindler (ed.) 1982.

————. 1987. Interpretive Ethnography of Education at Home and Abroad. Hillsdale, NJ: Lawrence Erlbaum Associates.

Spiro, M. 1956. Children of The Kibbutz. Cambridge, MA: Harvard University Press.

————. 1979. Gender and Culture: Kibbutz Women Revisited. Durham, NC: Duke University Press.

Sullivan, H. S. 1953. The Interpersonal Theory of Psychiatry. New York: W.W. Norton.

Young, F. 1965. Initiation Ceremonies. Indianapolis: Bobbs-Merrill.

10
Peer Socialization among Minority Students: A High School Dropout Prevention Program

Henry T. Trueba

This chapter presents and analyzes the ethnographic data collected in a dropout prevention program for high school minority students, from the perspective of educational anthropology as represented by the work of George and Louise Spindler since the 1950s (see, for example, G. Spindler 1955, 1974a, 1974b, 1977, 1982, 1987; Spindler and Spindler 1965, 1982, 1983, 1987a, 1987b, and 1987c). The Spindlers have made an important contribution to the study of minority students' integration into the school culture by pointing out the factors influencing these students' acquisition of skills, knowledge, and motivation necessary for successful schooling.

The underachievement of minority populations has been a serious concern in recent years and has been documented by many (Coleman et al. 1966; Carter 1970; U.S. Congress 1976; Jencks et al. 1972; Carter and Segura 1979; Ogbu 1974, 1978, 1987; Rueda 1983, 1987; Suarez-Orozco 1987, in press; Erickson 1984; and Trueba 1987a, 1987b, in press; among others). Some scholars have noted that very few Hispanics graduate in biology, physics, engineering, and mathematics (Burns et al. 1981; Brown and Stent 1977; Walker and Rakow 1985; Rakow and Walker 1985; Walker 1987). Educational research has demonstrated increasingly more sophistication and concern in the study of minority achievement and educational equity. The reasons are that minority populations are rapidly increasing, and efforts at resolving underachievement in minorities have failed. In an attempt to solve the problem of underachievement, some scholars have focused almost exclusively on the acquisition of English language skills (primarily standard forms).

Excellent research has been done on the linguistic dimensions of underachievement (see, for example, the work by Cummins 1976, 1978, 1981, 1983; Duran 1983; Heath 1983; Krashen 1980; Troike 1978; and Wong-Fillmore

1976, 1982a, 1982b.) This research, however, does not address the social and cultural knowledge, as well as the internalization of certain cultural values, which are essential for minority students to participate meaningfully and actively in the instructional process and in the culture of the school. Instead, we have been involved in numerous controversies about linguistic issues, such as the relative use of mother tongues in bilingual programs. The neglect of cultural issues affecting our understanding of other important organizational aspects of the instructional process as well as the significance of the home and community learning environments, are an example of misplaced and almost exclusive emphasis on language issues.

The sociohistorical school of psychology led by Vygotsky (1962, 1978) as represented by Neo-Vygotskians (Cole and D'Andrade 1982; Cole and Scribner 1974; Cole and Griffin 1983; Trueba et al. 1984, Wertsch 1981, 1985) has been highly instrumental in bringing back the importance of social and cultural dimensions of cognitive development and successful schooling. From this theoretical perspective, academic underachievement is not an attribute of the individual, but a sociocultural phenomenon related to social factors that isolate minorities. Cultural and psychological isolation prevents minority students from obtaining the experience, knowledge, and skills required for active participation in school activities that are the basis for cognitive development and academic success. Given, however, similar social constraints affecting all minority groups, we still have to explain why some groups react in ways that permit them to achieve academically higher than other groups (Spindler and Spindler 1978, 1987a, 1987b, and 1987c; DeVos 1980, 1983; Wagatsuma and DeVos 1984; Ogbu 1974, 1978, 1987).

DeVos (1983:137–143) suggested that minority differential achievement in response to similar social constraints be analyzed in four levels. The first level would explore the behavior of a minority group as a response or reaction to mainstream social behavior that is formally sanctioned by authorities and part of the social organization. The second explores the social role of minority persons and the patterns of social or ethnic interaction, adaptation or maladaptation, and social conflict. The third level focuses on the "self" as a participant in social interaction and examines the individual as he or she goes through the subjective experience of being a member of an ethnic/minority group and through adjustment processes, such as the "belonging and alienation" dilemma. In the fourth and final level one would study ego mechanisms in self-identification, mental health and maturation, psychosexual and cognitive development, and expressive emotional styles.

The impact of the peer reference group is uniquely strong for minority students because they often become socially alienated and distant from their home culture and family unit. Thus, peers' influence increases during the critical learning period in life (Spindler and Spindler 1987a, 1987b), that is, when a young person is attempting to internalize norms, values, and goals, to find emotional support, and to develop a positive self-identity. The conflictive interaction between family and peer group needs more attention if we want to understand the importance of peer socialization for academic achievement. Family cohesion for linguistic minorities is a function of many other social, economic, and cultural forces during the stages of adaptation and rapid change. Macrosociological trends based on economic and historical factors often lead to racial exploitation and discrimination of minorities in our society. Educational research has not paid enough attention to these factors during family and peer socialization processes. DeVos (1984:7) has written about ethnic persistence and role degradation of Koreans in Japan and suggests that the Marxist view of interracial conflict as "an extended form of class exploitation" disregards the important distinction between "a system of stratification based on expressive considerations and those [systems] based on instrumental concerns."

Social exploitation and discrimination, in some instances as a means to implement institutional policies, also takes place in schools when its representatives subject minorities to critical degradation incidents. These incidents have a profound impact on the personality structure of minority individuals and on the organization of extremely powerful peer socialization groups. Values, priorities, and behavior are normed by the peer group, as survival considerations take priority. Motivation to achieve in school and develop cognitively are subject to support and approval through interactional exchanges with peers. Some peer groups produce a weak individual in isolation and a strong member of the peer group with a clear conscience of collective power. Students' views of schooling, their experience as Chicano, Asian, black, or white low-income students, has important implications for our understanding of ethnicity and academic achievement, and consequently for educational reform. If we analyze the data from a vantage point of socialization for academic success or academic failure, and explore peer groups as agents of socialization, we may find the clue to achievement motivation. In other words, if peer groups can function as agents of socialization for academic failure, they could also operate as forceful socialization agents for academic achievement. More specifically, if critical degradation incidents seem to have a significant negative impact on minority students, a planned intervention to analyze such incidents could help these students re-evaluate their self-concept of their academic ability and motivation to achieve in schools. Furthermore, positive critical incidents could be created with the purpose of engaging ethnic minority students in active reconstruction of their self-concept and appreciation of current and potential personal achievements.

Based on the data gathered and analyzed in this study, could we argue that the influence of peer groups on minority individuals, in our case on the Mexican American youth studied here, is enhanced by their interpretation of their social exploitation and isolation experiences? If so, how are these experiences interpreted, and what are the mechanisms that translate experience into actual behaviors and attitudes? Can we explain the apparent rapid academic resocialization for achievement of these minority students primarily as the result of a new peer group influence? If so, what is the nature of this influence? How is this influence manifested? What types of processes of resocialization have the greatest impact on achievement attitudes?

Traditionally, most minority students' peer socialization has resulted in disengagement from academic activities, underachievement, and autonomy or separation from the family unit. Can a change in peer reference group explain the apparent reverse trend toward engagement in academic activities and toward family cohesion? If so, what is the impact of the new group, and how does the impact change predominant sociocultural trends?

In the final instance, the central question of the study is: How do we understand and explain the impact of well-planned educational interventions? Can we replicate them with similar results? More concretely, how do attitudes toward school and mainstream sociocultural values, on the part of the minority student, in clear conflict with the home cultural values, become negative through personal and vicarious experiences of degrading messages sent by the members of mainstream society to minorities? Is the educational philosophy and apparent intolerance for cultural diversity on the part of mainstream persons the cause or the result of stereotypical perceptions of minority students. How do these stereotypes prevail in spite of high academic performance of individual minority students? How do we attack the long-term problem of racism that is rooted in persistent cultural homogeneity? The focus of the analysis will be on the emic view of the predicament in which Chicano high school students find themselves, but its implications for the above questions will be attempted. This is an emic analysis of the way in which Chicano students "are handled" by the educational institution, as well as of the process of resocialization for achievement.

THE DROPOUT PREVENTION PROGRAM

During the summer of 1985 approximately 100 junior high school students from minority and low-income backgrounds were recruited to participate in a dropout prevention program sponsored by a California State College in the San Joaquin Valley, with monies from a prestigious foundation and local organizations. The recruitment was conducted by local organizations and the college, according to a specific set of criteria. Students were sought from those who, being "high risk" or potential dropouts, were free of drugs and criminal records. Also, during the interviews, those students who demonstrated the desire to engage in summer training programs were given preference.

The program lasted for approximately ten weeks (although originally it had been planned for six weeks, and the additional four weeks extended academic and nonacademic training). Sixty of these young adults attended all-day activities at the State College. In the morning they could choose either Computer Literacy and Basic Math classes, taught from 8:00 to 10:00 a.m., and either Public Speaking or Writing, taught from 10:00 a.m. to 12:00 noon. In the afternoon students were assigned jobs in various college offices. The other 40 students were involved in programs in local industries and school district offices four days a week. On Fridays they joined their peers at the State College for various activities. There was an English as a Second Language class available upon request, on a tutorial or quasitutorial basis for small groups of similar skill level.

All the instructors were college professors. There was one Anglo, one Chicano, and two blacks (one from Africa and the other from the United States). The program director was a Chicano faculty member. The second in command, called "Job-site Supervisor," played the role of assistant director in charge of counselors and tutors, and was a young Chicana who recently had obtained an M.A. Tutors/counselors were selected from among the graduate college students who had already been involved in working with high school students. The assistant director described the role of tutors as follows: "They were truly the backbone of the program. They worked very closely with the students, often on a one-to-one basis. The five tutors were expected to work with us full time." The senior tutor/counselor described his role as follows: "Tutors/counselors were each assigned to a specific classroom. They did their work during the class, during breaks, sometimes at lunch, or in the afternoon when students were at various job locations."

Because much of the impact of the program depended on the effectiveness of the tutor/counselor who served as the personal support and guide for a small group of students, the job became a 24-hour assignment. As the senior tutor/counselor described it,

We were all assigned our students and made ourselves available to them. There are still students, to this day, who are calling me at home, asking for advice. What the program did was to give support to these kids. A lot of them came from problem homes, with problems in all areas of family life. They wanted to say: "Just talk to me! Listen to me!" We were doing a lot of listening.

The assistant director did not anticipate the significance of the role played by tutors/counselors. She said in an interview (9/24/86): "Initially I thought the tutors were going to play a minimal role in impacting the students. As time went by, we realized they were having a much bigger impact than we thought."

One of the tutors described a series of critical incidents that demonstrates the nature of this process, from the standpoint of the minority high school students, and the impact of such incidents on the student's life.

We have a black girl, very tiny. She goes into the school system and is expelled from school. From there on, the counselor tells her: "You're a troublemaker." Soon a problem arises and she is out of school again. Now she says it was not her fault: "I did not do that." Once the student has been labeled in the record-keeping process, a student has no hope. Now the school counselor tells her: "Why even bother coming back to school." Let me give you a personal insight. I was once tutoring at my junior high school with the door open. Across the hall was a teacher yelling at the top of her lungs, "Get the hell out of my classroom, and don't ever come back again, because you are nothing." The kid sat down crying.

The testimonies from students themselves speak eloquently about the rituals of public degradation to which they are subjected in high school. But before I present some of these examples, there are testimonies indicating that even those counselors who seem to have some tolerance and sensitivity in dealing with minorities do not have the training, capacity, or human quality needed for the job. Sheer ignorance and neglect are not the only problems. Bad example and abuse are also present. A high school student described the following incident in high school:

The [older woman] counselor had a glass in her hand that looked like water. I asked if I could have a drink of water. I took a drink and it was vodka! She said she was going to retire soon. I was having family problems and I was cutting . . . I was really screwed up.

Another Chicano student relates this incident about another school counselor:

I may look like a student who doesn't like his classwork, who just messes off in class, but I'm not. Teachers just look at me and they say, "Oh, another mess off." I'm not dumb. They didn't care what was the result of my tests. I know I got a perfect score! It is like prejudice, but it's not prejudice . . . I just ignored it. I had this problem before. I had U.S. History, but somehow my teacher didn't like me, I don't know why. He told me I did not belong in that class. And I did good on the tests. History is my best subject. I felt like hitting him! He said I did not have what it takes to be a student there. I went to my counselor and told her. Same thing. But you see, that made me feel mad!

One of the program tutor/counselors summarized the high school administration's views of the minority students as follows:

From the administrators' standpoint these kids are a waste of time, they're worthless, they're failures. They would ask me: "Why are you wasting your energy on them?" My answer was: "That is my job, and they are worth it." But how many other people out there feel the same way?

STRATEGIES USED BY PROGRAM PERSONNEL

The general strategy, as described by the tutor/counselors, was to persuade the high school students that they were worthwhile and deserved attention, affection, and care from the director, instructors, tutors, and each other:

"I'm here, I care, and I'm here for you." That freaked a lot of students out. "How could anyone want to pay attention to me?" For some of the students it was a shock to know that someone cared and took a genuine interest in them.

Tutors/counselors often described a "total turnaround" reaction to some students. When the students gathered for the "graduation" ceremony at the end of the summer program they surrounded their tutors/counselors and hugged them. One of the tutors said:

I had tears in my eyes because all of my students gathered around me and they all gave me a hug, something they wouldn't even have thought about the beginning. It is that personal contact that translates into "I believe you care about me." One thing that I find is that humans need touch.

The performance of students in each of the classes was indeed outstanding. The reports from each of the college professors reflected a great deal of surprise and happiness on the part of the instructors and tutors. The actual ability to solve mathematical problems, the increased ability to write prose and poetry, speak in public, and work with computers increased above and beyond the expectations of college personnel. In ten short weeks there was a very intensive process of soul searching, peer interaction, and peer resocialization, under the guidance of skilled tutors/counselors. To illustrate the results, here are some excerpts from the testimonies given by students. One student expressed his satisfaction as follows:

I feel pretty good about myself, and I know what I'm going to do with my life. I already know what college I want to go to.... Nothing is stopping me. I got my own car. I got two jobs I can handle. As for career, I know I want to be a nurse, and nothing is going to change my mind.

Another student wrote in his journal:

Well, success is something you complete and you like. Failure is something you don't complete. Failure scares me because if I fail in school, then I'll never be able to succeed in anything in my life after that.... I won't feel good about myself.... I need to improve my study habits.

Another student:

I want to go to college because I want to be. I want to make something out of myself. I don't want to go through life like just another person, born and dead and nothing in between. There are a lot of people I know like that; they are not dead yet, when they die they will leave nothing behind. I want to leave something here to stay. If I am a writer, maybe people will read my books. That's why I want to go to college.

Another student:

I was thinking about college today and I was scared. When are you guys going to have your workshops? I need a boost.

The fear and ambivalence are often mixed with a realistic assessment of present conditions. A student wrote:

Well, I wasn't really too sure about this program. What I want to do is really to enroll in college.... I am going to push my kids to go to college. You see, my mom, she only went to college for like two or three months, and she dropped out. She had my older brother, and she never went back. I told her I was never going to go to college. And now that I'm here and I can see what it's like, I think I could give it a shot. I guess I can try it. I'm in school still, I'm working at a college, and God, my friends are married, pregnant, out of high school and they dropped out completely! I am glad I came here.

Discussing one of his crises and recognizing the worth of the program, a student said in one of the meetings:

Like Ray [one of the tutors/counselors] he's helped me with some problems. He gives a damn which a lot of people don't. I think this is neat! But others, the high school counselors, are a bunch of assholes. They didn't care. You'd ask them a question and they'd explained it the same way as before, you still couldn't understand, and they'd say: "Well, if you can't understand it by now, you must be stupid."

IDENTIFIED ACADEMIC PROBLEMS

In order to identify the areas of rapid improvement through the intensive summer academic resocialization and peer interaction, it is important to summarize, from my observations and the analysis of testimonies from the instructors and students themselves, the key areas of difficulties affecting academic performance of high-risk students. With respect to their overall adjustment to the formal academic (especially class-time) activities, there was some difficulty in understanding the transition from one section to another within the same subject. The confusion of contextual information made the subject difficult at times. Instructors had to insist on spelling out changes in activities and the relationship between activity and content in textbooks and exercises. Second, the time fragmentation from class to class and activity to activity seemed at times to prevent students from fully engaging in subjects previously perceived as traumatic. Third, the language used in some areas of the curriculum (math, computers) was not always clearly understood.

With respect to students' ability to process information received, some general problems existed.

1. Problems understanding abstract categories, concepts, and semantic domains as used by instructors.
2. Problems generated in writing abstract categories and procedural understandings grasped in class or during tutoring.
3. Unpredictable differences in ease or difficulty in retaining content. Some very difficult concepts are retained, some other relatively simple concepts are not retained.

4. Different rate of engagement and progress in academic subjects. Some students start out very slowly and progress quickly toward the end. Others were just the opposite.

These observations must be understood in the context of the overall intensive experience of working together in the college environment, under close supervision, and in a cooperative environment. While some students arrived with extremely serious economic and emotional problems, others were quite ready to engage in academic work. Some students continued to spend a great amount of energy overcoming the "degradation experiences" recently suffered in the high school and in previous educational and social experiences. Some students had an extremely difficult time accepting the fact that adults (the instructors or the tutors/counselors) cared for them and truly wanted to help them.

The development of these students' full potential and their subsequent incorporation into schools and society depends a great deal upon the ability of adults in the various social institutions (especially in schools) to also understand the nature of the impact that degradation processes have on these young adults, and to understand the possibility of resocializing them through experiences such as those illustrated here in the dropout prevention program.

A PSYCHOSOCIAL APPROACH TO RESOCIALIZATION

One could distinguish various stages in the process of socialization for failure of the minority students victimized through degradation events. Table 10.1 offers a brief presentation of these stages, divided into four interactional contexts: community, school, home, and self. These contexts reflect an attempt to distinguish the four analytical levels extending from macrosociological to micropsychological behavioral phenomena:

1. Institutional representatives (school personnel, for example) adopt philosophies and behaviors based on dominant cultural values that translate into degradation incidents for minority persons.

2. Degradation incidents (as described by students and tutors) lead minority persons to feelings of low self-esteem and negative attitudes toward the institution (in our case the school).

3. Minority persons search for support groups of victim-like persons, which further reinforce negative attitudes toward the institution and its representatives (school, teachers, counselors), as well as lack of self-esteem.

4. Lack of self-esteem and negative attitudes toward institutional representatives (teachers and counselors) prevent minority persons from entering the Zone of Proximal Development and establishing a learning relationship.

5. As minority persons remain away from the Zone of Proximal Development and are distanced from the institutional representatives, they either engage in learning marginally or refuse to participate at all.

6. As a result of this lack of meaningful participation, minority persons perform poorly

Table 10.1
Learning to Fail: Interactional Contexts and Socialization Stages

INTERACTIONAL CONTEXTS	STAGES OF SOCIALIZATION		
	ANTECEDENTS	CONSTRUCTION OF FAILURE	OUTCOMES
COMMUNITY	Pre-arrival trauma, loss separation, degradation and other critical incidents. Collective ethnic crisis and conflicting relationships	Collective, systematic and public abuse through "degradation events" internalized by ethnic group as "deserved."	Patterns of marginality reinforced by racist practices. Less participation in public interethnic activities.
SCHOOL	Isolation and degradation school experiences, peer social and cultural impact. Confusion about school personnel's roles and norms of behavior.	School viewed as part of hostile society. Resistance to engage in academic work. Peer pressure to view achievement as "selling out." Exposure to "degradation incidents."	Problem entering Zone of Proximal Development to do cognitive tasks. Traumatic communicative patterns. Cycle of stress, miscommunication and low academic performance. Deterioration of cognitive skills.
HOME	Collective previous experiences in home cultural environment contrasting with value of academic work.	Increasing sociocultural and emotional distance from adults at home. Emancipatory behavior and partial economic, social and emotional independence	Alienation from home, culture and loss of mother tongue. Selective acculturation. Tension between home and dominant cultures.
SELF	Confusion about self-identity and self-worth. Vague and pervasive fears and anxiety. Strong emotional need for peer support.	Identity crisis. Coping with stress and anxiety through withdrawal or uncommitted and unsuccessful participation in academic work.	Confusion, depression and less ability to deal with stress and to establish a learning relationship with teachers and high achieving peers.

210

Table 10.2
Learning to Succeed: Interactional Contexts and Stages of Socialization

INTERACTIONAL CONTEXTS	STAGES OF SOCIALIZATION	
	CONSTRUCTION OF SUCCESS	OUTCOMES
COMMUNITY	Community-based counseling, legal and mental health services, basic exposure to public institutions (banks, schools, hospitals, etc.) through literacy classes. Message: "America is multicultural and your ethnic community is part of America."	Selective assimilation patterns through active participation in interethnic public activities. Collective presence in various institutional positions and roles.
SCHOOL	Use of peer group to reinterpret degradation events and to create a climate of acceptance for cultural differences. Messages: "Minority students belong here and can achieve with peer support."	Acceptance of potential success of minority students on the part of school personnel and peer groups. Increasing influence of interethnic peer groups in support of academic success.
HOME	Reach out efforts to help parents become strong school allies. Friendly communication for the purpose of creating a support system for the minority student. Message: "You and your child belong in our school."	Selective adults support for student. Reorganization of home life style to help student engage in academic work and provide emotional support. Knowledge of the function of school and roles of school personnel.
SELF	On a one-to-one basis, reinterpret past experiences, overcome impact of degradation events, and engage in learning activities through personal relationships with teachers and peers. Discover actual and potential academic skills. Message: You can succeed if you are willing to seek help."	Redefinition of and acceptance of self. Control over stress and commitment to academic work. Increased cognitive and linguistic skills to articulate abstract thought. Social skills to handle academic problems and engage in learning relationships.

211

and are subjected to additional degradation events that tend to reinforce negative attitudes, decreased participation, and, in brief, perpetuate the cycle of academic failure.

If these hypothetical steps are correct, one must accept the intimate relationship between peer group interaction and academic achievement, and between the social interactional aspects of teaching/learning activities and the intrapsychological dimensions of personality structure and cognitive development. Both of these relationships have been emphatically pursued by Vygotsky (1962, 1978) and Neo-Vygotskians (Cole and Scribner 1974; Cole and Griffin 1983; Werstch 1985). Furthermore, if educators want to engage in educational reform, they must pay attention to important linkages between social and psychological processes associated with peer academic socialization. Also, we should take into consideration in our analysis the proposed social structural level (expressed in dominant educational philosophy and cultural values) and the interactional level of behavior expressed through specific degradation events and discriminatory practices.

Another consequence of accepting DeVos' theoretical frame and analytical levels for interdisciplinary approaches to the study of ethnicity and academic achievement is that educational reform must pay attention to resocialization processes through peer interaction. It stands to reason that if peer interaction is crucial for reinforcing negative attitudes toward self and school, one can construct and facilitate peer interaction to revalue oneself and develop positive attitudes toward school and schooling. In order to accomplish this purpose, one could speculate that minority students would have to be taken through precisely the opposite route that led them to underachievement. Table 10.2 illustrates the resocialization process for academic success summarizing the process and outcomes in four main interactional settings: community, school, home, and self.

Here are some possible steps, as inferred from the data presented above:

1. Minority students would be placed in social groups and one-to-one interactional settings (with tutor/counselor) in order to reevaluate and reanalyze degradation incidents and the consequences of low self-esteem and negative attitudes toward school. The intended result would be the will to take new risks in academic activities with the hope of succeeding.

2. Minority students would be exposed to a new learning environment in which individuals were respected and allowed to inquire without being ridiculed.

3. The positive experience of learning without degradation incidents, that is, of succeeding in handling specific areas of the curriculum, was created through explicit norms agreed upon between instructors of the entire group of students.

4. Over a period of several weeks the relationship between individual students, the instructors, and tutors/counselors resulted in a serious commitment to engage in learning activities and to succeed academically. At this point students were able to enter their Zone of Proximal Development.

5. Achievement gains reinforced by peer group support and personal guidance from instructor and tutors/counselors created success experiences that led to strong motivation to engage in academic activities and willingness to take higher risks, including that of entering college. Thus the cycle of social support and success would lead to increased cognitive development and academic achievement.

The data presented here seem to suggest the trend of reverse socialization from failure to success, in which peer group interaction is essential to restructure self-concept and engage in social ventures for academic achievement.

In an attempt to answer more directly the central research questions posed earlier, data analysis seems to indicate that while influence of the new peer group in the Dropout Prevention Program did enhance the academic resocialization of high-risk Mexican American youth, and that peers were instrumental in the reinterpretation of degradation incidents, the most crucial factor in changing students' attitudes toward school and academic achievement was the personal dyadic relationships these students established with counselors and professors. The dyadic relationships with other peers were also instrumental, but to a lesser extent. Consequently, one needs to examine peer group resocialization processes in conjunction with dyadic adult-peer and peer-peer relationships.

Indeed the most crucial mechanism in reversing the underachievement trend toward achievement motivation and self-confidence was the establishment of dyadic relationships with adults (teachers, counselors, ambassadors, etc.), but the advice and support of peer groups for the development of adult relationships was indispensable. In the final analysis, there existed a social network of peer relationships that provided information and emotional support leading to the establishment of youth-adult relationships. Furthermore, the cohesiveness of the new youth-adult relationships created a network of highly supportive groups, collectively strong in the face of the outside world composed of mainstream people. The influence from peers and adults on the individual was felt gradually, in subtle but powerful ways, step-by-step, opening up the possibility for each individual to take the risks in exploring new adult relationships and to make new attempts in the academic world. These risks are high for youth who have been degraded by adults in previous school encounters.

Traditional high school peer group activities produce a solidarity of Mexican American youth against "adult Anglo oppressors" who represent the system, the institution, and the entire mainstream sociocultural complex. It is understandable that Mexican American youth develop strong antagonistic feelings toward the entire cultural complex represented by white Anglo-Saxon adults. During the Dropout Prevention Program, which attempted to create a new learning environment, these feelings of hostility (see Hanna 1982:326-340) had to be reinterpreted and replaced in the new learning environment of solidarity between students (youth) and teachers (adults). Some of the instructors restructured the classroom interaction on the basis that teachers and all students constituted a single family, a strong and competent collectivity (of minorities), to compete with mainstream individuals in mainstream institutions. There was a new setting, with new relationships and new rules. Often this new collectivity opened the doors to new dyadic relationships and cooperative arrangements between peers and adults.

Can we replicate these types of interventions? It is possible, provided we adapt each intervention to the specific sociocultural setting and circumstances in which students and adults are involved. And yet, we cannot forget that sociocultural regional groups of mainstream persons tend to be extremely resilient to change (Spindler 1987). In other words, we can change a group of minority students and put them on the way to significantly better academic performance; but we cannot change prejudicial feelings and racist practices. As a consequence, part of the training of these individuals in planned interventions should be the follow up, from time to time, of strategies to deal with the organized persistent racism that is perpetuated in educational institutions.

Racial discrimination, as a concrete reality affecting human responses and personality characteristics in the educational setting, makes the significance of peer group influence and dyadic relationships on learning much more understandable. New peer groups and youth-adult relationships define priorities and the value of academic work, as well as the interpretation of its outcomes. Thus, peer resocialization and dyadic youth-adult relationships can be viewed both on a macrosociological level and by their micropsychological impact. These two aspects of resocialization are important for our understanding of racism in school and its consequences of alienation and underachievement in minority students.

REFERENCES

Brown, F. and Stent, M. (1977). Minorities in U.S. Institutions of Higher Education. New York: The Free Press.

Burns, M., Gerace, W., Mestre, J., and Robinson, H. (1981). The current status of Hispanic technical professionals: How can we improve recruitment and retention? *Integrated Education* 20(1-2):49-55.

Carter, T. (1970). Mexican Americans in School: A History of Educational Neglect. New York: College Entrance Examination Board.

Carter, T. and Segura, R. (1979). Mexican Americans in School: A Decade of Change. New York: College Entrance Examination Board.

Cole, M. and D'Andrade, R. (1982). The influence of schooling on concept formation: Some preliminary conclusions. *The Quarterly Newsletter of the Laboratory of Comparative Human Cognition* 4(2):19-26.

Cole, M. and Griffin, P. (1983). A socio-historical approach to remediation. *The Quarterly Newsletter of the Laboratory of Comparative Human Cognition* 5(4):69-74.

Cole, M. and Scribner, S. (1974). Culture and Thought: A Psychological Introduction. New York: Basic Books.

Coleman, J., Campbell, E., Hobson, C., Partland, J., Mood, A., Wenfield, F., and York, R.

(1966). Equality of Education Opportunity. Washington, DC: U.S. Department of Health, Education and Welfare.

Cummins, J. (1976). The influence of bilingualism on cognitive growth: A synthesis of research findings and explanatory hypotheses. *Working Papers on Bilingualism* 9:1–43.

————. (1978). Bilingualism and the development of metalinguistic awareness. *Journal of Cross-cultural Psychology* 9(2):131–149.

————. (1981). The entry and exit fallacy in bilingual education. *National Association for Bilingual Education Journal* 4(3):26–60.

————. (1983). The role of primary language development in promoting educational success for language minority students. In Schooling and Language Minority Students: A Theoretical Framework (pp. 3–49). Sacramento: Bilingual Education Office, California State Department of Education.

DeVos, G. (1980). Ethnic adaptation and minority status. *Journal of Cross-Cultural Psychology* 11:101–124.

————. (1983). Ethnic identity and minority status: Some psycho-cultural considerations. In A. Jacobson-Widding (ed.), Identity: Personal and Socio-cultural (pp. 135–158). Uppsala: Almquist and Wiksell Tryckeri AB.

————. (1984). Ethnic persistence and role degradation: An illustration from Japan. Paper read April, 1984 at the American-Soviet Symposium on Contemporary Ethnic Processes in the USA and the USSR. New Orleans, LA.

Duran, R. (1983). Hispanics' Education and Background: Predictors of College Achievement. New York: College Entrance Examination Boards.

Erickson, F. (1984). School literacy, reasoning, and civility: An anthropologist's perspective. *Review of Educational Research* 54(4):525–544.

Hanna, J. (1982). Public social policy and the children's world: Implications of ethnographic research for desegregated schooling. In G. Spindler (ed.), Doing the Ethnography of Schooling: Educational Anthropology in Action (pp. 316–355). New York: Holt, Rinehart and Winston.

Heath, S. (1983). Ways with words. Cambridge, MA: Cambridge University Press.

Jencks, C., Smith, M., Aclard, H., Bane, J., Cohen, D., Gintins, H., Heyrs, B., and Michaelson, S. (1972). Inequality: A Reassessment of the Effects of Family and Schooling in America. New York: Basic Books.

Krashen, S. (1981). The theoretical and practical relevance of simple codes in second language acquisition. In R. Scarcella and S. Krashen (eds.), Research in Second Language Acquisition (pp. 7–18). Rowley, MA: Newbury House.

Ogbu, J. (1974). The Next Generation: An Ethnography of Education in an Urban Neighborhood. New York: Academic Press.

————. (1978). Minority Education and Caste: The American System in Cross-cultural Perspective. New York: Academic Press.

————. (1987). Variability in minority responses to schooling: Nonimmigrants vs. immigrants. In G. Spindler and L. Spindler (eds.), Interpretive Ethnography of Education: At Home and Abroad (pp. 255–278). Hillsdale, NJ: Lawrence Erlbaum Associates.

Rakow, S. and Walker, C. (1985). The status of Hispanic American students in science: Achievement and exposure. *Science Education* 69(4):557–565.

Rueda, R. (1983). Metalinguistic awareness in monolingual and bilingual mildly retarded children. *National Association for Bilingual Education Journal* 8(1):55–68.

————. (1987). Social and communicative aspects of language proficiency in low-achieving language minority students. In H. Trueba (ed.), Success or Failure: Linguistic Minority Children at Home and in School (pp. 185-197). New York: Harper & Row.

Spindler, G. (1955). Anthropology and Education. Stanford, CA: Stanford University Press.

————. (1974a). The transmission of American culture. In G. Spindler (ed.), Education and Culture: Anthropological Approaches (pp. 279-310). New York: Holt, Rinehart and Winston.

————. (1974b). Schooling in Schoenhausen: A study of cultural transmission and instrumental adaptation in an urbanizing German village. In G. Spindler (ed.), Education and Cultural Process: Toward an Anthropology of Education (pp. 230-271). New York: Holt, Rinehart and Winston.

————. (1977). Change and continuity in American core cultural values: An anthropological perspective. In G. D. DeRenzo (ed.), We the People: American Character and Social Change (pp. 20-40). Westport, CT: Greenwood Press.

————. (1982). Doing the Ethnography of Schooling: Educational Anthropology in Action. New York: Holt, Rinehart and Winston.

————. (1987). Why have minority groups in North America been disadvantaged by their schools? In G. Spindler (ed.), Education and Cultural Process. Anthropological Approaches (pp. 160-172), 2nd ed. Prospect Heights, IL.: Waveland Press.

Spindler, G. and Spindler, L. (1965). The Instrumental Activities Inventory: A technique for the study of psychology of acculturation. Southwestern Journal of Anthropology (21(1):1-23.

————. (eds.). (1978). The Making of Psychological Anthropology. Berkeley: University of California Press.

————. (1982). Roger Harker and Schoenhausen: From the familiar to the strange and back again. In G. Spindler (ed.), Doing the Ethnography of Schooling (pp. 20-47). New York: Holt, Rinehart and Winston.

————. (1983). Anthropologists view American culture. Annual Review of Anthropology 12:49-78.

————. (eds.) (1987a). The Interpretive Ethnography of Education: At Home and Abroad. Hillsdale, NJ: Lawrence Erlbaum Associates.

————. (1987b). Instrumental competence, self-efficiency, linguistic minorities, schooling, and cultural therapy: A preliminary attempt at integration. Paper presented at the Conference on Educational Anthropology: Current Research and Implications for Instruction. University of California, Santa Barbara, May 16.

————. (1987c). Cultural dialogue and schooling in Schoenhausen and Roseville: A comparative analysis. Anthropology and Education Quarterly 18(1):3-16.

Suarez-Orozco, M. (1987). Toward a psychosocial understanding of Hispanic adaptation to American Schooling. In H. Trueba (ed.), Success or Failure? Learning & the Language Minority Student (pp. 156-168). New York: Newbury/Harper & Row.

————. (in press). In Pursuit of a Dream: New Hispanic Immigrants in American Schools. Stanford, CA: Stanford University Press.

Troike, R. (1978). Research evidence for the effectiveness of bilingual education. NABE Review 3:13-24.

Trueba, H. (ed.) (1987a). Success or Failure: Learning & the Language Minority Student. New York: Newbury House/Harper & Row.

_____. (1987b). Organizing classroom instruction in specific sociocultural contexts: Teaching Mexican youth to write in English. In S. Goldman and H. Trueba (eds.), Becoming Literate in English as a Second Language: Advances in Research and Theory (pp. 235-252). Norwood, NJ: Ablex.

_____. (in press). Raising Silent Voices: Educating the Linguistic Minorities for the 21st Century. Santa Barbara, CA: Newbury House/Harper & Row.

Trueba, H., Moll, L., Diaz, S., and Diaz, R. (1984). Improving the Functional Writing of Bilingual Secondary School Students. (Contract No. 400-81-0023). Washington, D.C.: National Institute of Education. ERIC, Clearinghouse on Languages and Linguistics, ED 240, 862.

U.S. Congress, Senate. (1976). Equal educational opportunity for Puerto Rican children. Hearings before select committee on equal educational opportunity. Ninety-first Congress, second session, part 8, 3683-3973.

Vygotsky, L. S. (1962). Thought and Language. Cambridge, MA: MIT Press.

_____. (1978). Mind in Society: The Development of Higher Psychological Processes, M. Cole, V. John-Teiner, S. Scribner, and E. Souberman (eds.). Cambridge, MA: Harvard University Press.

Wagatsuma, H. and DeVos, G. (1984). Heritage of Endurance: Family Patterns and Delinquency Formation in Urban Japan. Berkeley: University of California Press.

Walker, C. (1987). Hispanic Achievement: Old views and new perspectives. In H. Trueba (ed.), Success or Failure: Learning & the Language Minority Student (pp. 15-32). New York: Newbury House/Harper & Row.

Walker, C. and Rakow, S. (1985). The status of Hispanic American students in science: Attitudes. Hispanic Journal of Behavioral Sciences 7(3):225-245.

Wertsch, J. (1981). The Concept of Activity in Soviet Psychology. New York: M E. Sharpe.

_____. (1985). Vygotsky and the Social Formation of the Mind. Cambridge, MA: Harvard University Press.

Wong-Fillmore, L. (1976). The second time around: Cognitive and social strategies in second language acquisition. Unpublished doctoral dissertation, Stanford University.

_____. (1982a). Instructional language as linguistic input: Second language learning in classrooms. In L. Wilkinson (ed.), Communicating in Classrooms (pp. 283-296). New York: Academic Press.

_____. (1982b). Language minority students and school participation: What kind of English is needed? Journal of Education 164:143-156.

Selected Bibliography

Agar, M. (1980). *The Professional Stranger: An Informal Guide to Ethnography*. New York: Academic Press.

Alvarez, R. R. (1986). *The Lemon Grove Incident: The Nation's First Successful Desegregation Court Case*. San Diego Historical Society.

————. (1987). *Familia: Migration and Adaptation in Alta and Baja California, 1800-1975*. University of California Press: Los Angeles.

Anderson-Levitt, K. M. (1987). National culture and teaching culture. *Anthropology and Education Quarterly* 18:33-38.

Ansari, A. (1974). A community in process and in the dual marginal situation: The first generation of the Iranian professional middle class immigrants in the U.S. Unpublished doctoral dissertation, The New School for Social Research.

Balderrama, F. (1982). *In Defense of La Raza. The Mexican Consulate and the Mexican Community, 1926 to 1936*. Tucson: University of Arizona Press.

Bateson, G. (1972). *Steps to an Ecology of Mind*. New York: Ballantine.

Becker, H. (1953). The teacher in the authority system of the public schools. *Journal of Educational Sociology* 27:128-144.

Ben-Peretz, M. and Halkes, R. (1987). How teachers know their classrooms: A cross-cultural study of teachers' understanding of classroom situations. *Anthropology and Education Quarterly 18*, 17-32.

Berger, P. (1963). *Invitation to Sociology: A Humanistic Perspective*. New York: Anchor.

Berne, E. (1972). *What Do You Say after You Say Hello?: The Psychology of Human Destiny*. New York: Bantam.

Bogardus, E. (1934). *Mexicans in the United States*. Los Angeles: University of Southern California Press.

Borish, S. (1982). *Stones of the Galilee: A Study of Culture Change on an Israeli Kibbutz*. Stanford University, Department of Anthropology.

Cardenas, G. (1975). United States immigration policy toward Mexico: An historical perspective. *Chicano Law Review* (UCLA) 5(2), Summer.

Cole, M. and Griffin, P. (1983). A socio-historical approach to remediation. *The Quarterly Newsletter of the Laboratory of Comparative Human Cognition* 5(4):69–74.

Cummins, J. (1982). Tests, achievement, and bilingual students. *Focus* 9:1–7. Rosslyn, VA: National Clearinghouse for Bilingual Education.

————. (1983). The role of primary language development in promoting educational success for language minority students. In *Schooling and Language Minority Students: A Theoretical Framework* (pp. 3–49). Sacramento: Bilingual Education Office, California State Department of Education.

DeVos, G. (1983). Ethnic identity and minority status: Some psycho-cultural considerations. In A. Jacobson-Widding (ed.), *Identity: Personal and Socio-cultural* (pp. 135–158). Uppsala: Almquist and Wiksell Tryckeri AB.

Divine, R. (1957). *American Immigration Policy 1924–1952*. New Haven, CT: Yale University Press.

Doi, T. (1973). *The Anatomy of Dependence*. Tokyo: Kodansha International Ltd.

Eddy, E. M. (1985). Theory, research, and application in Educational Anthropology. *Anthropology and Education Quarterly* 16(2):83–104.

Ellis, A. (1980). *The Assimilation and Acculturation of Indochinese Children into American Culture*. Sacramento: Department of Social Services, State of California.

Erickson, E. H. (1950). *Childhood and Society*. New York: W. W. Norton.

Erickson, F. (1973). What makes school ethnography 'ethnographic'? [Council on] *Anthropology and Education Newsletter* 4(2):10–19. [Revised and reprinted in *Anthropology and Education Quarterly* 15():51–66. 1984.]

Erickson, F. and Wilson, J. (1982). Sights and sounds of life in schools: Research guide to film and videotape for research and education. Research Series No. 125). East Lansing: Institute for Research on Teaching, Michigan State University.

Faces are changing in San Francisco schools. (1980, May 5). *San Francisco Examiner*.

Feiman-Nemser, S. and Floden, R. E. (1986). The cultures of teaching. In M. Wittrock (ed.), *Handbook of Research on Teaching* (pp. 505–526). New York: Macmillan.

Fujita, M. (1977). The concept of "Amae" in Western social science. Unpublished master's thesis, Spring paper, Stanford University.

Garcia, M. (1982). *Desert Immigrants*. New Haven, CT: Yale University Press.

Geertz, C. (1973). *The Interpretation of Cultures*. New York: Basic Books.

Glaser, B. G. and Strauss, A. L. (1967). *The Discovery of Grounded Theory: Strategies for Qualitative Research*. New York: Aldine.

Goffman, E. (1961a). *Asylums*. New York: Anchor.

————. (1961b). *Encounters*. Indianapolis: Bobbs-Merrill.

Goodenough, W. H. (1976). Multiculturalism as the normal human experience. *Anthropology and Education Quarterly* 7(4):4–7.

Haro, C. M. (1977). *Mexicano/Chicano Concerns and School Desegregation in Los Angeles*. Los Angeles: Chicano Studies Center, UCLA.

Hoffman, A. (1977). *Unwanted Mexican-Americans in the Great Depression: Repatriation Pressures, 1929–1939*. Tucson: University of Arizona.

Jaeger, R. (ed.). (1987). *Complementary Methods for Research in Education*. Washington, DC: American Educational Research Association.

Jung, S., Phillips-Jones, L., Reynolds, D., and Eaton, M. (1982). *Evaluability Assessment of the Transition Program for Refugee Children*. Palo Alto, CA: American Institutes for Research in the Behavioral Sciences.

Lippitt, R. (1968). Improving the socialization process. In Clausen, J. A. (ed.), *Socialization and Society*. Boston: Little, Brown.

Lorenz, J. H. and Wertime, J. T. (1980). Iranians. In S. Thernstrom (ed.), *Harvard Encyclopedia of American Ethnic Groups* (pp. 521-524). Cambridge, MA: Harvard University Press.

Navarro, R. A. (1985). The problems of language, education and society: Who decides? In E. E. Garcia and R. V. Padilla (eds.), *Advances in Bilingual Education Research* (pp. 289-313). Tucson: University of Arizona Press.

Ogbu, J. and Matute-Bianchi, M. (1986). Understanding sociocultural factors: Knowledge, identity, and school adjustment. In *Beyond Language: Social and Cultural Factors in Schooling Language Minority Students*. Los Angeles: Evaluation, Dissemination and Assessment Center, California State University.

Philips, S. (1983). *The Invisible Culture: Communication in Classroom and Community on the Warm Springs Indian Reservation*. New York: Longman.

Pierce, D. C. (1983). A country of immigrants: Effects of and responses to the second wave of Indo-Chinese refugees into Orange County, 1979-1982. Unpublished doctoral dissertation. Washington, DC: George Washington University.

Rapson, R. L. et al. (1967). *Individualism and Conformity in the American Character*. Boston: D. C. Heath.

Rubin, J. (1981). Meeting the educational needs of Indochinese refugee children. Draft Paper. National Center for Bilingual Research.

Rueda, R. (1987). Social and communicative aspects of language proficiency in low-achieving language minority students. In H. Trueba (ed.), *Success or Failure: Linguistic Minority Children at Home and in School* (pp. 185-197). New York: Harper & Row.

Sabagh, G. and Bozorgmehr, M. (1987). Are the characteristics of exiles different from immigrants? The case of Iranians in Los Angeles. *Sociology and Social Research* 71(2):77-84.

Shweder, R. and LeVine, R. (eds.). (1984). *Culture Theory: Essays on Mind, Self, and Emotion*. Cambridge: Cambridge University Press.

Smith, L. M. (1979). An evolving logic of participant observation, educational ethnography, and other case studies. *Review of research in Education* 6:316-377.

Spindler, G. (1959). *The Transmission of American Culture*. Cambridge, Mass.: Harvard University Press.

_____. (1971). *Dreamers without Power: The Menomini Indians*. New York: Holt, Rinehart & Winston.

_____. (ed.). (1982). *Doing the Ethnography of schooling: Educational Anthropology in Action*. New York: Holt, Rinehart and Winston.

_____. (ed.). (1987). *Education and Cultural Process: Toward an Anthropology of Education*, 2nd ed. Prospect Heights, IL.: Waveland Press. (First Edition, New York: Holt, Rinehart and Winston, 1974).

Spindler, G. and Spindler, L. (1978). Identity, militancy, and cultural congruence: The Menominee and Kainai. *Annals of the American Academy of Political and Social Science* 436:73-85.

_____. (eds.). (1987a). *The Interepretive ethnography of Education: At Home and Abroad*. Hillsdale, NJ: Lawrence Erlbaum Associates.

_____. (1987b). Cultural dialogue and schooling in Schoenhausen and Roseville: A comparative analysis. *Anthropology and Education Quarterly* 18:3-16.

Spradley, J. P. (1980). *Participant Observation*. New York: Holt, Rinehart & Winston.

Taylor, P.S. (1928). Mexican labor in the United States: Imperial Valley California. University of California Publications in Economics 6(1). Berkeley: University of California.

Trueba, H. (ed.). (1987). *Success or Failure: Learning & the Language Minority Student.* New York: Newbury House/Harper & Row.

Varenne, H. (1977). *American Together: Structured Diversity in a Midwestern Town.* New York: Teacher's College Press.

Vygotsky, L.S. (1978). *Mind in Society: The Development of Higher Psychological Processes.* M. Cole, V. John-Teiner, S. Scribner, and E. Souberman (eds.). Cambridge, MA: Harvard University Press.

Wagatsuma, H. and DeVos, G. (1984). *Heritage of Endurance: Family Patterns and Delinquency Formation in Urban Japan.* Berkeley: University of California Press.

Warren, R.L. (1967). *Education in Rebhausen: A German Village.* New York: Holt, Rinehart and Winston.

_____. (1973). The classroom as a sanctuary for teachers: Discontinuities in social control. *American Anthropologist* 75:280–291.

_____. (1975). Context and isolation: The teaching experience in an elementary school. *Human Organization* 34(2):139–148.

Index

About the Editors and Contributors

HENRY T. TRUEBA, an anthropologist trained at Stanford and Pittsburgh, is currently the Director of Cross-cultural Studies at the University of California, Santa Barbara. He has recently published *Success or Failure: Linguistic Minority Children at Home and in School* (with S. Goldman), *Becoming Literate in English as a Second Language: Advances in Research and Theory*, and *Raising Silent Voices: Educating Linguistic Minorities for the 21st Century*. At present he is studying minority children classified as "disabled," and is exploring the process of socialization for academic success.

CONCHA DELGADO-GAITAN, trained in Educational Anthropology at Stanford and, with a broad experience in school administration, is the Associate Director of Cross-cultural Studies at the University of California, Santa Barbara. Her work focuses on literacy acquisition and the development of a supportive home environment for school achievement. Her ethnographic studies of children's transitions from home to school and of dropout phenomena led her to emphasize the need for adult mentorship and the education of minority parents. She is the author of many publications related to minority education, literacy and training of parents.

Robert R. Alvarez, Mexican Products

Steven Borish, Swarthmore College

Christine Robinson Finnan, Stanford University

Mariko Fujita

Diane M. Hoffman, American Institute for Research

Nancy H. Hornberger, University of Pennsylvania

Richard A. Navarro, Michigan State University

Toshiyuki Sano, Nara Women's University

Richard L. Warren, California Polytechnic State University

Harry F. Wolcott, University of Oregon